T0291217

The Lure of Economic Nationalism

The Lure of Economic Nationalism

Beyond Zero Sum

Kenneth A. Reinert

ANTHEM PRESS

Anthem Press
An imprint of Wimbledon Publishing Company
www.anthempress.com

This edition first published in UK and USA 2023
by ANTHEM PRESS
75–76 Blackfriars Road, London SE1 8HA, UK
or PO Box 9779, London SW19 7ZG, UK
and
244 Madison Ave #116, New York, NY 10016, USA

British Library Cataloguing-in-Publication Data
A catalogue record for this book is available from the British Library.

Library of Congress Control Number: 2023934489
A catalog record for this book has been requested.

ISBN-13: 978-1-83998-220-0 (Hbk)
ISBN-10: 1-83998-220-9 (Hbk)

This title is also available as an e-book.

Once again, to Gelaye, Oda and Ayantu

CONTENTS

Preface   viii

List of Abbreviations   x

1. Albert Hirschman's Forgotten Book   1

2. Power and Plenty   9

3. Industry and War   25

4. Zero-Sum Thinking   43

5. Battleground WTO   57

6. The Ethnicity Trap   77

7. The Brexit Blunder   99

8. Pandemic Nationalism   117

9. Techno-Nationalism   137

10. Beyond Zero Sum   157

Afterword   173

Bibliography   175

Notes   193

Index   219

PREFACE

In 2014, I began to write a book entitled *No Small Hope* about the universal provision of basic goods and services, drawing upon economics, ethics and human rights theory. In the middle of this project, the world began to shift. In 2016, the United Kingdom voted to leave the European Union and Donald Trump was elected president of the United States. Both these developments reflected economic nationalist and ethnonationalist political platforms. In 2018, I presented the *No Small Hope* book at the World Trade Organization's annual public forum. This was somewhat ironic because President Trump was beginning a full-scale assault on that institution, attempting to hobble the multilateral trading system he loathed.

About a year later, COVID-19 appeared on the global scene, setting off further expressions of economic nationalism, exacerbating an already fraught US–China relationship, and causing 15 million excess deaths worldwide. In the United Kingdom, Boris Johnson was "getting Brexit done," while Indian prime minister Narendra Modi was ramping up his ethnonationalist Hindutva movement. During 2020 and 2021, the pandemic ravaged the world, fraying economic relations. In January 2021, US president Trump attempted to overthrow the country's electoral process while Brexit came into effect. A little over a year later, Russia invaded Ukraine in another ill-considered nationalist spasm.

Whereas *No Small Hope* was a statement of what could be, this book is a statement of what is, and it is decidedly less hopeful. The main message is that economic nationalism is often a recipe for worsened economic welfare, strained international relations, enflamed ethnic tensions, global public health setbacks and reduced effective innovation. Behind economic nationalism lies a zero-sum mindset that misapprehends many realities and thereby sets back the important project of human flourishing. This zero-sum mindset, however, is an ever-tempting default that must be overcome for continued forward progress. This book argues that we must resist its lure and recognize the possibility of non-zero-sum outcomes as embedded in the principle of multilateralism. This lesson was painfully learned after World War II and unfortunately needs to be learned again.

Some small fragments of this book were published in editorial form in the US-based *The Hill*, and I would like to thank *The Hill's* Daniel Allott for his support in that process. Without implicating them, I would also like to thank my Schar School colleagues Des Dinan, Justin Gest, Mark Langevin, Jerry Mayer and J. P. Singh for comments on specific sections of the book.

As this book was going into press, I stumbled upon a statement by the trade economist and historian of economic thought Jacob Viner in his famous 1950 monograph *The Customs Union Issue*. Viner states: "The power of nationalist sentiment can override all other considerations; it can dominate the minds of a people, and dictate the policies of government, even when in every possible way [...] it is in sharp conflict with what [...] are in fact the basic economic interests of the people in question." These words reverberate today perhaps even more so than when they were first written.

Renewed hope requires that we go beyond zero-sum thinking, reembrace some degree of multilateralism, and attend to global public goods provision. I hope that, in some small way, this book makes these possibilities more likely.

LIST OF ABBREVIATIONS

AI	Artificial intelligence
ARIA	Advanced Research and Innovation Agency (United Kingdom)
ARPA	Advanced Research Projects Agency (United States)
ASCM	Agreement on Subsidies and Countervailing Measures
BATNA	Best alternative to a negotiated agreement
BJP	Bharatiya Janata Party (India)
CCP	Chinese Communist Party
COMAC	Commercial Aircraft Corporation of China
COVAX	COVID-19 Vaccines Global Access
CPAC	Conservative Political Action Committee (United States)
CPI	Parliamentary Commission of Inquiry (Brazil)
CSI	Coalition of Service Industries (United States)
DAO	Discrete analog and other (semiconductors)
DARPA	Defense Advanced Research Projects Agency (United States)
DFT	Development-facilitation tariff
DPA	Defense Production Act (United States)
DSU	Dispute Settlement Understanding
EC	European Community
ECJ	European Court of Justice
EDA	Electronic design automation (semiconductors)
EDPS	Environmentally displaced persons
EEC	European Economic Community
EIC	British East India Company
EMU	European Monetary Union
EU	European Union
FAO	Food and Agriculture Organization
FDI	Foreign direct investment
G7	Group of 7 (Canada, France, Germany, Italy, Japan, UK, US)
GATS	General Agreement on Trade in Services
GATT	General Agreement on Tariffs and Trade
GSP	Generalized System of Preferences

GVCS	Global value chains
ICT	Information and communication technologies
IP	Intellectual property
IPCC	Intergovernmental Panel on Climate Change
ITO	International Trade Organization
LCD	Liquid crystal display
LMICS	Low- and middle-income countries
MFN	Most-favored nation
MNE	Multinational enterprise
MPIA	Multiparty Interim Appeal Arbitration Arrangement
MTNS	Multilateral trade negotiations
NAFTA	North American Free Trade Agreement
NGO	Nongovernmental organizations
NICS	Newly industrialized countries
OIHP	Office International d'Hygiène Publique
OSEC	Organisation of Semiconductor Exporting Countries
PAHO	Pan-American Health Organization
PLA	People's Liberation Army (China)
PPE	Personal protective equipment
R&D	Research and Development
RCUK	Research Councils United Kingdom
RSS	Rashtriya Swayamsevak Sangh (India)
SMIC	Semiconductor Manufacturing International Company (China)
SNP	Scottish National Party
SOE	State-owned enterprise
SPRIN-D	Federal Agency for Disruptive Innovation (Germany)
TCA	(UK–EU) Trade and Cooperation Agreement
TEU	Treaty on European Union
TPP	Trans-Pacific Partnership
TRIPS	Agreement on Trade-Related Aspects of Intellectual Property Rights
TSMC	Taiwan Semiconductor Manufacturing Company
TTC	EU US Trade and Technology Council
UKIP	United Kingdom Independence Party
UNHCR	United Nations High Commissioner for Refugees
USMCA	United States–Mexico–Canada Agreement
VOC	Vereenigde Oost-Indische Compagnie (Dutch East India Company)
WHA	World Health Assembly
WHO	World Health Organization
WTO	World Trade Organization

Chapter 1

ALBERT HIRSCHMAN'S FORGOTTEN BOOK

In 1941, a little-known economist by the name of Albert Hirschman arrived at the University of California, Berkeley, on a fellowship. He was 25 years old and a Jewish German refugee. In the early 1930s, as Hitler rose to power, Hirschman had been active in the German Socialist Party but subsequently fled Berlin for Paris. From there, he went to study at the London School of Economics. Completing his studies at LSE, Hirschman went to Barcelona to fight in the Spanish Civil War. Then to Trieste, Italy, for doctoral work in economics and back to Paris to enlist in the French army. Peddling part of the way on a stolen bicycle, he later fled France over the Pyrenees and went on to Lisbon for his escape from European fascism.[1]

While in Berkeley, Albert Hirschman met his wife and wrote a book. He would go on to write many more books as he became increasingly famous, and this first book has been almost forgotten. It is entitled *National Power and the Structure of Foreign Trade* and represents a refugee economist's struggle with the economics of fascism. Indeed, the book was in part a response to Herman Göring's famous statement that "guns will make us powerful; butter will only make us fat." As such, it was a contribution to a centuries-long argument in economics between "power" and "plenty" and still has relevance for us today.

The objective Hirschman set out for himself in *National Power* was "a systematic exposition of the question of why and how foreign trade might become [...] an instrument of national power policy."[2] To address this, he engaged in novel statistical analysis of Nazi trade relations in the pursuit of national power. This analysis led him to the following conclusion:[3]

The Nazis have [...] shown us the tremendous power potentialities inherent in international economic relations, just as they have given us the first practical demonstration of the powers of propaganda. It is not possible to ignore [...] these relatively new powers of men over men; the only alternative open to us is to prevent their use for the purposes of war and enslavement and to make them work for our own purposes of peace and welfare.

Consequently, Hirschman called for "a frontal attack upon the institution which is at the root of the possible use of international economic relations for national power aims—the institution of national economic sovereignty."[4] His ultimate policy conclusion was that, given the power aspects of international trade, trade autonomy must be limited and placed in an international institutional framework.[5] Sovereignty needs to give way a bit for "peace and welfare."

Such an effort was to soon take place but not because of Hirschman's book.[6] The process began in 1945 when the United States proposed the establishment of an International Trade Organization (ITO). This led to 23 countries meeting in Geneva to sign a General Agreement on Tariffs and Trade (GATT) based on a draft of the ITO charter. The ITO charter itself was finalized in 1948 at a meeting of 56 countries in Havana, Cuba, but in 1950, the United States walked away from the ITO plan. The world was left with a trade agreement, but no legal international organization to go along with it, and an improvisational GATT Secretariat grew around the GATT. Nonetheless, Hirschman's vision of placing trade sovereignty within an international institutional framework was partially realized.

Despite its incomplete start, the GATT had some real success. Between 1946 and 1994, it provided a forum for numerous "rounds" of multilateral trade negotiations (MTNs). These GATT-sponsored rounds reduced tariffs among member countries in many sectors. As a result, the weighted-average tariff on manufactured products imposed by high-income countries fell from approximately 20 percent to approximately 5 percent.[7] This process and the GATT's multilateral institutional structure were historically unprecedented.

In 1995, the GATT became the World Trade Organization (WTO), realizing the original ITO idea. The WTO took its place alongside two other international organizations created in the aftermath of the war that Albert Hirschman escaped, namely the International Monetary Fund and the World Bank. These entities provided an institutional structure for an evolving global economy: the WTO in the realm of trade, the IMF in the realm of monetary affairs and the World Bank in the realm of development finance. Given their inevitable imperfections, it is important to remember that they are all products of war and were devised in the hope of preventing future catastrophes, both economic and political.

There is also a recognition that, despite whatever reduction in protection achieved under the GATT/WTO system, its real benefits have been the ones anticipated by Albert Hirschman in *National Power*, namely, the global public good of a rules-based structure for trade relations. These benefits include transparency, predictability, the support of positive sum, cooperative outcomes and the availability of dispute settlement mechanisms when necessary. These institutional intangibles have been the real contribution of multilateral trade cooperation but are nonetheless currently under threat.[8]

The last round of MTNs, the Doha Round launched in 2001, was a famous failure. This seems to have been the result of institutional overreach. The Doha Round involved an unprecedented number of countries and maintained the goal of a complete package ("single undertaking") that all members would agree to (no "variable geometry"). That is why it became known as the "first truly global trade negation in history."[9] Further, it attempted to address the thorniest issue, agriculture, that has vexed the GATT/WTO from the beginning.

There have been small wins in MTNs, most notably the 2013 Trade Facilitation Agreement, which entered into force in 2017 and helps to enhance customs procedures, including in low-income countries. More importantly, the WTO intangibles are still immensely important, the most notable of which is dispute settlement. Indeed, it is not an exaggeration to say that the WTO dispute settlement system is the most well developed and robust on the planet. Unfortunately, beginning in 2017, it fell into the sights of the US Trump administration and was significantly undermined. The Trump administration's strategy was to starve via veto the WTO Dispute Settlement Body of the staff it needed to function, namely members of its Appellate Body. By the very end of 2019, this entity no longer had enough members to operate, and a transparent system that had worked well for a quarter century in more than five hundred cases ceased to function. In the words of trade economist, Chad Bown, Trump "shot the sheriff."[10] Whether this damage can be undone is still a question at the time of this writing.

It is also important to remember that the WTO dispute settlement system was largely designed *by* and *for* the United States. The US government wanted such a system to protect its gains in trade in services and intellectual property (IP), two new areas of agreement it pushed into the WTO. It subsequently used this system in more than a hundred cases. Nonetheless, President Trump's trade negotiator, Robert Lighthizer, had a long-standing dislike of it. Lighthizer often referred to the WTO as a "litigation society" despite his own career litigating on the behalf of US industries, notably the US steel industry. His real issue was not the litigation itself but who was winning and losing in specific cases.[11]

The US Trump administration had also substantially increased tariffs on steel and aluminum by claiming *national security* concerns. The WTO and former GATT do make provisions for this, but members had long avoided invoking this language because they knew that it would throw open doors that best remain closed.[12] Significant tariffs were imposed on Canada, for example, a long-standing ally. Although this was not a violation of WTO rules per se, it was a provocative violation of WTO traditions. In these and other ways, including a US–China trade and technology war, the long-standing institutions of the multilateral trading system had come under sustained attack from self-described economic nationalists.

With the beginning of the COVID-19 pandemic, the year 2020 saw an increased turning away from multilateral cooperation with renewed nationalist sentiments, including economic nationalism. For example, the US-based nationals security analysts Colin Kahl and Thomas Wright refer to this recent period as an "international experiment" in the form of: "What would happen in a global crisis if world politics was dominated by nationalist governments that refused, or were unable, to cooperate with one another?."[13] The answer, unfortunately, was 15 million excess deaths.[14]

In this book, we take a careful look at economic nationalism to understand both its history and its current revival. We do so in a number of different contexts, from trade and industrialization to ethnicity and the COVID-19 pandemic. Currently, there are myriad calls for a revival of nationalisms around the world as a way of restoring mythical pasts, and these calls have economic elements. This book will argue that economic nationalism is in many ways misconstrued and self-defeating as a means to enhance national welfare. As we will see, in both its emphasis on ethnicity and tendency to neglect public health issues, it can be quite dangerous.

Economic Nationalism

Economic nationalism has a centuries-long pedigree. A set of writers in the sixteenth and seventeenth centuries set out a system of economic nationalist policies that became known as *mercantilism*. There are current disagreements about how to best interpret mercantilism but considering it a form of economic nationalism is something of a consensus. A careful consideration of this body of writing finds that it has echoes up to the present era. That is one reason that, in the early 1940s, Hirschman began his book with a consideration of mercantilism. We will do the same here but also consider the post-mercantilist economic nationalism of Friedrich List, the role of industry in economic nationalist ideology and modern techno-nationalism.

Beyond these historical precedents, we need a contemporary definition of economic nationalism. To do so, we first need to define "nationalism." One definition is that "nationalism is an expression of a constructed societal identity."[15] That seems to move us in a relevant direction. Political scientist

George Crane emphasizes that the content of nationalism is both "variable" and "malleable" to the extent that it often takes the form of what has been called "imagined communities."[16] According to Crane, national identity is not just constructed but continually *reconstructed*, drawing upon "a variety of resources, economic memories as well as socio-cultural narratives."[17] It can therefore be historically incorrect and even intentionally false.

What about the term "economic nationalism"? As it turns out, it can mean a few different things. In the field of economics, economic nationalism is usually associated with protectionism, state-directed industrial investment and technology development, the shunning of multilateral commitments and zero-sum narratives that tie them together.[18] These elements still have important relevance today but are increasingly seen as limited by researchers outside of economics.[19] Here, we want to relax these limitations to some degree and engage with these noneconomist researchers. In doing so, however, we will not necessarily adopt all the same terminology as these researchers do.[20]

One of the founders of the field of international political economy, Robert Gilpin, states that economic nationalism consists of the idea that "economic activities are and should be subordinate to the goal of state-building and the interests of the state."[21] This definition has been questioned because it confounds the state with the nation. While the state is an administrative apparatus, the nation is an imagined community, and the difference proves to be important. As stated by George Crane, "the imaginings of the economic nation, while certainly shaped by state action, are not wholly determined by the state. Nation may have a life of its own."[22] Political scientist Derek Hall tries to overcome this conundrum by stating that economic nationalism "refers to the goal of promoting the survival, strength, and prestige of the state and/or the nation in a competitive international system."[23] However, as we will see, this avoids what proves to be an important distinction.

One of the main points of the recent political economy research on economic nationalism is that it can be compatible with many different policy regimes, from "protectionist" to "free trade."[24] To again quote Derek Hall, "there is no reason why liberalization cannot be promoted for reasons of national power and prestige."[25] This perspective has had the salutary effect of expanding our scope of how economic nationalism can express itself in different times and places. A second point is that national contexts still matter, and they do. This is widely recognized by economists, if not by the authors of popular books on globalization.[26] To state it simply, globalization has not erased countries to no less nations.

Expanding our concept of economic nationalism beyond the traditional realm of economists is important. But there is also a risk of the concept becoming both too narrow and too expansive. Regarding the former, a recent statement is that: "Where there is a state, there is—at least one—nation. Where there is a nation, there is nationalism."[27] In truth, however, there are *many* more nations than states, and it is important to remember this. Further, some virulent nationalisms turn on their own citizens, casting them as members of a different nation that does not "belong." Uighur concentration camps in China and Rohingya refugees from Myanmar are just two contemporary examples of this.

Indeed, Albert Hirschman was not the only German refugee to arrive in California in 1941. Another of his fellow refugees that year was Theodor Adorno, scholar, pianist, musicologist and coauthor of a famous book entitled *The Authoritarian Personality*.[28] Whereas Hirschman was interested in investigating the economic features of fascism, Adorno and his colleagues were interested in its social psychological features, particularly its intolerance of ambiguity and its propensity to discriminate against out-groups.[29] In asserting the role of the "nation," political entrepreneurs often embrace these tendencies in the form of ethnonationalism.

Regarding the tendency for the new research to become too expansive, the concept of economic nationalism is sometimes stretched to the point of being nearly commensurate to what we would normally call "governance." For example, this takes place under the term "nationalizing mechanism" introduced by political scientist Andreas Pickel.[30] While this idea is quite evocative, we will take a slightly more focused approach in this book. We will extend far beyond standard economics but will also stay within some thematic and analytical bounds.

Given these considerations, it is not possible to provide a completely fixed definition of economic nationalism. For our purposes in this book, however, we will use the following working definition:

Economic nationalism consists of the ideas that a socio-political defined "nation" is best supported by protectionism, domestically supported manufacturing and technology, the rejection of multilateralism, the deployment of zero-sum narratives, and in some circumstances, ethnic discrimination in support of the conception of the nation.

Political scientist Eric Helleiner states that "economic nationalism remains alive and well in today's global economy" (p. 226).[31] Indeed it does. We will see that economic nationalism is about national power through both economic and psychological means. Economic power is an inescapable fact of human affairs, both national and international. Handled well, it can be a benign force. Handled badly, as it often is, it is a source of harm and even violent conflict.

Alternatives

One recurring theme is that nationalism and, therefore, economic nationalism are inevitable. The argument is that there are just no practical alternatives, and to pretend otherwise is naïve and unrealistic. This book attempts to question this default posture. It calls for a renewed commitment to multilateralism, an end to the obsession with industry over services, the promotion of open innovation systems, an embrace of civic nationalism as an alternative to ethnonationalism and a full engagement with global public health. This posture runs counter to current political trends, but the book does not apologize for it.

Consider first the renewed commitment to multilateralism. Multilateralism and multilateral institutions are the bane of economic nationalists and are increasing under attack. But they are the very things that help to prevent the conflagrations that drove Albert Hirschman to write his book. They therefore deserve our respect and support. This book will attempt to show why this is so in multiple contexts, not least the global response to the COVID-19 pandemic.

As we will see, there is also a persistent overlap between economic nationalism and ethnonationalism, which combine in what has been called the "new nationalism" based on identities. An alternative to this is the idea of civic nationalism, a notion that appears to be as unpopular as it is relevant.[32] However, given the violent threats and actual violence associated with ethnonationalism, both historically and in the contemporary era, it appears to be the only ethical and practical alternative.[33] Consequently, this book will argue strongly on its behalf.

Another important phenomenon emphasized in this book is the ability of both nationalism in general, and economic nationalism in particular, to *distract*. What really matters in the end is countries' abilities to provide the necessary basic goods and services to their citizens in support of their well-being.[34] When economic nationalism takes hold, and in particular when ethnonationalism is inflamed, these important provisioning processes are often downplayed and even forgotten altogether. Worse still, caught up in their distractions, economic nationalist leaders can fail to respond effectively to crises, even exacerbating them, as the COVID-19 case makes clear.

The alternative promoted here is to keep a sharp focus on what really matters, the actual economic and general welfare of all citizens and to engage in serious policy discussions on how to further these ends within national and multilateral systems. To do this, however, we need to go beyond the zero-sum thinking that characterizes economic nationalism. Given the multiple challenges of the contemporary era, avoiding the lure of economic nationalism and getting *beyond zero sum* are critically important. To do this requires a focus on basic economics, reimagining nationalism as civic nationalism, taking global public health policy seriously and reengaging with multilateral institutions. These are the elements that support economic and human welfare, and their not-always-casual dismissal by economic nationalists has always been a grave mistake.

Chapter 2

POWER AND PLENTY

Approximately three centuries before Albert Hirschman wrote *National Power and the Structure of Foreign Trade*, another book was written on the same subject. The author was Thomas Mun, a wealthy merchant trader born in 1571. Mun's early career was in the Mediterranean trade, particularly in Italy. These trade interests led to his becoming a very rich man. As a result of his commercial experience and his wealthy stature, in 1615, Mun became a director of the British East India Company (EIC), and he spent the rest of his career advocating on its behalf. In 1622, he was also appointed to a British government commission on international trade and thereby brought the interests of the EIC directly into government.

The EIC had its origin in a meeting that took place in London in September 1599. Present at that meeting were a group of traders, most notably the auditor of the City of London, Sir Thomas Smythe, as well as explorers, including William Baffin of Baffin's Bay fame.[1] Their purpose was to request a royal charter granting them monopoly rights to trade, and they were quickly successful in this aim, the charter being granted in 1600. This set in motion a long series of events in which the EIC would expand into Asia with the largest private army in the world.

Along with his dedicated service to the EIC, Thomas Mun became the best-known member of a group of individuals who wrote on economic affairs in Europe during the sixteenth and seventeenth centuries. Their body of work became known as *mercantilism*. What exactly mercantilism was has been a matter of extensive debate and substantial disagreement to the present day. The prominent historian of economic thought, Henry William Spiegel, referred to the mercantilist idea as "economic warfare for national gain."[2] If that put it too strongly, mercantilism was most certainly a form of economic nationalism. Consider another description from the economic historians Ronald Findlay and Kevin O'Rourke:[3]

> The prevailing mercantilist doctrine of those times viewed the struggle for wealth as a zero-sum game, and each of the powers looked upon its colonies as suppliers of raw materials and markets for manufacturers of

the "mother country" alone, with foreign interlopers to be excluded by force if necessary. [...]

Most of the rivalries of the age of mercantilism were about which national company could gain control of a given market or trading area. [...] The aim was to exert monopoly control over a given trade, thus gaining monopoly profits, which in turn would increase the state's financial ability to successfully wage war, thus enhancing its mercantilist trade objectives.

This was the context in which Mun developed his ideas. He died in 1641, and in 1664, his work *England's Treasure by Forraign Trade* was published by his son. Indeed, Mun wrote the book as a letter to his son. It was quite the letter![4]

Mun begins *England's Treasure by Forraign Trade* by extolling the virtue of merchants whose private gains he equates with the public good. Centuries before "What is good for General Motors is good for America," there was "What is good for the East India Company is good for England." However, Mun took great pains to explain and prove his point. The main reason to support merchant interests was their "bringing Treasure into the Kingdom."[5] By "treasure" Mun meant precious metals or gold, but the means of getting these was indirect and occurred through international trade. As Mun stated, "we have no other means to get Treasure but by foreign trade, for Mines we have none which do afford it."[6]

Mun explains the process many times in his book, but his most famous statement is: "The ordinary means [...] to increase our wealth and treasure is by Foreign Trade, wherein we must ever observe this rule; to sell more to strangers yearly than we consume of theirs in value."[7] Mun returns to this point again and again. Here is just one other statement: "All Nations (who have not Mines of their own) are enriched with Gold and Silver by one and the same means, which is [...] the balance of their foreign trade."[8] This was Mun's central point, one mistakenly embraced by some modern economic nationalists.

How does this work? If a country exports more overall than it imports, then the payments to this country in precious metals exceed the country's own payments to other countries in precious metals, so there is a net inflow of precious metals. Ever the member of the wealthy class, Mun emphasized that this increased balance of "treasure" would also increase land values, increasing the incomes of landowners. What would happen to poor laborers and yeomen was mostly outside of his inquiry.

Importantly, Mun did not fall into the trap of focusing on *bilateral* balances of trade. Rather, he focused on England's *overall* balance of trade across all its trading partners ("the whole trade of the Realm for Exportations and Importations"). He was also aware that trade in services mattered, particularly shipping, the primary tradable service of his day. In these two respects, this seventeenth-century merchant was conceptually far out in front of many twenty-first century politicians who focus on bilateral balances of trade in goods alone.

There was one way that all of this could go awry, however, and this is what Mun referred to as the "canker of war." He saw Spain as having fallen into this trap, dispersing its treasure abroad to pay armies throughout its empire rather than keeping it at home. Ironically, Great Britain would soon be doing the same in its own empire, mostly guided in this endeavor by Mun's EIC.

Toward the end of his famous book, Mun begins to assess the "power" and "plenty" of "this Kingdom," Great Britain, introducing what would become enduring themes.[9] In doing so, however, he turned his attention to the Dutch and to fish.

His Majesty's Seas

Mun felt that the Dutch had a few things over the British. They smoked less, for one. More generally, Mun bemoaned in Britain "the general leprosy of our Piping, Potting, Feasting, Fashions and mis-spending of our time in Idleness and Pleasure" and the fact that these had "made us effeminate in our bodies, weak in our knowledge, poor in our Treasure, declining in our Valor, unfortunate in our Enterprises, and condemned by our Enemies."[10] In short, he turned to the cultural explanations of national decline used by nationalists to this day. But then he got back to the matter of fish.

Regarding the "Hollanders," Mun stated:[11]

It seems a wonder to the world, that such a small Country, not full so big as two of our best Shires, having little natural Wealth, Victuals, Timber, or other necessary ammunitions, either for war or peace, should notwithstanding possess them all in such extraordinary plenty, that besides their own wants (which are very great) they can and do likewise serve and sell to other Princes, [...] which by their industrious trading they gather from all quarters of the world.

How did they do this? By "fishing in His Majesty's Seas of England, Scotland, and Ireland,"[12] this "being indeed the means of an incredible wealth."[13] It was this "Golden Mine" that supported Dutch success, and Mun wanted to take it away. Indeed, he wanted to take away their ships as well. He was ready for the "canker of war" against this enemy because "in truth

[…] there are no people in Christendom who do more undermine, hurt, and eclipse us daily in our Navigation and Trades, both abroad and at home."[14]

Mun would eventually get his wish. Between 1652 and 1674, the two rivals fought three bloody wars, partly over Dutch access to "His Majesty's Seas," and with a steady improvement in British naval dominance. During these wars, "large and powerful fleets with thousands of sailors and soldiers clashed on the North Sea and in the English Chanel."[15] Subsequently, Mun's vision of dominance over the Dutch would find purchase in the world of British policy in the hands of Sir George Downing, a formidable character.

Downing is famous for buying New York from the Dutch and for 10 Downing Street in London, but he began his career as the son of Puritan preachers active in the Massachusetts colony. He graduated from Harvard in 1642, the year after Mun died and, for a short while, served as Harvard's first tutor. He subsequently returned to England and began a military career in 1647. He was active in military intelligence and served in Parliament. He also served as ambassador to The Hague from 1661 to 1665, all this initially in service to the controversial Oliver Cromwell and then to Charles II after the restoration of the monarchy.[16] While ambassador to The Hague, he was paid by the EIC to support its interests, "double-dipping" as it were.

Downing himself is controversial in many respects, but he carried the ideological torch for Mun, and his experience with the Dutch was instrumental. As an observer put it, "Downing's lasting contribution to England's economic destiny was that he brought to bear his observation of Dutch economic practice on English economic theory and policy."[17] More generally, another observer states that "his utter ruthlessness and lack of scruple did nothing to detract from his practical effectiveness."[18] He was thus a formidable figure with great impact.

Besides himself, Downing had one central allegiance, and that was to Britain's "national fiscal and military power."[19] Downing understood that military power rested upon taxation, something he learned from the Dutch. He also supported the naturalization of Dutch citizens with manufacturing talent and experience to relocate to England, an early form of high-skilled migration. But it was in the areas of trade and colonial policy where he really left his mark.

Economic historians Ronald Findlay and Kevin O'Rourke describe Downing as "an ardent believer in the doctrines of Thomas Mun" and as "the father of mercantilist practice in England."[20] He was behind the 1651 Navigation Act, revised in 1660 and subsequently, as well as the Staples Act of 1663. These Navigation Acts were complicated, but in essence, they required that all goods imported into England to be on English ships or on ships from the country of origin. Shipping within the Commonwealth was also to be exclusively on English ships. In a step further, the Navigation Acts required certain colonial products to be exported to England alone, from where they could be reexported. The historian Gijs Rommelse states that "in the 1660s, English mercantilism stretched out its arms like an octopus creating an efficient lobby that could influence politics on every level."[21] A primary target of all of this was, of course, the Dutch.

Having helped guide the Navigation Acts through Parliament and having served in The Hague, Downing became commissioner of customs in 1671. He held that position until his death in 1683. Downing is now remembered both for his lack of principles and for wedding mercantilism to what has been called the British "fiscal-military state."[22] One observer states that "if Downing was godfather of anything, it was not a London street but the British state."[23] In his ardent economic nationalism, he left quite the legacy.

Commerce and Conflict

But what of the Dutch? Unlike the English, they wrote relatively little about mercantilism, putting their efforts into practice with ruthless efficiency. The Dutch began their rise at the very end of the sixteenth century in the form of what economic historians Ronald Findlay and Kevin O'Rourke term a "merchant oligarchy." In their words, "the main asset of the upstart republic was its economic system, certainly the most productive and efficient in Europe."[24] There was more behind their success than "fishing in His Majesty's Seas," including high-value agriculture, shipping and textile manufacturing concentrated in the city of Leyden. Moreover, international commerce was baked into the seventeenth-century Dutch government.

The Dutch countered England's EIC in 1602 with its own trading company, the Vereenigde Oost-Indische Compagnie (VOC) with a monopoly on all trade east of the Cape of Good Hope. Many if not most of the government's regents owned stakes in the VOC, thereby merging public and private interests. By mid-century, the VOC dominated trade between Europe and Asia and trade within Asia as well. It was initially led by the ruthless Jan Pieterszoon Coen who made the famous statement that "we cannot make war without trade nor trade without war." *The Economist* describes the success of the VOC as follows:[25]

> By 1670 it was the richest corporation in the world, paying its shareholders an annual dividend of 40% on their investment despite financing 50,000 employees, 30,000 fighting men and 200 ships, many of them armed. The secret of this success was simple. They had no scruples whatsoever.

This lack of scruples reached the "spice islands" of Asia in 1604, subsequently and most notably on the Banda archipelago in the current Indonesian province of Maluku. Here, Coen engaged in a campaign of ethnic cleansing to secure clove production, described in brutal detail by Giles Milton in his book *Nathaniel's Nutmeg*.[26] During this period, the VOC and the EIC were in extreme conflict with each other over the spice trade, culminating in the Dutch torture and execution of British nationals in the 1623 Amboyna Massacre.

The Anglo-Dutch commercial conflict played out in many regions, however. While the Asian spice race was the most famous, other conflicts took place in the Caribbean, the Baltic, the Mediterranean and even the Muscovy trade via the northeast passage and the port of Arkhangelsk. In the case of Asia, the commercial rivalry is represented by the number of ships sailing around the Cape to Asian markets. This is shown from one historical source in Figure 2.1. As we are taught in grade school, the Portuguese were the first movers into Asia, accidentally reaching Japan in 1543 and giving the world *tempura*. Anglo-Dutch trips around the Cape came later, at very end of the sixteenth century. The Dutch quickly became dominant, leveraging their original comparative advantage in shipping, with the VOC alone ultimately accounting for about half of all Europeans travelling to Asia. However, the British asserted their own shipping capabilities. Consequently, the shipping conflict that began in "His Majesty's Seas of England, Scotland, and Ireland" extended into Asia.[27]

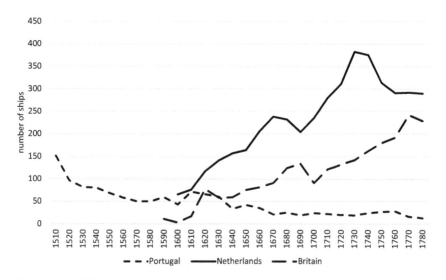

Figure 2.1 Ships on the Cape Route. Source: de Vries (2003).

Throughout most of the seventeenth century, as summarized by the historian Gijs Rommelse, "merchants and companies from both countries competed for every major trade both within and outside Europe. The English governments were eager to defend and advance economic interests and the Dutch leaders were prepared to respond by force."[28] Like with mercantilism in general, there are arguments among researchers regarding mercantilism's relevance to the Anglo-Dutch conflict. However, Rommelse comes firmly down on the side of the relevance of mercantilist ideology in this history:[29]

> There is an abundance of source material, political and diplomatic, as well as economic, that suggests that commercial competition was the prime factor in Anglo-Dutch relations. Arguably, political ideology played a part in Anglo-Dutch relations. The ideology, however, was very much connected to the emerging notion of the interest of the state. English political ideology was heavily coloured by anti-Dutch rhetoric in mercantilist pamphlet literature. [...] The mercantile rivalry between both countries is still fundamental for understanding the three (Anglo-Dutch) wars, but analyzing the political process, the strategic situation, and the organization and practices of mercantile interest groups is essential for understanding how mercantile competition could lead to war.

The Dutch were able to exert monopoly control over cinnamon, cloves, nutmeg and mace (but not pepper) through their ruthlessness and lack of concern for human life. The Dutch subsequently took control of Ceylon in 1638 and Jaffna in 1657. Economic historians Ronald Findlay and Kevin O'Rourke describe the first 50 years of the VOC as a "remarkable success," if the violent subjugation of Asian peoples can be called a "success."[30] But after 1663, the British began to attack Dutch settlements along the African coast. In 1664, British Parliament voted in favor of war spending, and war was declared in 1665. This was followed by the 1667 Peace Treaty, signed in the Dutch town of Breda, which slightly relaxed the Navigation Acts in the Dutch favor. While the British consequently gained traction in the New World, the Dutch did so in the East Indies. This was the high-water mark of Dutch colonial and commercial activities.

Despite the Treaty of Breda, a last round of Anglo-Dutch war began in 1672. Notwithstanding the intervention of France on the British side, this conflict ended in a draw. But during the eighteenth century, the VOC's profits declined relative to those of the EIC, and the VOC entered a slow, downward decline. As described by *The Economist*:[31]

As early as the end of the 17th century, careful analysis of the books shows that its volume of trade was reducing every year. [...] By 1735, dwindling spice income had been overtaken by textiles in the company's profit column. In 1799, the most vicious robber baron of them all met its final end. The VOC went bankrupt.

Despite the demise of the VOC in 1799 and the EIC in 1874, economic warfare for national gain lived on. But there was one important volley directed at mercantilism in the war of ideas, namely that of Adam Smith, and his influence was profound.

Enter Adam Smith

Adam Smith introduced the notion of "mercantilism" or the "mercantile system" as a formal idea in his *The Wealth of Nations* published in 1776. Smith's conception of mercantilism reflected Mun's ideas about "treasure" and was given in his famous statement: "That wealth consists in money, or in gold and silver, is a popular notion which naturally arises from the double function of money, as the instrument of commerce, and as the measure of value."[32] Smith disputed this notion.

While there have been protracted debates over Smith's characterization of mercantilism and its focus on precious metals, he was firmly against monopolistic trading companies such as the EIC and VOC.[33] Smith spent a good deal of time examining the use of "exclusive companies" and other trade regulations in the colonies of the type favored by Sir George Downing. In his careful understatement, Smith notes:[34]

Of the greater part of the regulations concerning the colony trade, the merchants who carry it on, it must be observed, have been the principal advisors. We must not wonder, therefore, if, in the greater part of them, their interest has been more considered than either that of the colonies or that of the mother country.

Indeed, this is what seemed to irk Smith most about mercantilism. He states that many European colonial projects were based on "folly and injustice." Even in the case of Britain, Smith advocates that is "should voluntarily give up all authority over her colonies."[35] As we know, that process took a great deal of time.

There is a modern interpretation of mercantilism that suggests that it was mostly about expanded liberty and trying to achieve full employment.[36] There is also an argument that mercantilists (at least of the "early" sort) contributed to a series of institutional reforms such as an increased role for private property, an incipient patent system and a decreased role of the crown vis-à-vis Parliament and merchants.[37] Much of this line of thought is focused on reforms *within England itself,* forgetting the colonial projects, and is therefore incomplete.

Ironically, this point was first made in 1883 by the British historian J. R. Seeley in his book *The Expansion of England.* In addressing the "prodigious greatness" of his country, Seeley discusses liberty but then turns his attention to "the simple obvious fact of the extension of the English name into other countries of the globe, the foundation of Greater Britain."[38] He states:[39]

> There is something very characteristic in the indifference which we show towards this mighty phenomenon of the diffusion of our race and the expansion of our state. We seem, as it were, to have conquered and peopled half the world in a fit of absence of mind. [...] We constantly betray in our modes of speech that we do not reckon our colonies as really belonging to us [...] (We) make too much of the mere parliamentary wrangle and the agitations about liberty. [...] We ought to beware of putting England alone in the foreground and suffering what we call the English possessions to escape our view in the background of the picture.

The tendency noted by Seeley to focus on liberty and ignore colonial projects reached a sort of apex in the career of John Stuart Mill. Mill, the philosopher, political economist and author of *On Liberty,* spent his career working for Mun's cherished EIC. Liberty, it seems, was fine for the English, but not for the subjects of the colonial empire.[40] Indeed, Mill was less progressive on this issue than Smith had been.

Smith was also a general proponent of "free trade," and this reflected tendencies in mercantilism as well. As described by the Indian economist P. J. Thomas, beginning toward the end of the seventeenth century, mercantilist policy "entered a [...] remarkable phase" that involved "vigorous protection of what were regarded as national industries against unfair competition from foreign countries."[41] Thomas also notes that the arguments were "fought on the now familiar lines of protection versus free trade," and we will return to this issue below.[42] By and large, Smith came down on the "free trade" side.[43]

If Adam Smith's *The Wealth of Nations* can be read as an anti-mercantilist work, Smith was nevertheless in agreement with Mun on one thing, namely, the Navigation Acts. Smith, like Mun before him, was supportive of the "monopoly of trade of their own country" but stated his support in terms of national defense.[44] In what was to become a famous sentence, Smith stated that "as defense [...] is of much more importance than opulence, the act of navigation is, perhaps, the wisest of all the commercial regulations of England."[45] To state this another way, in the balance of power and plenty, Smith was ultimately on the side of power.

This is a conundrum for Smith's criticism of mercantilism because, in practice, the defense argument proves to be very elastic, and we will encounter it at many junctures in this book. It is, indeed, a centerpiece of economic nationalism. The colonial projects to which Smith objected, along with their monopolization practices, were justified in terms of national defense. Neomercantilist policies in the contemporary era are also justified in these terms. In invoking the national defense argument, Smith undermined his criticism of mercantilism.

Looting India

Josiah Child was a successful merchant who became a director of the EIC in 1677. In 1681, he rose to the rank of governor. In his trajectory from merchant to EIC heavyweight, he followed the path of Thomas Mun. He also followed in Mun's path in writing his own mercantilist tract entitled *A New Discourse of Trade* in 1692. The historian of economic thought Henry Spiegel says that the influence of this work "was almost as great as Mun's."[46] Indeed, it was printed numerous times through 1804. Child also had an eye on Holland, as did Mun, but sought to emulate its success.

A New Discourse of Trade relaxed Mun's balance of trade doctrine, perhaps because the EIC was at that time contributing to a deficit rather than a surplus.[47] Child is also known as the "liberal mercantilist," and indeed a few of his ideas in this realm foreshadow those of Adam Smith. However, any liberal sentiments that Child possessed stopped at the water's edge. He was a full-on imperialist with designs for the Britain's Asian and North American enterprises, and his reign at the EIC set in motion the EIC's ultimate conquest of India.

As part of the spice race with the Dutch described above, the EIC had established a station or "factory" in Surat in 1607. This proved to be an important port on the West coast of India, to ultimately be supplanted by Bombay (Mumbai) after 1670. On the East coast, similar stations were established in Madras in 1639 and Calcutta in 1690. The subsequent history of the EIC is gruesomely described by William Dalrymple in his book *The Anarchy*. Most notable initially was the conquest of Bengal by Robert Clive in 1757. Clive had started out his career as an EIC accountant, but his daring and ruthlessness led him to be the governor of Bengal. As Dalrymple states:[48]

We still talk about the British conquering India, but that phrase disguises a more sinister reality. It was not the British government that began seizing great chunks of India in the mid-eighteenth century, but a dangerously unregulated private company headquartered in one small office, five windows wide, in London, managed in India by a violent, utterly ruthless and intermittently mentally unstable corporate predator—Robert Clive.

Clive literally looted Bengal, returning to Britain in 1760 with his riches packed into a ship to pursue (buy) a career in Parliament. Power and plenty are not everything, however, and he died by suicide at age 49 in 1774.

Clive was replaced by Warren Hastings, a sort of anti-Clive. A hardworking and almost scholarly individual, he became an Indophile and set to limit the looting of Bengal. Nonetheless, he left an EIC administrative state in Bengal built on coercive revenue collection. Hastings was, in turn, replaced by Charles Cornwallis who was fresh from his famous surrender to General George Washington at Yorktown, and after Cornwallis came Richard Wellesley. Piece by piece and battle after battle, the Mughal Empire was incorporated into the EIC with the Mughal emperor Shah Alam ultimately placing himself and his reduced empire under British (EIC) protection in 1804, the year after the final printing of Josiah Child's *A New Discourse of Trade*.

To emphasize again, Britain's activities in India during the seventeenth and eighteenth centuries were not those of the British government but of the EIC. The activities there were carried out with a vast private army in what Dalrymple calls "the supreme act of corporate violence in world history."[49] The EIC's private army was not just one of the largest in the world but twice the size of the British army. Any liberal pretensions within England itself were put paid by private, corporate conquest and plunder.

One must also remember that India possessed a long-standing advantage in cotton textiles across the entire range of quality, an advantage that stretched back to ancient times. Via numerous intermediaries, including multiple European companies, these textiles served markets the world over, including Britain, naturally expanding the monetary (silver) base of the Mughal economy.[50] Beginning in about 1670, these textiles began to be part of the EIC's trade in increasing numbers of arrangements of what we would now call contract manufacturing and had detrimental impacts on the British woolens sector. The woolens issue was debated in Parliament, a debate in which Josiah Child took part, and coalesced in the "calico controversy" of 1696–1700. Ironically, many mercantilists argued on the protectionist side and against the EIC, ridiculing Josiah Child in the process. The Indian economist P. J.

Thomas summarizes the protectionist view as follows, an argument made in various forms to this day:[51]

> In brief, the weaver's contention was that all their ills were due to the East India trade, and that the Company sent out artificers and patterns to India and thereby taught the people there to make stuffs suited to the English market, and that the goods so brought supplanted the use of English manufactures both at home and abroad.

Josiah Child and other EIC mercantilists were on the side of "free trade," albeit in a limited manner. Child recognized the imperfect substitutability between woolens and cottons, stating "at this rate, the brewers may be opposed to the vintners." The mercantilists opposed tariffs on imports of calicos but insisted on the EIC monopoly of the trade. Indeed, with its ultimate conquest of the Mughal Empire, the EIC ended up monopolizing what had been a very competitive sector in India, to the detriment of the Indian producers. This is exactly what Adam Smith disapproved of, and the hypocrisy did not go unnoticed by the protectionist side.[52]

Parliament considered bills to prohibit calico imports in 1696, 1697 and 1699 to address the "groans of the poor weavers." The ultimate Act of 1700 prohibited the import of calicos for domestic use. Any imported calicos were to be warehoused, printed if not so already, and reexported. While the calico printing industry benefitted (copying techniques from India), calicos found their way into the English market by one way or another and competed with English woolens abroad. Meanwhile, domestic demand for calicos continued unabated. There was, it seems, no holding back the calico tide.

Until there was. The woolen weavers continued to agitate and found success in 1720 when not only the importation of unprinted cotton was prohibited but the very wearing of cotton. This followed a series of violent protests by the weavers, sometimes targeting individual calico wearers but ultimately targeting the EIC and the calico printing industry. In the words of the Indian economist P. J. Thomas, "everything was subordinated to the interest of the woolen industry, which was then universally regarded as the palladium of English prosperity."[53] Eventually, the woolen palladium was replaced by a cotton palladium as English industrialist learned to do what their Indian counterparts had been doing for millennia and to do it better.

By the nineteenth century, the calico crisis would be affecting Bengal as a result of three things: EIC monopolization of previously competitive markets, protection against calicos in the British market and innovation on the part of British cotton manufacturers. After the EIC had consumed the Mughal Empire, it next consumed the Bengali textile industry.[54] Economic nationalism, EIC style, had a real success in South Asia. In the end, however, the period's colonial conflicts would be settled through the second hundred years' war, a worldwide conflict of England with the Dutch and French, a lengthy and fraught process of decolonization, including the eventual takeover by the Crown of the EIC in 1858, which forced an end to John Stuart Mill's career. Mun's beloved EIC would cease to exist in 1874.

Giving Mercantilism Its Due

Having taken a somewhat critical tone to mercantilism, it is worthwhile to pause for a moment to give it its due. Mercantilism did contain some important insights that extended beyond what some modern economic nationalists can muster. While the mercantilist emphasis on the balance of trade and, more broadly, economic nationalism was misplaced, modern assessments of the school of thought have revealed that it was engaged in real economic analysis. Key concepts uncovered by mercantilist writers included balance of payments accounting, trade in services, preliminary monetary theory, aggregate employment and exchange rate determination. These were valuable contributions.

The famous trade economist and historian of economic thought, Jacob Viner, showed how Mun drew attention to nontangible items in the balance of payments, including trade in services and what would now be called net income and net transfers. Mun also discussed trade policies, including the exemption of export taxes on what we would now call re-exports, and he developed a simple model of exchange rate determination. There was therefore more in his writings than the balance of trade doctrine and bashing the Dutch.[55]

Although mercantilist writings were a clear case of special pleading or early corporate lobbying, they were also more than that. They contained elements of liberal economic policy (at least domestically) and went beyond international economic policy into public finance.[56] Other contributions were support of property rights, including patents, two fundamental institutions of market systems.[57] While we should never lose sight of the main thrusts of mercantilist thinking, we should also acknowledge its variations and that some of these had lasting value.

Relevant Alternatives

As part of their consideration of mercantilism, Ronald Findlay and Kevin O'Rourke pose the following important question:[58]

One has to ask, what was a realistic counterfactual for an individual European nation state choosing to unilaterally embrace peaceful free trade? In the absence of anything resembling an effective collective security mechanism, or a clearly defined hegemonic power, military defeat and exclusion from foreign markets seems [...] as plausible an answer as any.

This observation is right on the mark. It is easy to be critical of mercantilist thought and practice, but the absence of a relevant alternative might have made these the only possible default. It turns out, however, that there were a few things afoot that were somewhat non-mercantilist in nature. An important one was the Methuen Treaty of 1703 between England and Portugal, negotiated on the British side by John Methuen. There were actually two Methuen treaties, one for power and another for plenty. The latter is the one we want to focus on here.

The Methuen Treaty on trade was known as the Port Wine Treaty and addressed trade between England and Portugal, which had been a thorny issue for decades.[59] Methuen had previously served in a post in Lisbon and consequently knew the diplomatic territory well. He had family connections in the English textile sector and had a personal interest in Portuguese wines. These were the very subjects of the treaty, which granted preferential access for British cloth exports in Portugal in return for preferential access for Portuguese wines in England.

The impact of the Methuen Treaty seems to have been positive but limited.[60] It became immortalized, however, in the theory of comparative advantage developed by the British economist, David Ricardo in 1817, set out in terms of cloth and wine trade between England and Portugal. In the careful analysis of trade economist Roy Ruffin, it took Ricardo "two weeks of intense thought" to come up with this theory, but it would become perhaps the most important cornerstone of international economics and perhaps in the entire history of economic thought.[61]

Ricardo, a previous stockbroker, was very much aware of the "real world," but he thought in abstract terms, and in his development of the comparative advantage idea, he introduced a few critical abstractions. First, he envisioned a national labor market with a constant amount of employment. Second, he did not concern himself with the national balance of payments, putting himself in a realm far removed from mercantilism. Third, he assumed that productive factors do not move between countries. Each of these assumptions has been subsequently relaxed in modern trade theory.

Ricardo's insight was that, in this sort of world, the *relative* efficiencies or costs of production among countries matter more than the *absolute* efficiencies or costs, and he set out an example of this in terms of the Methuen Treaty. The implications have been succinctly summarized by the trade economist Douglas Irwin:[62]

The key idea behind comparative advantage is that every country, no matter how advanced or behind it might be in the productivity of its labour compared to other countries, would be able to engage in beneficial trade with other countries. A country with a productivity advantage over other countries would not export everything, but only those goods in which it had a comparative advantage. Thus, paradoxically, an advanced country would find it advantageous to import goods even if it could produce those goods more efficiently than other countries. Conversely, countries behind the technological frontier [...] could still export goods in which (their) comparative disadvantage was the least and import goods in which its comparative disadvantage was the greatest—and benefit from doing so.

The key thing to note about the comparative advantage idea is that trade based on relative efficiencies turns out to be *mutually* beneficial, not zero sum, and that such trading relationships can be supported through agreements among countries. Economic theory and international institutions can come together to support non-zero-sum outcomes.

That said, Ricardo's comparative advantage notion has become known as a "difficult idea."[63] It is also an idea routinely criticized by economic nationalists. We need to be clear that Ricardo was talking about non-zero-sum outcomes at the national level. Subsequent economic analysis has shown quite clearly that such mutual national gains are fully compatible with winners and losers *within* countries.[64] International trade is therefore always a distributional issue, something that even the mercantilists knew quite well, no less modern trade theorists.

In the contemporary era, a realistic counterfactual exists, and it is a multilateral one. While it has many antecedents, including the famous Cobden–Chevalier Treaty of 1860 between England and France, it was the post-1945 era that made this option a reality. And it was the United States as a global power that helped to both develop the multilateral system and to maintain it, mostly for its own interests. In the trade realm, this multilateral system was first embedded in the GATT, which was later folded into the WTO. This system is with us today but is increasingly under threat.

The role of Ricardo's idea of comparative advantage in this multilateral development was captured by trade economist Jonathan Eaton: "Ricardo's message was an element in the development of a view of the world that took a universal rather than solely national perspective on welfare. [...] Keeping this message alive poses a major challenge to trade economists."[65] Indeed, mercantilist thinking has an almost everlasting, intuitive appeal and is invoked by economic nationalists to this day. There is reason for this. As stated by the Indian economist P. J. Thomas, "the core of mercantilism is the strengthening of the State in material resources; it is the economic side of nationalism."[66] We first need to more fully examine this "strengthening of the State in material resources," and we then need to examine zero-sum thinking in more detail.

Chapter 3

INDUSTRY AND WAR

After the mercantilist era, economic nationalism became intertwined with industry or manufacturing, and the two have been remained so ever since. This fact was not lost on one of the founders of the field of modern political economy, Robert Gilpin, who notes:[1]

> For several reasons, the foremost objective of nationalists is industrialization. In the first place, nationalists believe that industry has spillover effects (externalities) throughout the economy and leads to its overall development. Second, they associate the possession of industry with economic self-sufficiency and political autonomy. Third, and most important, industry is prized because it is the basis of military power and central to national security in the modern world.

As we will see in this and subsequent chapters, these perspectives on manufacturing are limiting and tend to lead to conflict, something that Gilpin also notes. Further, the focus on industry turns out to be somewhat misplaced, and we need to take some time to see why.

What became known as the "Industrial Revolution" first took place in Britain or, more precisely, in the north of England. The initiating sector was the one we discussed in the previous chapter, namely, cottons. The initiating innovation was the flying shuttle, which, beginning in 1735, doubled productivity in weaving. Subsequent innovations took place in spinning. It is worth remembering that, up until the mid-eighteenth century, China and India accounted for approximately one-third and one-quarter, respectively, of global manufacturing output.[2] Britain was playing catch-up but did so in a manner that surpassed these two previous loci of global manufacturing expertise. Eventually, these innovations had significant growth and wage effects in Europe. Exactly when this took place is a matter of debate, but it is located somewhere in the mid-nineteenth century.

Recall from Chapter 2 that the woolens sector in Britain successfully agitated for protection from cotton goods. This increased the incentives for domestic cotton goods production and innovation, including the introduction of a cotton–linen blend known as fustian that escaped the ban on cotton products. Steam power became central to the innovation processes as well. Importantly, innovations were not confined either to specific products or to specific countries. As noted by economic historians Ronald Findlay and Kevin O'Rourke, "the technical innovations that were first made in cotton were applied to the woolen, linen, and silk industries as well."[3]

Further, despite efforts to limit technological diffusion via bans of machinery exports, the new technologies began to spread within Europe. This can be seen in Figure 3.1 for a small set of European countries (plus India and the United States) in terms of a measure of per-capital industrialization. The leading technology was weaving, and the technological diffusion within Europe depended on British exports of cotton yarn.[4] One important exception to increased industrialization was India which experienced a *deindustrialization* process under British colonial rule. The centuries-long, leading cottons producer in the world lost its manufacturing glory.[5]

It is important to state that the Industrial Revolution that took place in Britain drew upon the mercantilist trading structures discussed in Chapter 2. This included the import of cotton from colonies, in particular cotton produced in the New World using slave labor. Indeed, estimates are that between 70 and 80 percent of American export commodities were produced by Africans during the nineteenth century.[6] The Industrial Revolution was therefore dependent on slave labor applied to significantly expanding

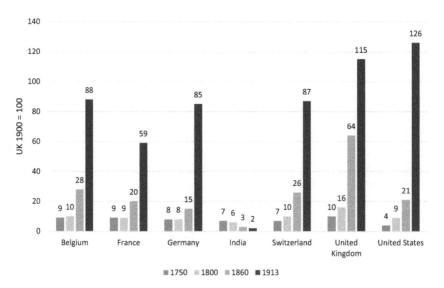

Figure 3.1 Comparative per-capita industrialization. Source: Bairoch (1982).

land resources in the Americas. Further, on the export side, approximately one-half of the additional output produced by Britain was exported, including to the Americas. Mercantilist-inspired trade, slavery and the Industrial Revolution went together, and Britain's empire, most importantly its naval prowess, played an important role.

List's National System

Scholars of economic nationalism often explicitly cite the German writer Friedrich List as one important intellectual touchstone. For example, Eric Helleiner states that "List certainly deserves a prominent place in the intellectual history of economic nationalism because he was one of the first thinkers to express very eloquently the core belief of economic nationalists: that the economy should serve nationalist goals."[7] Assessing List is therefore an important part of assessing economic nationalism.

Friedrich List was born in 1789 in Württemberg, Germany, and had careers both in the kingdom's civil service and at the University of Tübingen.[8] He was an early advocate of a customs union among German states, what was to become the Zollverein in 1834. Unfortunately, his advocacy earned him a prison term, and he was ultimately forced to leave Württemberg. Rejected in Paris as well, he fled to the United States in 1825.

In the United States, List became active in coal mining and in a German language newspaper. More importantly, he was sponsored by the Pennsylvania Association for the Promotion of Manufacturing Industry. In about 1828, he began to write essays advocating protection of manufacturing and the building of railroads, with an eye to his native Germany. According to one researcher, "List was not a professional scholar of political economy but a publicist whose self-proclaimed goal was to influence the economic policies of what he called 'second- and third-rate industrialized nations' like the USA, Germany, France and Russia in their endeavor to catch up with Britain."[9]

Just how they were to catch up was a matter of some importance to List, and he took this question quite seriously. He gathered his essays in a book published in 1841 as *The National System of Political Economy*, which was subsequently published in English. In this work, he considers Germany in its relationship to Britain as one of inequality, an inequality that must be addressed:[10]

Modern Germany, lacking a system of vigorous and united commercial policy, exposed in her home markets to competition with a foreign manufacturing power in every way superior to her own, while excluded at the same time from foreign markets by arbitrary and often capricious restrictions, and very far indeed from making that progress to industry to which her degree of culture entitles her, cannot even maintain her previously acquired position, and is made a convenience of (like a colony).

He also considers Germany as especially deserving of correcting this inequality. In his words:[11]

> If any nation whatever is qualified for the establishment of a national manufacturing power, it is Germany; by the high rank which she maintains in science and art, in literature and education, in public administration and in institutions of public utility; by her morality and religious character, her industry and domestic economy; by her perseverance and steadfastness in business occupations; as also by her spirit of invention, by the number and vigour of her population; by the extent and nature of her territory, and especially by her highly advanced agriculture, and her physical, social and mental resources.

In his policy confrontation with Britain, List also pushes back on British economic thought. While he recognizes the validity of what he calls the "popular school" of "cosmopolitical economy," he emphasizes the important of "true political or national economy" that focuses on catch-up with Britain. In the catch-up process, "those nations which feel themselves to be capable [...] of developing manufacturing power of their own must adopt the system of protection as the most effective means for this purpose."[12] Along with the "system of protection," List's other central idea is "productive power." List sets this idea in opposition to Smith's division of labor and includes in it nearly everything else that we would, in the current era, describe as technology, institutions and culture. List criticizes Smith for the division of labor idea being vague, but his own productive power notion suffers from an even greater lack of specificity.[13]

For List it is manufacturing that unleashes productive power, including in agriculture and services. In one of many examples, he states that "manufacturing power developed in all its branches forms a fundamental condition of all higher advances in civilisation, material prosperity, and political power in every nation."[14] Indeed, List maintains a stages theory of economic development, with the pre-manufacturing stage being "barbarous." Moving from the barbarous state to increased amounts of productive power and "civilisation" is of utmost importance to List.

What List calls for is what we now refer to as *infant industry protection*, and List's suggestions in this regard are quite valid. He specifically calls for protection that is targeted, is phased out and has a terminal date. As we will see,

this is entirely consistent with current economic thinking on the infant industry policy, and we will return to this policy suggestion below.

As one researcher notes, List's "efforts to raise collective German tariffs on
British goods bore no fruit during his lifetime."[15] List died of his own hand in
1846, but we see from Figure 3.1 that, by 1860, manufacturing capacity had
nonetheless begun to increase across Europe via technological diffusion. It
was only where Britain's imperial grip was the strongest, in India, that it was
able to prevent this process from taking place. Indeed, as Germany developed
in the mid- to late-nineteenth century, it was largely due to this technological
diffusion and the German education system rather than from protection.[16]

Among researchers impressed with List's ideas, a great deal has been made
of the following quote by Adam Smith:[17]

Were the Americans, either by combination or any other sort of violence, to stop the importation of European manufactures, and, by thus
giving a monopoly to such as their own countrymen as could manufacture the like goods, divert any considerable part of their capital into
this employment, they would retard instead of accelerating the further increase in the value of their annual produce, and would obstruct
instead of promoting the progress of their country towards real wealth
and greatness. This would still be more the case, were they to attempt,
in the same manner, to monopolize to themselves the whole exportation
trade.

There are several points to be made here.

First, Smith uses the terms "monopoly" and "monopolize." As discussed
in Chapter 2, these are primarily employed regarding mercantilist colonial
practices. His aversion to monopoly is the main theme of his criticism of
colonialism, including in the Americas. For this reason, it is possible to see
this paragraph in this more general context: Smith strenuously opposed the
monopolization of trade and colonial domination.[18]

Second, Smith's comment is made in a chapter dedicated to the issue of the
allocation of scarce capital across agriculture, manufacturing and services
(what he terms "wholesale trade"). His caution is stated as follows.[19]

The country [...] which has not capital sufficient for all those three purposes, has not arrived at that degree of opulence for which it seems
naturally defined. To attempt [...] prematurely and with an insufficient
capital to do all three, is certainly not the shortest way for a society [...]
to acquire a sufficient one. [...] It is likely to increase the fastest, therefore, when it is employed in the way that affords the greatest revenue to

all the inhabitants of the country, as they will thus be enabled to make the greatest savings.

What Smith is suggesting here is that capital be employed where it will have the greatest *returns* in a particular place and time. His assessment in 1776 was that this was in agriculture in America. Smith's observation is that agriculture "does not admit of so many subdivisions of labour as manufactures" and that, consequently, "the improvement of productive powers of labor in this art, does not always keep pace with their improvement in manufactures."[20] Nonetheless, in his view "the most opulent nations [...] generally excel all their neighbors in agriculture as well as in manufactures." It is therefore clear that he (rightly) views agriculture as an activity subject to innovation.

Third, Smith was emphasizing the search for high *value added*. This is an important concept lost on many to this day. Indeed, the preference for specific sectors in economic development is nothing more than a heuristic for the real determining factor, value added, and the way it is affected by technological change. To assert that value added is to only be found in manufacturing is just that, an assertion. It must be held up to scrutiny in specific times and places. Indeed, List himself recognizes the importance of "progress in manufactures, agriculture, and trade" and was very much aware of innovations in agriculture.[21] We address the issue of value added in stages of manufacturing below.

Fourth, contemporary research has revealed the central importance of agricultural development to growth and even to successful manufacturing development. Britain in the Industrial Revolution is often referred to as the first newly industrialized country or NIC. Subsequently, the post–World War II growth trajectories of the East Asian NICs were exclusively attributed to manufacturing and manufactured exports. However, Japan, Taiwan and South Korea each pursued their development strategies "walking on two legs," that is, on both agriculture and manufacturing.[22] This aspect of their development is consistently ignored.

On another point, List differs from much contemporary economic nationalism in that he supports "the immigration into our country of workmen, talents, and capital."[23] Indeed, he sees immigration as a key element in Britain's success since the twelfth century. As we will discuss in Chapter 6, modern economic nationalism, including that inspired by List, is often ethnonationalist and therefore anti-immigrant. In this way, modern economic nationalists cherry-pick from List's policies.

In some important ways, List was not so different from Albert Hirschman in his call for the subjection of national sovereignty to a global system of rule of law discussed in Chapter 1. Indeed, current multilateralists would not find too much to object to in the following statement that trade restrictions[24] cannot be dispensed with until this conflict of national interests shall cease, in other words until all nations can be united under one and the same system of law. Thus the question as to whether, and how, the various nations can be brought into one united federation and how the decisions of law can be invoked in the place of military force to determine the differences which arise between independent nations, has to be solved concurrently with the question of how universal free trade can be established in the place of separate national commercial systems.

What a contemporary multilateralist would add to this, however, is that "universal free trade" is not the real objective but rather a rules-based trading system, of the sort we now have (ever imperfectly) under the WTO. We return to this issue in Chapter 5.

In other ways, List helped to sow the seeds of Albert Hirschman's exile. This is the dark side of List's writings that the current List revival often ignores. For example, List's conception of nationality extends to the acquisition of colonies. He states:[25]

A nation in its normal state possesses one common language and literature, a territory endowed with manifold natural resources, extensive, and with convenient frontiers and a numerous population. [...] It must possess sufficient power on land and at sea to defend its independence and to protect its foreign commerce. It will possess the power of beneficially affecting the civilization of less advanced nations, and by means of its own surplus population and their mental and material capital to found colonies and beget new nations.

Writing in a century after Adam Smith, List is much less enlightened on the matter of colonies and seems to have been quite resistant to the emancipation of slaves.[26]

But there is more. List is explicitly in favor of German expansionism in Europe:[27]

By its Zollverein, the German nation first obtained one of the most important attributes of its nationality. But this measure cannot be considered complete so long as it does not extend over the whole coast, from the mouth of the Rhine to the frontier of Poland, including Holland and Denmark. A natural consequence of this union must be the admission of both these countries into the German Bund and consequently into the German nationality, whereby the latter will at once obtain what it is now in need of, namely, fisheries and naval power, maritime commerce and colonies.

The man who hired Albert Hirschman at the University of California, Berkeley, economist John Bell Condliffe, was very much aware of this *Mitteleuropa* tendency in List, writing that "Bismarck, and later the Nazis, could find in List's writings authority for practically all of their policies."[28] This is not a positive legacy but nonetheless represents a recurring tendency of economic nationalism.

The Historical Record

In his well-received book *Kicking Away the Ladder* (a title taken from List's *National System*), the economist Ha-Joon Chang considers cases of nineteenth-century growth in multiple countries. In the case of the United States in the nineteenth century, Chang suggests that economic historians see tariff protection as beneficial to growth. The evidence seems to be otherwise, however. In particular, the work of trade economist and economic historian Douglas Irwin suggests that there is little reason to think that tariff protection played a role in nineteenth-century US growth.[29] Indeed, much of the growth in the United States at that time can be attributed to the *services sector* rather than to protected manufacturing.[30] List and his followers seem to have got the US case wrong.

Regarding List's own Germany, Chang acknowledges that infant industry protection does not seem to have been important. He explicitly states that "tariff protection actually played a far less important role in the economic development of Germany than in that of the UK or the USA," and he cites several more important policies (e.g., education and social policy).[31] Nonetheless, he states that "the importance of tariff policy [...] for the development of heavy industries at that time should not be underestimated."[32] Again, the evidence is much more mixed. For example, the analysis by economic historian Stephen Broadberry suggests that the successful long-run economic performance of both the United States and Germany relative to Britain is, once again, mostly due to improvements in productivity in *services* rather than manufacturing.[33]

Further, the nineteenth-century link between tariffs and growth is weaker than Chang suggests. As a general principle, correlation is not causation, but even the correlation has been questioned. Chang cites the work of economic historian Kevin O'Rourke on this issue, but subsequent work by Douglas Irwin has seriously questioned the initial results.[34] Irwin shows that the initial results are largely due to the land-abundant countries Argentina, Canada and the United States that pursued revenue-generating tariffs. With these outliers removed, the correlation largely disappears.

We can get a visual sense of this in Figure 3.2. One main message in List's *The National System* was that protection would help Western Europe catch

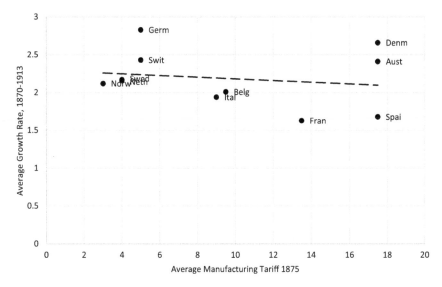

Figure 3.2 Tariffs and growth in Western Europe, 1870–1913. Sources: Average tariffs from Findlay and O'Rourke (2007), Table 7.3. Average growth rates from Maddison (2001), Table A1-e. Britain, with a tariff rate of zero and a growth rate of 1.90, is excluded since it industrialized earliest. Labels for Sweden and the Netherlands overlap in the figure.

up with Britain. Figure 3.2 considers tariffs and rates of growth in Western Europe from 1870 to 1913. It plots growth over this period against available tariff rates in 1875. This is far from a valid, econometric exercise, but there seems to be little reason to suppose that tariff protection helped in Western European growth during this period. In the current period, evidence suggests that tariffs are actually bad for growth.[35]

What does not receive a lot of attention in Chang's *Kicking Away the Ladder* is the half-century, import substitution era of Latin America, roughly from 1940 to 1980. List-style infant industry protection was pursued with the goal of developing a manufacturing base in the region. Latin American governments did not abide by List's suggestion that the tariffs involved be explicitly temporary, but the historical experience was not positive for import substitution as a development policy. The intellectual underpinnings of infant industry protection were provided by Raul Prebisch's United Nations report *The Economic Development of Latin American and Its Principal Problems*, written in 1950. By 1963, he had written a follow-up report stating the following:[36]

An industrial structure virtually isolated from the outside world thus grew up in our countries. [...] The criterion by which the choice was determined was based not on considerations of economic expediency, but on immediate feasibility, whatever the costs of production. [...] Tariffs have been carried to such a pitch that they are undoubtedly—on an average—the highest in the world. It is not uncommon to find tariff duties of over 500 percent.

As is well known, the proliferation of industries of every kind in a closed market has deprived the Latin American countries of the advantages of specialization and economies of scale, and owing to the protection afforded by excessive tariff duties and restrictions, a healthy form of internal competition has failed to develop, to the detriment of efficient production.

Even researchers largely sympathetic to the infant industry protection notion conclude that this era was quite ineffective for Latin American economic development, worsened income distribution and set the stage for Latin America's debt crisis in the 1980s.[37] In a well-known consideration, the development economist Henry Bruton draws us back to what spread the Industrial Revolution throughout Europe and the later East Asian success story, namely, *learning*.[38] No amount of infant industry protection will succeed without it, but taking the learning process seriously leads us in very different directions than those suggested by most contemporary economic nationalists.

More success for infant industry protection is found in East Asia, and Chang recognizes this. Importantly, he also explicitly recognizes the role of technological learning. His statement that successful East Asian development "is fundamentally due to activist industrial, trade and technology policies by the state" is very much in keeping with research on East Asian development.[39] But left out, again, is rural development and land reform, which played an indispensable role in each of these countries, as well as explicit education strategies. These factors, rather than infant industry protection per se, are what distinguished East Asia from Latin America.[40] In downplaying them, economic nationalists misrepresent East Asian economic history.

Infant Industry Protection in the WTO

As previously stated, List's conception of infant industry protection was very modern, one that would pass muster in today's policy discussions. In the case of his highly favored Germany, he recommended: "A moderate protective duty of about twenty-five percent, during the next five years, which could be maintained for a few years at that rate and then be lowered to fifteen to twenty percent, ought to completely accomplish this object."[41] The question is how to evaluate this policy proposal in the twenty-first rather than the nineteenth century.

Among contemporary defenders of List, the WTO does not rank very high as a valuable international institution. Consider again Ha-Joon Chang's *Kicking Away the Ladder* in which he asks: "Is it fair to say that the WTO agreement puts restrictions on the ability of developing countries to pursue activist [...] policies is only a modern, multilateral version of the 'unequal treaties' that Britain and other (developed countries) used to impose on semi-independent countries?"[42] He does not answer this question, suggesting that the answer is indeed "yes."

Regarding recommended policies, at the very end of his book, Chang suggests that "WTO rules and other multilateral trade agreements should be rewritten in such a sway that more active use of infant industry promotion tools (e.g., tariffs and subsidies) is allowed."[43] But he does not inquire into what the actual rules *are* or specifically *how* they should be rewritten. This is the case for many current writers in List's tradition. Given the centrality of this policy to the current economic nationalist project, this oversight is significant.

Infant industry protection in the WTO was introduced in its origin as the GATT in Article XXVIII, and this article was revised in the 1950s at the request of "developing" countries. Currently, infant industry protection is covered in GATT94 Article XVIIIa and XVIIIc, GATT94 being the version of GATT covering trade in goods that was updated in 1994 as part of the establishment of the WTO. In principle, these articles allow for infant industry protection "to promote the establishment of a particular industry with a view to raising the general standard of living." Any measures taken under this article must be notified, negotiated and, potentially, compensation provided. Partly because of these required procedures, the provisions have not received much use.

A broader issue is the relevance of infant industry protection in the current era. As a general principle, it is not clear that infant industry protection is the most efficacious way forward. For example, trade economist Patrick Messerlin states:[44]

The transitory handicap faced by domestic firms can be related to a host of causes: scale economies, imperfect information and knowledge about the production process, product characteristics or market features, differences in market maturity, absence or insufficient quality of domestic inputs, etc. Tariffs or other trade barriers are unlikely to be the best means for addressing these issues. For example, trade policy limits the market for infant firms to the domestic market, certainly the worst way to reap scale economies, especially in the poorest countries where markets are tiny. It cannot help firms acquire the information and knowledge that foreign firms may have. It has no reach to the input markets (such as capital or skills).

These are relevant concerns, and it is fair to say that the trade policy and trade law research on a more development-friendly WTO have expanded far beyond infant industry protection.[45] The entire trade and development discourse has moved on to issues such as participation in global value chains (GVCs), IP and trade facilitation. Nonetheless, what if we were to take the infant industry idea seriously?

Trade lawyer Yong-Shik Lee has developed a proposal for reforming Article XVIII into a development-facilitation tariff (DFT).[46] The DFT proposal envisions a tiered set of maximum tariffs by GDP per capita measures such as those maintained by the World Bank. A country invoking the DFT would be required to submit an infant industry promotion plan with scheduled reductions over time, and this plan would be subject to public hearings to promote transparency. "Developing" countries with a great deal of manufacturing capacity (e.g., China) would be excluded. The purpose of the DFT proposal is to remove the burden of negotiations and compensation, as well as potential retaliation of affected exporters that are not in agreement. Given that Article XVIII has rarely been invoked, this proposed reform is worth considering. To date, economic nationalists have not done so.

List and War

For Adam Smith, the military is an awkward necessity to which he does not ascribe much value. For List, the subject is a bit more complicated. In some passages, he describes war for what it is, a drain on economic resources with little good associated with it. In other passages, however, he strikes a different tone. For example, he states:[47]

And power is more important than wealth. That is indeed the fact. Power is more important than wealth. And why? Simply because national power is a dynamic force by which new productive resources are opened out, and because the forces of production are the tree on which wealth grows, and because the tree which bears the fruit is of greater value than the fruit itself. Power is of more importance than wealth because a nation, by means of power, is enabled not only to open up new productive resources, but to maintain itself in possession of former and of recently acquired wealth and because the reverse of power—namely feebleness—leads to the relinquishment of all that we possess, not of acquired wealth alone, but of our powers of production, of our civilization, of our freedom, nay, even of our national independence, into the hands of those who surpass us in might.

Here List states three times that, in the balance of power and plenty, he values the former over the latter. Indeed, for List and some of his followers, there is a link between war and manufacturing. List himself was very much concerned about national preparedness and self-sufficiency in times of war. There is a quotation often attributed to List that states: "War or the very possibility of war makes the establishment of a manufacturing power an indispensable requirement for a nation of the first rank."[48] Here List describes a clear relationship between industry and war. If the "very possibility of war" makes industry a necessity, war also supports industry. List writes that:[49]

The equipment of armies [...] may [...] under certain circumstances, very greatly conduce to increase of the productive powers of a nation. Strictly speaking, material wealth may have been consumed unproductively, but this consumption may, nevertheless, stimulate manufacturing to extraordinary exertions, and lead to new discoveries and improvements, especially to an increase of productive powers. This productive power then becomes a permanent acquisition; it will increase more and more, while the expense of war is incurred only once for all.

Recall from Chapter 2 that the historian of economic thought, Henry William Spiegel, referred to the mercantilist idea as "economic warfare for national gain."[50] To some degree, this also partly applies to the "neo-mercantilist" List, but he also has the opposite message of "warfare for national economic gain" that resonates to this day.[51]

We have already mentioned the connection between List and the *Mitteleuropa* idea. Indeed, an early book on the subject states that "Friedrich List was universally celebrated by the (German) wartime writers as the oldest prophet of *Mitteleuropa*" and that "the wartime *Mitteleuropa* authors promptly enshrined List. *The National System* appeared to foreshadow a modern war economy."[52] Another author notes that List's "conception of Germany included Belgium, the Netherlands, Denmark and Sweden, even though they were nations in their own right, since they were small and had no right to exist."[53] Indeed, at the end of his life, he advocated an alliance between Germany and his nemesis, Britain. In his proposed pact, List included the agreement that Germany would "dominate the Balkans and Central Europe. How this was to be achieved was the main preoccupation of List for many years."[54] In List,

Bismarck was to find a kindred spirit.[55] With his ill-advised 2022 invasion of Ukraine, so did Vladimir Putin.[56]

List's ideas on industry and war spread far and wide, including to Japan. As stated by political scientist Meredith Woo, "The Meiji oligarchs [...] were assiduous students of the Prussian military state."[57] Indeed, representatives of the Japan's Meiji government were sent to Germany to study its manufacturing sector and military. Beginning in the 1870s, a List-inspired ideology of *fukoku kyōhei* (rich nation, strong army) and *shokusan kōgyō* (industrial promotion) were developed, and these diffused among Japanese government officials.[58] Unfortunately, manufacturing in Meiji Japan was a military affair. As one Japanese writer put it in 1922:[59]

> In Japan (military) industry has the greatest influence on the general industry of the country. [...] But that is not all. The advancement of science and arts, the diffusion of education, the protection of laborers—in these matters also, the military industry of Japan has been an important factor. In short, the degree of development of a nation's military industry not only tells the strength of its military preparations but also serves as the indicator of the progress of its general industry and its economic status, as well as the grade of its civilization.

As a result of this List-inspired policy posture, two centuries of peace for Japan came to an end. As stated by Richard Samuels in his book *Rich Nation, Strong Army*, the *fukoku kyōhei* ideology "brought war and devastation" to Japan and Asia.[60] This was not a positive legacy.

In one review of nationalism and violence, the conclusion was that "the increased lethality of twentieth wars" should be attributed to "technology rather than nationalism."[61] What this view ignores is that technology and nationalism can form a unified whole in what has been called the "techno-military paradigm," and this paradigm has been associated with manufacturing in the minds of both politicians and policymakers.[62] Consider, for example, the contemporary US journalist Michael Lind who calls for a merging of international trade and national security policies with trade policy serving national security goals. For example, Lind states that "any country which hopes to be an independent great power must be able to obtain and maintain its own state-of-the-art manufacturing sector." He continues:[63]

> Many of the same factories that produce capital goods or civilian consumer goods can be converted to produce weapons. It is thus not enough for rival powers to monitor each other's standing armies, navies, fleets and stocks of weaponry; they must also monitor the overall industrial

capacity of their actual or potential rivals. Industrial capacity, in turn, has to be defined broadly to include the entire economy of the rival state—not only its factories, but also its infrastructure, energy and telecommunications system, resources, workforce and financial system.

This is a vision, described by Lind as a "new economic nationalism," in which entire economies are pitted against each other and domestic manufacturing sectors are "the basis of national military power." The link between industry and war established by List is alive and well nearly two centuries after he published *The National System*.[64] Unfortunately, it is entirely misguided.

Manufacturing and Services

Regarding the service sector and the knowledge economy, Michael Lind states that "a country cannot defeat its enemies with cat video apps." This is cute but totally misleading. As we have seen, even in the nineteenth century no less in the contemporary era, overall economic progress has reflected productivity increases in services. As stressed by many economists, the important factor here is *producer* or *intermediate services*.[65] The types of producer services that can support manufactured exports are transport and logistics services, telecommunications services, electricity services and financial services. Commercial banking and insurance services can also be relevant here. Indeed, there is a great deal of research in what has become known as the "servicification" of manufacturing.

Consider, for example, the trade economist Rupa Chanda, who states that "manufacturing firms today are buying and producing more services than ever before and are also selling and exporting more services which are embodied in their products. [...] Services are becoming important as both inputs and outputs for manufacturing."[66] Countries that ignore these long-standing trends risk being caught behind both a conceptual curve and empirical reality. This new reality even has implications for export competitiveness, a perennial occupation of economic nationalists. First, there are exports of services themselves, recognized by the mercantilists of the seventeenth century but often ignored today. Second, exports of goods are very much reliant on services. In fact, the export of *manufactured* goods is *dependent* on the *services* sector, including trade in services.[67]

Even if we accept Lind's zero-sum military approach to economics (and we should not), military preparedness and operations, like manufacturing, are entirely dependent on services. In the words of one researcher, these include "the construction, maintenance and operation of military bases; equipment maintenance; food service; transportation; communications and IT support;

and supply chain management."[68] Neglect of these factors led to the failures of the Russian army in Ukraine at the beginning of their 2022 invasion. The fact is that, along with the "servicification" of manufacturing, there is the "servicification" of the military. Although economic nationalists might not recognize this, effective military planners do.[69]

Recall from the beginning of the chapter that there was a distinction between spinning and weaving in the Industrial Revolution. This is an early example of a value chain. Currently, much of the global economy consists of or is influenced by GVCs, the series of tasks involved in developing, assembling, selling and serving a product. We also talked about the importance of value added for long-run economic development. Given the complexity of contemporary GVCs, it is important to ask where most of their value added is to be found. As it turns out, it is not always in the assembly or manufacturing stage but rather "upstream" and "downstream" from assembly in services of various kinds.[70]

Observations such as these were generalized into a visual depiction by Stan Shih, the founder and CEO of the Taiwanese company Acer. Shih proposed what was to become known as the "smile curve." This curve is depicted in Figure 3.3 and plots tasks or stages of production in a GVC along the horizontal axis and value added on the vertical axis. The smile curve suggests that the greatest value added is to be found in upstream tasks such as research and development (R&D), branding and design, as well as in downstream tasks such as distribution, marketing and after sales service. The smallest amount of value added is often to be found in the manufacturing or assembly stage of the GVC.

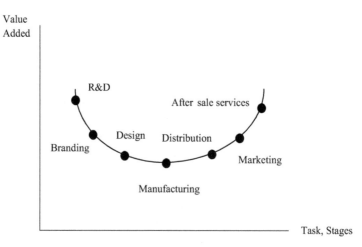

Figure 3.3 The smile curve. Source: Adapted from Gupta (2017).

Why does the smile curve matter? Economic nationalists in high-income countries mistakenly focus on manufacturing and assembly as the great hope for economic revival. This is often contained in the lament that "we don't make anything anymore!" While it is true that much of the "making" has moved to low- and middle-income countries (LMICs), this is not necessarily a bad thing from a value-added point of view. For example, the economist Enrico Moretti has stated that "more assembly jobs in China and more customer assistance jobs in India ultimately mean more R&D jobs in America as well as more jobs for the professionals—advertisers, designers, analysts, accountants—who cluster around high-tech companies."[71] Moretti also offers evidence that what he calls "innovation" jobs at the ends of the smile curve have significant multiplier effects for local services, multiplier effects that are approximately *three times those of traditional manufacturing*.

The other implication of GVCs and the smile cure has been pointed out by international economists Robert Johnson and Guillermo Noguera and in a separate article by Robert Koopman, Zhi Wang and Shang-Jin Wei.[72] This is the fact that GVCs and their distributed tasks imply that trade in value added values can differ significantly from gross trade values. Consequently, the gross value, bilateral trade balances that economic nationalists tend to highlight can be a misleading guide to the more realistic, value-added trade balances between countries. We will return to this issue in Chapter 5.

Conceptually, then, it is important to expand our scope beyond manufacturing and industry, to free ourselves from the predilections of Friedrich List, and recognize the empirical realities of not just modern economies but even those of the past. If the world List invoked ever existed, it is long past. Nonetheless, zero-sum thinking is a recurrent trap, and one that we need to take seriously. This is our next task.

Chapter 4

ZERO-SUM THINKING

Behind mercantilist and neo-mercantilist policies is the implicit notion that international economic transactions tend to be *zero sum* in nature. In many expressions of economics nationalism, for example, exports are a win, while imports are a loss. This formula is largely at variance with the results of international economics, but this kind of *zero-sum thinking* seems to be hardwired into human psychology. As it turns out, this is a field of inquiry in psychological sciences, and it shows that zero-sum thinking, if not universal, is a very real phenomenon with implications for understanding economic nationalism.

Game theory has been one of the most fundamental developments in the social sciences, and it had its origin in a paper by the mathematician John von Neumann on two-person, zero-sum games.[1] In zero-sum games, the available resources and rewards are fixed, and one person's gain is another's loss. Subsequently, however, this original contribution was generalized to the possibility of non-zero-sum games by von Neumann and Oskar Morgenstern in their book *Theory of Games and Economic Behavior.*[2] In this more general context, resources and rewards can increase, and there are win-win outcomes that can be achieved via cooperation.

Among researchers across many different fields, actual zero-sum games are considered to be *rare*. The problem is that even if a game is non-zero sum, it can be *perceived* as zero sum, limiting win-win outcomes and cutting off cooperative strategies.[3] The possibility and perhaps prevalence of this zero-sum bias has profound implications. As stated by one set of researchers:[4]

Misappraisals of a situation or domain as zero-sum even when it is objectively and explicitly non-zero-sum are far from rare. These misappraisals bear critical implications because the strategies that are appropriate in real zero-sum situations (e.g., aggression instead of cooperation) can be detrimental in non-zero-sum situations—leading to worse social and economic outcomes for all concerned.

Economic nationalism is largely a zero-sum enterprise, and it can dramatically shape impressions and beliefs at both the individual and collective levels. This can have significant impacts in the form of lost potential gains in international economic relations and even in domestic political coherence. We will explore some of these implications in this chapter.

Market Transactions

Basic economics shows that, under a set of assumptions, market transactions provide gains for participants. These transactions also tend to provide positive social welfare.[5] There are indeed some important conditions where this does not occur, but it is the general case. For example, one set of researchers who investigated the psychology of zero-sum thinking began with this idea, noting:[6]

> Buyers do not buy something they value less than their price, and sellers do not sell something they value more. Within this range between the buyer's maximum and the seller's minimum, both parties benefit from the transaction. [...] Although people are not fully rational, they are not fools either: Absent coercion or deception, we rarely cede something we value highly for something we value less.

To be a bit more formal, on the seller side, there is a minimum willingness to accept, say P_S, while on the buyer's side, there is a maximum willingness to pay, say P_B. When $P_S < P_B$, there is room for negotiations or market transactions. The buyer's maximum willingness to pay is above the seller's minimum willingness to accept, and there are net gains to be made via market transactions.[7] This is the general case.

That said, coercion and deception are more common than we usually admit. Forced labor still exists, criminal market transactions are not unusual, and relevant information can be missing in some important instances. In such cases, there is no relevant "range" between buyer and seller that has real meaning. Outside of coercion and deception, however, there is. The misperception of these potential mutual gains can lead to zero-sum thinking or, as it is sometimes called, *win-win denial*. These same researchers suggest that zero-sum thinking in economic matters is actually "endemic," so it is worth considering this possibility in some detail.[8]

The Economic Psychology of International Trade

The potential "range" between buyers and sellers, the potential market gains for participants, applies to international markets as well, that is, to international trade. This appears in the form of demonstrated "gains from trade" among countries. We mentioned in Chapter 2 that Ricardo's principle of comparative advantage is known as a "difficult idea." While economists tend to complain about people's lack of appreciation of it, they often forget that it is indeed *difficult*.[9] Researchers working in economic psychology do not make this mistake. Here is one example:[10]

> Ricardo's theory is not obvious. [...] Hence it would be understandable if its implications were not clear to all lay-people, and it is possible that anti-trade attitudes might result from a failure to comprehend it. It is difficult to comprehend because it requires consideration of two ratios. It says, in essence, that everyone is better off if everyone does what they are *relatively* most efficient at doing.

Those who teach principles of economics can attest to this fact. What is sometimes called "ratio reasoning" is indeed difficult for many students, and a lack of understanding of comparative advantage does seem to be implicated in attitudes against trade.[11] The subject is also muddied by economists themselves who apply the gains from trade outside of its appropriate realm, to international financial transactions and the protection of IP, in an overall support of broad economic globalization.[12] Ricardo's difficult idea is actually more narrowly cast.

If Ricardo's idea is difficult (and it is), then individuals might (and do) engage in what psychological scientists call "heuristic substitution." This is the tendency to replace a difficult question by an easier one.[13] For example, neo-mercantilists' notions of a country as a business and exports as sales become the default easier problem. Unfortunately, this easier problem is often misleading because countries are not businesses. Nonetheless, this kind of heuristic substitution underlies much of economic nationalist agendas.

There is also the issue of dynamics. At a fundamental level, international trade is about *change*. As amply demonstrated by economic historians Ronald Findlay and Kevin O'Rourke in their book *Power and Plenty*, these changes are relentless and go back millennia to ancient times. There is just no getting around them. However, in the transition from the mercantilist era to the era of the steamship and the reduced transportation costs in the nineteenth century, domestic politics in response to trade-induced changes became more important. In their words:[14]

> Before 1815, [...] international trade had been seen by governments as the means of extracting rents, by driving a wedge between the prices paid to producers in one location and those paid by consumers in another. The question then was who was going to get these rents, and

[...] the result was international competition between overseas trading companies, and frequent warfare in the age of mercantilism. Trade-related conflict was thus inherently *inter*national in nature. Cheaper transportation and intercontinental trade in competing goods implied that the politics of trade would now also involve *intra*national conflict, between those groups in society who gained as a result of international trade and those who lost.

In other words, with the advent of the steamship, no less the more recent container ship and airfreight, the *domestic politics of trade* began to matter. The international economist and economic historian Barry Eichengreen makes a similar argument in the realm of international finance. In the move from the nineteenth to the twentieth century, defending the fixed exchange rate pegs of the former century became increasingly difficult. While capital controls initially held off the reckoning, eventually domestic politics began to matter for international finance as well as international trade.[15]

As these new political voices began to surface, the way that individuals *think* about international trade increasingly began to matter, and economic psychology gives us some further insights into how this thinking might affect the politics of trade. These insights also shed light on why heuristic substitution is part of economic nationalism.

A first insight is that there might be an inherent resistance to change, namely the *status quo effect*. The status quo effect is a concept from decision-making research and refers to situations in which decision-makers tend to overvalue the current situation relative to available alternatives.[16] Empirically, the effect appears to be real, and there are alternative explanations for it. It can reflect rational decision-making in the face of risk, uncertainty and transactions costs, or it can reflect cognitive misperceptions (loss aversion and anchoring). It can also stem from psychological commitment to past decisions and their sunk costs, as well as to regret avoidance.

A second insight is that perceptions of *fairness* matter and that fairness is often interpreted in terms of reciprocity. Further, this reciprocity can be interpreted in bilateral terms where imports from a particular country are "unfair" unless that country is also a market for exports. Further, such considerations can be more important than positive economic welfare effects (gains from trade).[17] As we will see, however, when reciprocity is applied to bilateral trade balances, it can lead policies astray.

We see that international trade always involves a challenge to the status quo. More fundamentally, it involves winners and losers. The status quo effect can act as a norm against any changes that might cause harm or unfairness, including a psychological resistance to the harm and perceived unfairness caused by trade-induced economic changes.[18] It is human nature to expect that changes to the status quo norm to be addressed through some sort of reciprocal notion of fairness. Consider the following description of reciprocal fairness by trade economist Steven Suranovic:[19]

> Reciprocity fairness can be separated into two distinct categories. Actions which have beneficial effects upon others and which are reciprocated with beneficial responses will be called positive reciprocity fairness. Actions which have negative effects on others which are reciprocated with harmful responses will be labeled negative reciprocity fairness. An important aspect of reciprocity fairness is that the size of the two effects should be approximately equal in value. In other words, if person A takes an action which has an effect upon person B of value X, then it is reciprocally fair for B to take an action that will have an effect upon A, with value approximately equal to X. This is valid whether the value X is positive or negative.

If this notion of fairness is operant, and if imports are heuristically viewed as a harm, then it is short step to neo-mercantilist policy proposals and concern with bilateral trade balances. This then becomes a reference point for economic nationalists alleging mistreatment by other countries.

Finally, there is also the possibility that zero-sum thinking can coalesce into *zero-sum belief*, a possibility considered in cross-cultural psychology. One set of researchers defined zero-sum belief as "a general belief system about the antagonist nature of social relations, shared by people in a society or culture and based on the implicit assumption that a finite amount of goods exists in the world, in which one person's winning makes others the losers, and vice versa."[20] While such a belief operates at the individual level, it can also become socially generalized into what is known as a *social axiom*, an untested belief about the world acquired through social interaction.[21] When this takes place, zero-sum beliefs become more firmly entrenched in societies, are difficult to dislodge and spill over into policymaking.

There is a final point to make regarding zero-sum thinking as it applies to international trade. We have discussed the principle of comparative advantage as a difficult idea. As it turns out, however, not all international trade is based on comparative advantage. There is also a great deal of trade based on product differentiation and economies of scale. In some notable cases, this results in two-way trade *within* sectors, an outcome that is not always well recognized by policymakers. Further, this two-way or *intra-industry trade* requires fewer economic dislocations than trade based on comparative advantage.[22] Two-way trade within sectors is also positive sum because it enlarges the range of products available while generally imposing fewer adjustment costs on the countries involved. The application of zero-sum thinking to this prominent type of trade is therefore even more misplaced than for trade based on comparative advantage.[23] But again, the concepts are difficult and subject to heuristic substitution.

Trade Balances and Zero-Sum Thinking

In open-economy macroeconomics, a country's overall trade balance is a result of the balance between aggregate domestic investment and aggregate domestic savings.[24] The overall trade balance is therefore a macroeconomic variable largely unaffected by trade policies. Trade policies can affect how this trade balance is apportioned among trading partners, but not the overall balance itself. This is another "difficult idea," along with Ricardo's principle of comparative advantage. Zero-sum thinking often ignores this difficult idea and uses a country's overall trade balance as a measure of success or failure and as a measure of "fairness."

There is a second List-inspired step to this logic, and this is to go further and substitute the balance of trade in *goods* for the overall trade balance because goods represent "industry," and services are therefore less important. A relevant example of this is the Trump administration in the United States. Upon entering into office in January 2017, President Trump issued an executive order calling for a report on "significant trade deficits." This executive order stated:[25]

> For many years, the United States has not obtained the full scope of benefits anticipated under a number of international trade agreements or from participating in the World Trade Organization. The United States annual trade deficit in goods exceeds $700 billion, and the overall trade deficit exceeded $500 billion in 2016.

The implied cause of these deficits was not macroeconomic balances but unfair trade policies:

> The United States must address the challenges to economic growth and employment that may arise from large and chronic trade deficits and the unfair and discriminatory trade practices of some of our trading partners. Unfair and discriminatory practices by our trading partners can deny Americans the benefits that would otherwise accrue from free and fair trade, unduly restrict the commerce of the United States, and put the commerce of the United States at a disadvantage compared to that of foreign countries.

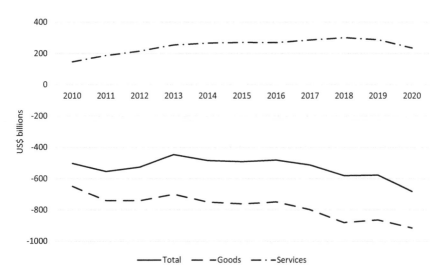

Figure 4.1 United States' trade balance, 2010–20. Source: https://www.census.gov.

It is worth assessing this policy stance in the light of the actual trade balance of the United States during the Trump administration. We can see this in Figure 4.1. The first thing we see is that, during the Trump administration, the overall trade balance *worsened*. Given the strong protectionist measure enacted during this administration to be discussed in Chapter 5, how was this possible? The answer is macroeconomic. The signature piece of legislation of the Trump administration was a tax cut, which reduced aggregate domestic savings (via reduced government savings) and therefore contributed to an expanded overall trade deficit as suggested by basic macroeconomic principles.

Disaggregating, the beloved trade in goods balance worsened as well. Given that this was perhaps the most important economic variable in US president Trump's worldview, this fact is notable. It is also notable that the balance of trade in services, on a long-term upward trend before the Trump administration, also worsened, contributing to a more precipitous decline in the overall balance.

The Trump administration's executive order's first call for action on the part of the US government was as follows:

Assess the major causes of the trade deficit, including, as applicable, differential tariffs, non-tariff barriers, injurious dumping, injurious government subsidization, intellectual property theft, forced technology transfer, denial of worker rights and labor standards, and any other form of discrimination against the commerce of the United States or other factors contributing to the deficit.

Each of these targets was a trade or trade-related policy of some kind. Each might have had relevance in the trade policy realm and could have been reasonably investigated. But they were not relevant to the overall trade balance of the United States. The lesson here is that misconstrued, zero-sum thinking is no match for economic realities. Indeed, as seen in Figure 4.1, it can fail even by its own standards.

Insights from Negotiations Theory

Along with the potentially difficult nature of the comparative advantage and balance of trade ideas, further insights regarding zero-sum thinking can be found in negotiations theory. Here the "range" between "buyer" and "seller" discussed above becomes a "zone of agreement."[26] Negotiation theorists often use a market transactions analogy even when they are considering negotiations outside of the market context. If the "buyer" and "seller" can reach an agreement, there are mutual gains to be achieved in the general negotiations case.

This economic view of negotiations lets us know what *should* happen. What happens in practice can be another and more complicated matter.[27] There are potential roles for both parochialism and constituencies. Each of these impacts the ability to effectively engage in the zone of agreement. Parochialism is another term for in-group bias, something we will take up when we consider ethnicity in Chapter 6. It can involve individuals cooperating with other individuals who they perceive as being "like them." This cooperation can increase the chances that zones of agreement will be recognized among like individuals. But it can motivate individuals to agree to things *outside* of zones of agreement, that is, to go against their own self-interest. This phenomenon has applicability to international, religious and ethnic conflict, particularly when resources are *perceived to be* scarce.[28] In such cases, zero-sum thinking reinforces itself.

There is a bit of a potential irony here. Individuals can *claim* to be operating for their own self-interest, but they interpret this self-interest in terms of a reference group, people "like them." Sometimes researchers refer to this as an "illusion," but it is salient, nonetheless. Such parochialism helps to explain a great deal regarding economic nationalism. In the trade context, for example, negotiators have cultural biases that become relevant.[29] They bargain for perceived in-groups in their own countries rather than for overall economic welfare.

Constituencies also turn out to be problematic for reaching non-zero-sum outcomes in zones of agreement. Politics relies on constituencies, and in the realm of international economic relations, the system of constituencies can be quite complex. As it turns out, however, constituencies can get in the way of positive outcomes. In the words of one set of researchers:[30]

> The pressure generated by constituencies toward loyalty, commitment, and advocacy of a particular position may not be in the best interest of either the constituency or the negotiator. Empirical evidence suggests that as a negotiator's commitment to an audience increases, his or her ability to perceive alternative proposals as worthwhile and to make concessions in the best interest of that constituency is significantly decreased.

Constituencies in international economic relations can include firms (including multinational enterprises (MNEs)), lobbying groups (representing firms in particular sectors), political parties and movements and even foreign governments. Their multiple nature can make international negotiations difficult. Further, within constituencies, the above-mentioned perceptions of *fairness* seem to matter a great deal, and this becomes important in the politics of international trade. As we stated, fairness in trade is often tied to reciprocity, and reciprocity is often set out in neo-mercantilist terms: if a country is to agree to import from another country, it must also be allowed to export to it. The requirements of perceived fairness and reciprocity can even lead to a country rejecting trade opportunities that might benefit it.[31] Further, fairness might need to be purely symbolic and even performative to past political muster.[32]

Trade economists Bernard Hoekman and Michel Kostecki have given us a useful typology of multilateral trade negotiations.[33] These MTNs are multi-issue, multistage, multiplayer, repeated games that take time to conclude successfully. They are therefore *complex*. Relatedly, *cognitive complexity* has been found to be important to find cooperative solutions in such negotiations.[34] In the absence of cognitive complexity, the default is "distributive bargaining," where the pie is fixed and there are only win–lose outcomes. It turns out that the distributive bargaining default is quite common, even among negotiators. The search for win-win outcomes is known as "integrative bargaining" and is critical to many kinds of negotiations, even ones that are not too complex.

The degree of cognitive complexity helps to determine whether negotiations fall into the distributive bargaining or integrative bargaining realms. Consider the description from one set of research psychologists:[35]

> Distributive bargaining, which is governed in large part by gamesmanship, nerve, and aggressiveness, is affected by personality factors that influence social interaction but not by problem-solving ability and

planfulness. In contrast, integrative bargaining, which is governed primarily by problem solving, is affected by enhanced understanding, creativity, and care. [...] The relative emphasis on tactics in distributive bargaining and problem solving in integrative bargaining seems to drive which individual differences are most important to understanding the influence of bargainer characteristics on negotiation outcomes.

Given the qualities of trade negotiations (multi-issue, multistage, multiplayer, repeated games), cognitive complexity characterized by problem-solving is a prerequisite for success, while gamesmanship and aggressiveness is a recipe for failure. As we will see in the next chapter, cognitive complexity has been in short supply in recent years. In particular, the Trump administration in the United States embraced distributive bargaining with a vengeance, perceiving integrative bargaining as too "soft." It is difficult not to conclude that the personality traits of that administration, in combination with a particular political psychology, supported that posture.

The Corporate Strategy Perspective

In 2000, *New York Times* editorialist Thomas Friedman published *The Lexus and the Olive Tree: Understanding Globalization*. He followed this up in 2005 with *The World Is Flat: A Brief History of the 21ˢᵗ Century*. To say that these books were well received is an understatement. For some years, they were the bibles of the globalization crowd, although one hears less about them now than then. Unfortunately, the books were *misleading* on many accounts, combining fascinating anecdotes with exaggerated claims that painted a distorted view of the global economy. Consequently, despite their popularity, international economists largely ignored them.

Corporate strategist Pankaj Ghemawat did not ignore them and emphatically stated his objections to them. Ghemawat stresses that, in response to the intellectual fad of seeing the world as "flat" and distance as irrelevant, corporations began to overly focus on expanding global operations to reap economies of scale, taking care to adjust to the local environment in each destination country, a process known as localization. In his words, "in many if not most cases, companies see globalization as a matter of taking a superior (by assumption) business model and extending it geographically, with necessary modifications, to maximize the firm's economies of scale" in a process of what might be called corporate imperialism.[36]

What this leaves out is a "strategy of differences" that is attuned to the myriad differences among countries, from labor costs to cultural and institutional differences. Regarding Friedman's assertion of global "flatness,"

Ghemawat states that it is "simply the latest in a series of exaggerated visions that also include the 'end of history' and the 'convergence of tastes.'"[37] If the world is indeed not "flat" (and it emphatically *is not*), then corporations can and perhaps should recognize and leverage differences.

Interestingly, Ghemawat relates the strategy of differences to Ricardo himself and his difficult idea of comparative advantage, stating:[38]

Greater managerial sensitivity to comparative advantage would [...] help sharpen the location strategies of multinational firms. Focusing on comparative rather than absolute advantage could help counter the tendency to focus on "one best place" in the world for producing or sourcing a product or component. [...] And broadening firms' locational consideration sets [...] can also boost development opportunities in countries that tend to get overlooked.

How is this related to zero-sum thinking? A frontier model of exploiting scale economies, while relevant to some extent, involves a somewhat zero-sum calculation: one firm's scale economies take place at the expense of another's. The search for differences of many kinds among locations opens the door to an expanded set of potentially mutual gains. The fact that a leading corporate strategist is making these sorts of arguments suggests that they might be worth considering.

Although not specifically addressed by Ghemawat, as we will see in Chapter 9 on techno-nationalism, the strategy of differences will also prove to be important for the concept and practice of *open innovation*. This refers to firms increasingly recognizing differences in technological capabilities across firms in different countries and leveraging them via cooperative R&D projects for mutual gains. Given the increasingly important role of knowledge in modern economies, open innovation is an important component of international economic relations.

The Military Analogy

As we saw in Chapter 3, economic nationalism and its emphasis on manufacturing capacity as a measure of economic power has a military flavor to it. This might be because economic nationalism and attitudes toward the military share a tendency to zero-sum thinking. As it turns out, there is empirical evidence for this, once again from the field of psychology. For example, one set of research psychologists has shown that levels of militarization across countries are positively correlated with a measure of zero-sum thinking.[39] It is not hard to imagine that the preference for distributive bargaining over integrative bargaining, associated with zero-sum belief systems, plays a role in this.

Yet the application of zero-sum thinking to military affairs is now seen as relic of the past with little current applicability. Consider, for example, the reflections of US colonel Christopher Holshek who has a 30-year career with the US military. In analyzing that military institution, he notes the "incongruities of its overwhelming national security, hard-power psychology."[40] He states:[41]

> In the 21st century, coercive power is losing both its dominance and appropriateness. Hard power is more threats-based, resource-intensive, zero-sum, reactive, and short term (i.e., tactical). [...] Soft power, in turn, is more suitable to collaborative, human security settings. It is community-based, largely resident in civil society and the private sector, and is more adaptable, economical, [...] and durable (i.e., strategic).

It is easy to see how hard power is associated with the zero-sum psychology of distributive bargaining, while soft power is associated with the win-win psychology of integrative bargaining and cognitive complexity. Holshek's association of tactical with the former and strategic with the latter is notable in the US context, because even those positively disposed toward the US military have noted its "persistent strategy deficit."[42] In other "great power" context, this strategic deficit was also on dramatic display during Russia's 2022 disastrous invasion of Ukraine. Regarding Putin's decision to invade, one observer stated that "a master tactician but inept strategist, he made his most powerful miscalculation."[43]

A relevant factor here is *hostile attribution bias* in which zero-sum thinking makes is more likely to interpret a situation as hostile even when it might not be.[44] This can even have the impact of reducing cognitive and social resources allocated to assessing the situation and tilting the balance away from soft power and cooperation and toward hard power and conflict. Correcting these deficits across countries would require abandoning zero-sum thinking, recognizing integrative bargaining and utilizing cognitive complexity to reduce the threat of unnecessary wars and their profound economic disruptions.

Democratic Processes

We mentioned in Chapter 1 the work of Theodor Adorno who coauthored *The Authoritarian Personality*. In this book, Adorno and his colleagues address the social psychological features of fascism, particularly its intolerance of ambiguity and its propensity to discriminate against out-groups. Indeed, there is a troubling link between zero-sum thinking and authoritarianism that poses an ongoing threat to democratic processes. The problem is that democratic processes and representative government depend on a degree of non-zero-sum mindsets. While electoral outcomes appear to be zero sum, representative government as a whole is not. Consider one set of researchers:[45]

> Meaningful differences in values, priorities, and approaches to policy notwithstanding, residents and citizens in a society ultimately have far more interests that are shared rather than opposed. Operating from this basic principle, a non-zero-sum view of political efficacy relies upon serving these shared interests through both cooperation and negotiation.

Despite this, there is an unfortunate tendency for zero-sum thinking to undermine the democratic processes of representative government. This can happen through a process of the projection of zero-sum mindsets to both situations and political opponents that reduces the space for political negotiation, the rejection of possible policies where some degree of consensus is to be found, and the potential intensification of violent rhetoric.[46] Zero-sum mindsets have been implicated in a lack of commitment to voting rights and the legitimacy of political violence.[47] More generally, it appears to undermine *trust* upon which representative governments depend. This possibility has been well described by the same set of researchers:[48]

> First, in a zero-sum world, everyone is a rival. That is, if another person's success requires your failure and you expect most people to seek their own success, then this entails that they seek your harm. Since perception [...] is the primary driver to trust, a bias toward perceiving rivalry and hostility should also bias one away from trust. Second, another essential feature of the zero-sum world is the belief in limited goods, or fixed scarcity. If one tends to see resources a relatively fixed, then one may also systematically underestimate the possibility of growth. While beliefs about the nature of scarcity should not directly influence the beliefs about the trustworthiness of others, it may alter the calculus of trusting behavior by reducing the perceived incentives for trust.

The problem here is that successful representative governments (as well as successful economies) depend on trust. This, of course, was the main point of political scientist Frances Fukuyama's famous book on this issue. In that book, he states that "in all successful [...] societies [...] communities are united by trust."[49] When this trust erodes from zero-sum thinking and distributive

political bargaining, this also erodes representative government and successful, thriving economies.

An Intuitive Appeal

What are we to make of research into zero-sum thinking? From several perspectives, there appears to be an intuitive or heuristic, win–lose default that is
often operable, even when the prospects are win-win. This can limit potential
economic gains. This win–lose default is also often a heuristic for fairness. For
this reason, one set of researchers concluded that there is reason to think that
mercantilist thinking is widespread because "it maintains an intuitive psychological appeal."[50] We need to recognize and confront this intuitive appeal.

   We also need to be careful about what we are saying and not saying in this
chapter. In our critique of zero-sum thinking, we are not saying that there
are not both winners and losers from expanded international trade. The
local losses involved from expanded international trade are significant and
can extend to economically ravaged communities around the world. As will
see, however, the policies (and non-policies) of zero-sum thinking, economic
nationalists are often wide off the mark, do little to help these communities
and often enflame ethnic tensions. There are much better ways forward, but
these require the cognitive complexity of real policy analysis.

Chapter 5

BATTLEGROUND WTO

The WTO sits on the edge of Lake Geneva in a building that once housed the International Labor Organization and the United Nations High Commissioner of Refugees (UNHCR). We said a few words about it in Chapter 1. It has the distinction of coming under criticism from all points along the political spectrum. This criticism began with the political left in the 1990s who were outraged by certain rulings that affected environmental policies and spread to labor interests who were concerned about trade and wages in manufacturing. It has now moved to the political right in the form of new economic nationalists who, at times, appear to be bent on destroying the institution and its rules-based global trading regime.

Few WTO critics take the time to try to understand it. Despite many flaws, it is an international trade institution that embodies the important principle of *multilateralism*. As such, it is a response to the tendency toward zero-sum thinking and distributive bargaining discussed in the preceding chapter. What exactly is multilateralism? International relations scholar John Ruggie emphasizes that "multilateralism refers to coordinating relations among three or more states in accordance with certain principles."[1] Understanding these principles is important.

In his investigation of multilateralism, Ruggie begins with Nazi Germany and Albert Hirschman's *National Power and the Structure of Foreign Trade* discussed in Chapter 1. He emphasizes that the trade relations pursued by the Nazi government were *bilateralist*. Here is his description:[2]

> The essence of the German international trade regime was that the state negotiated "reciprocal" agreements with its foreign trading partners. These negotiations determined which goods and services were to be exchanged, their quantities, and their price. Often, Germany deliberately imported more from its partners than it exported to them. But it required that its trading partners liquidate their claims on Germany by reinvesting there or by purchasing deliberately overpriced German goods. Thus, its trading partners were doubly dependent on Germany.

This is not multilateralism. In the WTO, any bilateral agreement on trade in a particular good is generalized to *all members* through what is known as the *most-favored nation* (MFN) principle. If Japan lowers a tariff on Indonesia's exports of lumber, it must also lower its tariff on the exports of lumber from all other member countries. MFN is a core principle of multilateralism that allows countries to escape the confines of bilateralism.

MFN was a feature of British commercial agreements in the nineteenth century, most famously in the Cobden–Chevalier Treaty of 1860. Recall from Chapter 2 the Methuen Treaty of 1703 between England and Portugal. This agreement was one of "exclusive advantage" in which Britain reduced tariffs on Portuguese wine while maintaining tariffs on French wine. In the Cobden–Chevalier Treaty, England and France committed themselves to extend to each other any tariff concessions they made to third parties. This was a trade policy revolution in the form of MFN.

The Cobden–Chevalier Treaty set the stage for several additional treaties in Western Europe, scaled back mercantilist trade privileges and supported Western European trade expansion in the latter half of the nineteenth century. This treaty has been the subject of rather extensive research, nearly all of which suggests that it was central to forming a network of approximately fifty bilateral treaties in European countries. The evidence that the Cobden–Chevalier Treaty ushered in an era of "free trade" or that it increased overall trade volumes in Western Europe is contested, and perhaps rightly so. However, the evidence that it had a positive effect in those specific sectors that were covered by the network of trade agreements is stronger.[3] Further, the network structure supported trade liberalization through the outbreak of World War I. As described by trade economist and economic historian Douglas Irwin, for example:[4]

> During 1860–1913, world trade relations centered around a network of bilateral trade treaties containing the MFN clause. Each country was generally free to set and change its tariff code so long at it adhered to the MFN clause. These arrangements arose without multilateral cooperation. Yet despite the lack of any oversight mechanism or any institutional basis, this regime [...] brought about relatively low trade barriers—almost exclusively tariffs, with an absence of quantitative restrictions, voluntary restraint agreements, exchange controls, and the like—and very little discrimination.

Importantly, the Cobden–Chevalier Treaty became a model for MFN treatment in the 1947 GATT and subsequently the WTO.[5] MFN is institutionalized in Article I of the GATT that famously states:

Any advantage, favour, privilege or immunity granted by any contracting party to any product originating in or destined for any other country shall be accorded immediately and unconditionally to the like product originating in or destined for the territories of all other contracting parties.

The genius of GATT Article I is that it creates network effects across the entire membership of the GATT/WTO system, institutionalizing the Cobden–Chevalier innovation. The multiple, positive effects of the MFN principle have been identified by trade economists Bernard Hoekman and Michel Kostecki:[6]

It ensures that deals that are struck between two countries to lower tariffs are not undone subsequently by one of the parties offering better terms to another country. [...] Most favoured nation also reduces overall negotiating costs—once a negotiation has been concluded with one country, the results extend to all. [...] Most favoured nation also provides smaller countries with a guarantee that larger countries will not exploit their market power by raising tariffs against them in periods when times are bad and domestic industries are clamouring for protection, or alternatively, give specific countries preferential treatment for foreign policy reasons.

But there is more. The multilateral trading regime is also *rules based*. Even a quick dabble into the goings-on of the WTO reveals that it all comes down to agreed-upon *texts* (and their interpretation). These multiple texts specify a system of conduct that all members agree to follow. They include allowed safeguard measures, transparency procedures and effective dispute settlement. The whims of particular WTO members are constrained by these rules. It is not an exaggeration to say that these features make the WTO a unique international institution, one that has done much to ensure a reasonably functional international trading system.

The US Imprint

As previously stated, the WTO and its GATT predecessor are multilateral institutions, forged in the dying days of World War II. A main protagonist in the move toward multilateralism was the United States, and this support for multilateralism was not just confined to trade. As emphasized by Ruggie and others, after 1945, the United States assisted in the development of many multilateral institutions and organizations. Ruggie states that "for American postwar planners, multilateralism in its generic sense served as a *foundational architectural principle* on the basis of which to reconstruct the postwar world."[7] Indeed, the term associated with the efforts of the United States in this period is "open" rather than "closed," and this represented a "new thinking" about international economic relations.[8] Multilateralism at that time was largely an American construction.

Further, if one examines the subsequent history of the GATT/WTO system, it becomes clear that it was largely designed *by* and *for* the United States. The WTO is sometimes described as a "tripod" with the three legs being trade in goods, trade in services and trade-related IP. Regarding trade in goods, early on, the United States insisted on violating basic GATT principles to subsidize agriculture and has been doing so ever since. If, say, Thailand was to subsidize its electrical machinery sector, it would be caught afoul of a WTO violation, but the US can and does subsidize its agricultural sector with abandon. The European Union (EU) does the same under its Common Agricultural Policy.

Turning to services, the WTO's General Agreement on Trade in Services (GATS) was explicitly written to support the US-based Coalition of Service Industries (CSI), which began in 1982 to lobby strenuously for the inclusion of the GATS in the institution. The US Trade Representative introduced the issue at that time and was equally aggressive in its support.[9] The purpose of the GATS was to support the US financial, telecommunications and business/professional services sectors. The non-negotiable position of the United States was that trade in services be included as part of the 1995 agreement establishing the WTO. It naturally prevailed, and the US services sector has benefitted ever since. Indeed, in a speech in 2003, US trade representative Robert Zoellick reiterated the US interest in continued services trade liberalization at a meeting of the CSI.[10]

The WTO Agreement on Trade-Related Aspects of Intellectual Property Rights (TRIPS) was also explicitly written to support US economic interests. This began in 1974 with an Advisory Committee on Trade Policy Negotiations headed up by the CEO of the US pharmaceutical company Pfizer. The advisory committee was followed by the Intellectual Property Committee of US-based multinationals that authored a position paper under the direction of IBM.[11] Many prominent international economists correctly argued that IP protection had no place in the WTO, but they were ignored. The inclusion of IP as part of the WTO was another nonnegotiable position of the United States, and it again prevailed. Given the radically broad scope of the agreement, across IP of all kinds, US businesses have reaped significant benefits.

Finally, there are the dispute resolution provisions of the WTO. These were also written with US interests in mind, namely, to enforce the expected US wins in services and IP. While it is true that other WTO members have successfully brought dispute settlement cases against the United States, the United States has also had many significant victories, including against China.[12] In writing the dispute settlement agreement, the United States inadvertently created the most robust dispute settlement system in the world, one that could be effectively used as a model for other realms of conflict. The past claim by US president Trump that "We lose the lawsuits, almost all of the lawsuits in the WTO" was *entirely false*.[13] Nonetheless, US economic nationalists often make that claim for political effect.

Evidence

Is there any evidence that the GATT/WTO system has been helpful as a trade institution? International economists have a general sense that membership in the previous GATT and current WTO has tended to have a positive effect in international trade. There has been some empirical dispute on this matter, however. In a famous research article, economist Andrew Rose provides evidence that GATT/WTO membership per se has had very little impact on overall trade levels, but that the WTO's Generalized System of Preferences (GSP) does.[14] These results had some impact.

There are several issues that arise in Rose's research. First, he examines overall levels of trade in goods, not in specific sectors or trade in services. Second, while membership in the institution does not affect overall trade in goods, an aspect of the institution (GSP) does. Third, subsequent research has largely overturned Rose's initial results with evidence that the GATT/WTO has indeed contributed to expanded global trade. There are several statistical issues behind these different results, but the subsequent studies do seem more valid than the initial study.[15] That said, this issue is probably best seen as one of necessarily mixed results at this juncture.

But the question as to whether WTO membership increases trade or not might be the wrong one. As several researchers have pointed out, the real issue at hand is the overall institutional regime and the relative certainty it provides vis-à-vis potential trade wars. As stated by one team of researchers, for example, "the main value of the WTO—and the real risk of its deterioration—lies in cooperation and conflict avoidance, a value that goes well beyond a simple calculation of rising or falling trade costs."[16] Any historical analysis of trade wars would suggest that this is indeed the correct, broader perspective, and that protecting the global public good of the trading regime is of utmost importance to maintaining global welfare.

The Dragon in the Room

In 2001, after 15 years of fraught negotiations, China joined the WTO, and things have not been quite the same since. It is important to remember that, in the bilateral trade relationship between China and the United States, the United States began granting China MFN status in the 1980s, so China's WTO membership was not as dramatic a change as sometimes alleged. One thing that did change was the reduction in uncertainty regarding the application of MFN to China, as well as the network effects across the entire WTO membership.[17]

It is clear that China's accession to the WTO helped to facilitate an unprecedented expansion of exports to the rest of the world, what one set of researchers called "among the most significant events in international trade in recent decades."[18] It is important, however, to put this expansion in some context. While it was large in absolute value, it was not necessarily large relative to China's GDP. We can begin to get a sense of this in Figure 5.1, which plots exports as a percent of GDP for China, Germany, the United Kingdom and the United States. We can see that, after 2001, China's exports as a percent of GDP grew significantly from 20 in 2001 to 36 in 2006. At this peak, it was still below Germany's 41 percent. Thereafter, China's exports as a percent

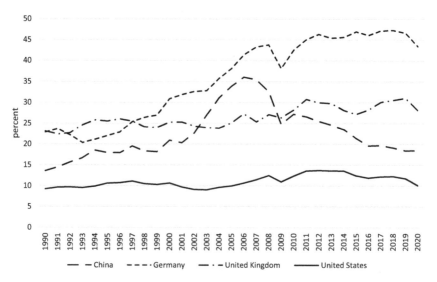

Figure 5.1 Exports of goods and services as a percent of GDP. Source: databank. worldbank.org.

of GDP declined, while Germany's increased. In 2020, China's exports as a percent of GDP were 18.5 percent, below where they were in 2001 and much closer to the United States' 10 percent than Germany's 43 percent and the United Kingdom's 28 percent.

It is also worth recognizing that a significant amount of China's exports reflects imports of intermediate products that are assembled, often for MNEs from other countries, including the United States and EU member countries. Statistics on trade in value added compiled by the Organization for Economic Cooperation and Development show that the foreign value-added content of China's exports was 26 percent in 2005, declining to 10 percent in 2016.[19] So the peak in exports as a percent of GDP was also a peak in the use of imported intermediate goods in producing those exports. Consequently, China's value-added exports are much less than its gross exports, as is the bilateral value-added trade deficit of the United States with China.[20] Using the gross value, bilateral trade deficit of the United States with China as a political measure of "unfairness" is therefore misleading.[21]

Despite this context, one of the most contentious issues in China's membership in the WTO has been its impacts on labor markets in the United States. This connection was made almost immediately, but it was not until the research of economists David Autor, David Dorn and Gordon Hanson in 2013 that real evidence began to emerge.[22] This work looked at the 1990–2007 period and attributed one-quarter of the decline in US manufacturing employment to import competition from China. A subsequent study with some of the same researchers put the figure at 10 percent for the 1999–2011 period.[23] This became known as the "China shock." These studies spawned many more, with varying results, most of them negative, including for the EU.[24]

There are also relevant considerations regarding what economists refer to as "general equilibrium effects." First, countries export as well as they import. This side of the story was addressed by Robert Feenstra and his colleagues. As it turns out, US exports rose significantly throughout this period as well, including to China, and these researchers have shown that the employment gains from this increase in exports are of the same order of magnitude as the employment losses on the import side.[25] From the US employment perspective, the China shock might have been less shocking than previously thought. We do need to be careful here because workers gaining jobs in export-competitive sectors will not necessarily be those losing jobs in import-competing sectors. Therefore, the rough offset of job gains and losses is compatible with a significant amount of labor market dislocation. Nonetheless, gains in export-related jobs are significant, and the China shock appears to have ended in the late 2000s.[26]

Second, the manufacturing sectors affected by imports from China are only part of the US economy. For example, one thorough study found that workers affected by imports from China tended to locate to construction and services sectors, which in turn benefited from lower intermediate input costs due to these imports.[27] Indeed, some studies find that, given the extent of labor market flexibility in the United States, the overall employment effects of the "China shock" are actually positive for this reason.[28]

Despite these important employment issues, a great deal of attention regarding China's WTO membership has focused on the role of its state-owned enterprises (SOEs). In the WTO China accession report, a Chinese government representative is quoted as saying that:[29]

> State-owned enterprises had been reformed by a clear definition of property rights and responsibilities, a separation of government from enterprise, and scientific management. A modern enterprise system had been created for the state-owned sector, and the latter was gradually getting on the track of growth through independent operation, responsible for its own profits and losses. A nationwide unified and open market system had been developed.

Unfortunately, it is not clear that this had been actualized 20 years later, no less at that time. For example, writing in 2021, Petros Mavroidis and André Sapir concluded that "twenty years after its accession to the WTO, China is still a socialist country. The Chinese state continues to maintain a heavy hand in the country's economy and, consequently, its trade regime."[30] With SOEs in China accounting for approximately 25–30 percent of GDP, this point of view clearly has some validity, complicating China's role in the WTO.[31]

As Mavroidis and Sapir point out, however, the WTO's dispute settlement system has been open to treating Chinese SOEs as "public bodies" and thus actionable under its Agreement on Subsidies and Countervailing Measures (ASCM). This offers a narrow pathway to addressing some of the issues that have arisen regarding Chinese SOEs. This approach was generally supported by the US Obama administration's Trans-Pacific Partnership (TPP) in its Chapter 17. Unfortunately, in a fit of pique, US president Trump withdrew the United States from the TPP on his first day in office. Nonetheless, and with characteristic inconsistency, his administration strengthened the TPP Chapter 17 for inclusion in his modified North American Free Trade Agreement (NAFTA) known as the United States–Mexico–Canada Agreement (USMCA). Revisiting Chapter 17 of the TPP might play an important role in future trade negotiations.

Short of that, WTO actions have made it clear that the details of the China's Protocol of Accession are "justiciable." In other words, within the WTO, China can be held to account for the commitments it made in these protocols above and beyond standard WTO agreements. These apply to trade in goods, trade in services and IP protection (including technology transfer). Combing through the Protocol of Accession and holding China accountable to it would be a good first step to addressing the dragon in the WTO room. Unfortunately, as we will see, that is not what happened during the US Trump administration and the subsequent Biden administration.

Regarding China's behavior within the WTO, it is widely recognized among trade policy professionals that, when it suffers a loss in the WTO dispute settlement process, China mends its ways *in each instance*.[32] Its record is better than that of the EU and the United States. This suggests first that it is a "good citizen" within the WTO and second that, in instances where it violates WTO provisions, the dispute settlement process can be effectively used against it.

Threats from Within

Despite the WTO's significant contribution to maintaining an open trading system, as well as to global and US prosperity, beginning in 2017, the US Trump administration did everything in its power to undermine it. It even threatened to withdraw from it altogether, a sort of trade tantrum. Short of this, it sabotaged the very WTO dispute settlement system the United States designed. The main motivation here seems to have been not practical but ideological, a loathing of all things multilateral. Under the influence of this ideology, the creator became the destroyer.

The Trump administration rejected multilateralism in favor of aggressive bilateralism, including against longtime allies such as Canada and Western European countries. Trade economists Chad Bown and Douglas Irwin note that President Trump "made economic nationalism a centerpiece of his agenda in office" and viewed trade relationships as a zero-sum, win–lose game.[33] This economic nationalistic ideology was expressed most forcibly by its resort to national security arguments to justify its trade policies, particular in the case of increased tariffs on steel and aluminum.

GATT Article XXI allows WTO members to take "any action which it considers necessary for the protection of its essential security interests." Traditionally, this article was only invoked on *rare occasions*. For if the WTO ever ruled that this was a legitimate form of protection, the floodgates would be opened. But if it ruled that it was an illegitimate form of protection, some leading members such as the United States might just leave the organization altogether. It is a no-win situation for the WTO and its members. As one trade law scholar put it, "for decades, Article XXI [...] lay like a dormant dragon beneath the mountain, still dangerous but fallen out of memory."[34] The Trump administration revived this memory.

A key issue regarding Article XXI is whether any WTO member can simply claim any national security interest it perceives as legitimate ("self-judging") or whether the WTO can assess the legitimacy of claimed security interests ("justiciable"). These issues remain unresolved, but the increased interest in this path to protection will force their consideration by the WTO with no real satisfactory outcome. From a multilateral perspective, this is a dangerous game, but dangerous games can be real temptations for aspiring economic nationalists.[35] Ironically, the original US intention in developing Article XXI was to *limit its use*. As the same trade law scholar put it, US Department of State "officials believed it was better to tear down walls by opening trade than to use the concept of national security to build them up."[36] This sensibility has now been abandoned.

In 2018, the US Trump administration increased tariffs on steel imports by 25 percent and on aluminum imports by 10 percent. Certain countries were exempt, including Canada and Mexico, but the Trump administration later reimposed the tariffs on Canada more than once, significantly alienating a long-term ally and deliberately insulting its prime minister in the process. These tariffs were imposed under Section 232 of the 1962 Trade Expansion Act, the national security provision. Awkwardly, the US Department of Defense was not at all convinced of the national security argument, noting that it only required 3 percent of total US production of steel and aluminum for national security purposes.[37] Even the US Department of Commerce reports on steel and aluminum that were used to justify the national security argument acknowledged this as well.[38]

The Trump administration went even further, defining national security in terms of economic security. This is exactly what previous US administrations had avoided because it opens the door for other countries to do the same. The EU, Canada, Mexico, Japan, South Korea and Turkey all rejected the national security arguments and retaliated. Reactions like this are exactly why WTO members have avoided using Article XXI to support protection, but the damage was done.

Regarding the Trump administration's "self-judging" of its national (economic) security argument, there are good reasons to be skeptical. For example, renowned trade lawyer Yong-Shik Lee's analysis suggests that the arguments used to defend it fell short. At the most basic level, the administration did not show that the domestic sector was unable to meet defense needs. Further, it did not consider less trade distorting approaches to meeting defense needs, and it did not demonstrate that imports could not fulfill defense needs if the domestic sector was unable to do so. In sum, the Trump administration "failed to provide a reasoned and adequate explanation of whether the tariffs are necessary to protect essential national security interests, including national defense requirements, under Article XXI."[39]

It is worth remembering that the national security argument applied to US steel and aluminum is an *old* argument. Consider the comments on steel made by Harry Johnson, a noted international economist, in a discussion of economic nationalism in "developing" countries in 1965:[40]

> In regard to the choice of industries to be fostered by development policy, there is a marked tendency to regard certain industries as strategic. [...] In the earliest stages of development, a steel industry is generally regarded as the *sine qua non* of economic development, even though [...] the world steel industry has tended to suffer from chronic overcapacity rather than excessive pressure of demand.

We can see that a nationalistic theory applied to LMICs in the 1960s was invoked for the United States in the late 2010s, with overcapacity having characterized the industry for all the decades in between. It is indeed striking how patterns of thinking tend become locked in with little critical thinking, but critical thinking is not always a priority of economic nationalists, particularly of the performative variety. Indeed, when he was a presidential candidate, Donald Trump already had the US steel sector in mind. At a campaign stop in Pittsburgh, he stated: "Today I am going to talk about how to make America wealthy again. We are going to put American-produced steel back into the backbone of our country. This alone will create massive numbers of jobs."[41] Despite this claim, the idea of the steel sector creating a "massive" number of jobs was just a fantasy. Let us see why.

Figure 5.2 plots employment in *all metals manufacturing* in the United States as a percent of all employment. There is indeed a downward trend, but it started in 1990 at *less than 1 percent*. In 2020, the entire metals manufacturing sector composed one-quarter of 1 percent of total US employment with the steel sector at one-fifth of 1 percent. Note however that the *output* of metals manufacturing had not fallen. The sector had instead become more productive.

There is also the matter of the economy-wide effects of protecting metals sectors, the above-mentioned "general equilibrium" effects. First, steel and aluminum were an unfortunate focal point because they are intermediate inputs into so many other sectors. Protecting steel and aluminum raises their domestic prices and increases costs in these downstream sectors. This is the

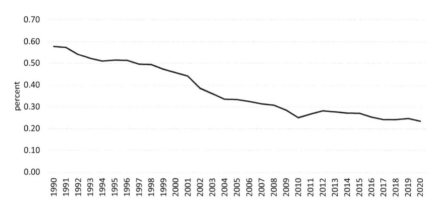

Figure 5.2 Metals manufacturing employment as a percent of total US employment. Source: US Bureau of Labor Statistics.

reason that most economic simulations of steel tariffs do not find any increase in overall employment and sometimes find an actual decrease.[42] Tariffs on intermediate inputs have also been identified as bad for growth across many countries and over time.[43] In the run-up to the Cobden–Chevalier Treaty of 1860, Napoleon advocated eliminating tariffs on wool and cotton imports because these intermediate goods were "indispensable to industry."[44] In ignoring the same regarding aluminum and steel, the Trump administration's preferred trade strategy was less enlightened that that of the nineteenth century.

What about the argument that "we don't make anything anymore?" We can get a sense of this in Figure 5.3, which considers the entire US manufacturing sector as percent of total US employment. This has been on a downward trend since the 1940s, from about one-quarter of all employment to about 8 percent. This is not unusual but rather completely in line with most other high-income countries. Trying to leverage the entire manufacturing sector to "make American wealthy again" would make more sense than focusing on the metals sector alone, but it is still only 8 percent of employment and 10 percent of total GDP. That does not mean total output is falling, because productivity is increasing (approximately fivefold since the early 1980s in the case of US steel).[45]

What US Trump administration did with its steel aluminum tariffs was to throw the world trading system in disarray, alienate political allies, and begin a trade war to protect one-fifth of 1 percent of US employment. Why? It seems to have been a case of *economic nostalgia*, a type of heuristic substitution discussed in Chapter 4. Steel is an iconic, if increasingly insignificant, sector of the US economy and therefore symbolic of an idealized era when "life was better."[46] As one trade law scholar put it:[47]

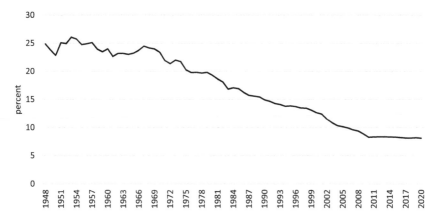

Figure 5.3 Manufacturing employment as a percent of total US employment. Source: US Bureau of Labor Statistics.

There is [...] a political and social element to this nostalgia. It is not just that an earlier era had more factory employment, but that society was different as well. [...] The political promise to restore the employment status of "big, strong guys" in industries such as steel [...] is, in part, about restoring a previous social order in which these men dominated.

The Trump administration had its sights on more than steel and the WTO. It also began to selectively attack the preferential trade agreements the United States had committed itself to. As previously stated, on President Trump's first day in office, he withdrew the United States from the TPP. He derided NAFTA as the "worst trade deal ever" even though it was forward looking for its time. But his update of NAFTA, aside from slightly increasing rules of origin for automobiles, drew from the language of the TPP, and with a few small tweaks, NAFTA went from being the worst to the best. Something illogical and ideological was clearly at play here.[48]

Then there was China, discussed above, a selected target of US president Donald Trump. Economist Peter Navarro had caught candidate Trump's eye or rather the eye of his son-in-law Jared Kushner. Navarro was coauthor of the book *Death by China*, and this book reached Kushner's attention.[49] As a result, despite a lack of background in trade policy, Navarro was given a position in the Trump administration. The resulting policy pursued by that administration is described by trade economists Chad Bown and Douglas Irwin:[50]

This is not protectionism in the sense of trying to help a domestic industry in its struggle against imports. The goal is much broader and more significant: the economic decoupling of the United States and China. That would mark a historic fragmentation of the world economy. [...] Such a separation would have foreign and national security implications well beyond the economic consequences.

The Trump administration's complaints against China were, in the main, legitimate. As previously discussed, they included theft of IP, subsidies to SOEs and forced technology transfers. The EU and Japan had identical concerns, and some of these concerns could have been addressed at the WTO. Rather than work with the EU and Japan or work within the WTO, however, the Trump administration chose unilateral tariff retaliation with President Trump famously stating: "Remember I am a Tariff Man. When people or countries come in to raid the great wealth of our Nation, I want them to pay for the privilege of doing so. It will always be the best way to max out our economic power." This is language that the mercantilists would have understood. The Tariff Man was a seventeenth-century man.

The Trump administration imposed increased tariffs on US$50 billion of imports from China. China, of course, retaliated, sparking a trade war. The Tariff Man claimed that "trade wars are good and easy to win."[51] They are not, and subsequent events proved Trump wrong. China increased tariffs on just under US$200 billion worth of US goods, targeting the agricultural sector. In what has been described as one of the largest trade measures in history, the Trump administration in the end placed tariffs on US$350 billion of imports from China and was forced to bail out US farmers with over US$20 billion in support.[52] But as the trade economist Douglas Irwin reported, it "compensated them for only a fraction of their financial losses."[53] To no surprise, in 2020, the WTO ruled the unilateral tariffs imposed by the United States on China violated the MFN principle.

As shown by trade economist Chad Bown, the "success" that the Trump administration claimed under the "phase-one deal" reached with China in early 2020 was completely illusory. Under this "deal," China agreed to increase its imports of US$200 billion of US goods over 2017 levels, distributed over manufacturing, services, agriculture and energy. It represented a managed trade process, and never fully bore fruit, falling far short of the targets. As of the end of 2021, China had not even reached 60 percent of its committed imports. And given the decline in China's imports from the United States, relative to baseline projection, China actually bought *none* of the additional exports.[54] The "phase-one deal" was a complete failure.

There is also the issue of who paid for Trump's trade war. President Trump himself repeatedly claimed that the tariffs were paid by China directly to the US Treasury.[55] While this is a remote theoretical possibility in the economics analysis of tariffs, it requires very unusual assumptions. Not surprisingly, subsequent economic analysis suggests that the bulk of the costs were absorbed by US households and firms in the realm of billions of US dollars per month.[56] Once again, President Trump's economic nationalism was misguided.

The subsequent US Biden administration largely sailed in the Trump administration's wake, changing the tenor of its trade policy but not much of its substance. While it tried to avoid antagonizing allies and removed the objection to naming a new WTO director general, it continued to block appointments to the WTO's Appellate Body, vaguely citing "systemic concerns" and validating this serious attack on the world's trading regime.

It is true that the first refusal to appoint a member of this body took place in three instances under the US Obama administration. However, as emphasized by trade law scholar Henry Gao, each of these cases was eventually resolved and alternative candidates appointed.[57] What the Trump administration did was entirely different and resulted in the Appellate Body ceasing to function altogether. At the time of this writing, there is a makeshift Multiparty Interim Appeal Arbitration Arrangement (MPIA), but this has several significant limitations, including its voluntary nature and limited membership reach.[58]

There are of course, valid questions regarding the Appellate Body and its functioning, but to effectively eliminate it altogether in the hopes of some future redrafting of the Dispute Settlement Understanding (DSU) under which it operates is counterproductive. Calls for reform of the DSU are entirely legitimate but taking the system hostage to press for reforms is not.[59] The US trade representative Katherine Tai's 2021 statement to the WTO that "reforming dispute settlement is not about restoring the Appellate Body for its own sake" did not bode well for the DSU.[60]

The Biden administration also did not fully repudiate the Section 232 national security approach to tariffs. In the case of the steel tariffs, this appears to have been a nod to union voters in the United States. More specifically the American Iron and Steel Institute, the Steel Manufacturers Association and the United Steelworkers made their positions clear to Biden administration officials. The Biden administration responded, eschewing concerns of the rest of the US manufacturing sector that had to use more expensive steel. A misconstrued economic nationalism prevailed.

A Return to Multilateralism

At the end of an assessment of the Trump administration's trade policies, *The Economist* asks a simple and important question: "What if the president had not threatened American allies, and instead focused energies on tackling

China's subsidies?"[61] Similarly, trade economists Chad Bown and Douglas Irwin suggest that "a better response would (have been) to identify specific instances in which China has violated international agreements and then join with trading partners and allies to file cases at the WTO."[62] Indeed, before destroying the dispute process of the WTO, the Trump administration barely used it to confront China. Nationalistic ideology and a preference for political drama over results prevailed.

As part of the negotiation process of the previously discussed Cobden–Chevalier Treaty between England and France, Richard Cobden wrote the following to Michel Chevalier:[63]

I should be glad to see a removal of impediments which our foolish legislation interposes to the intercourse between the two countries. I see no other hope but in such a policy for any permanent improvement in the *political* relations of France and England. [...] The *people* of the two Nations must be brought into mutual dependence by the supply of each other's wants. There is no other way of counteracting the antagonism of language and race. It is God's own method of producing an entente cordiale, and no other plan is worth a farthing.

This was a nineteenth-century expression of the hope of multilateralism via MFN. It is one that needs to be revived in the current era. On the matter of how to achieve this, there are many contradictory voices, but the objective of doing so remains paramount.

In the past, the multilateral system was politically maintained by what was called "the Quad," consisting of Canada, the EU, Japan and the United States. This then shifted imperfectly to a "new Quad" consisting of Brazil, the EU, India and the United States. As evidenced by the failed Doha Round of multilateral trade negotiations, the new Quad never quite functioned effectively enough with the interests and approaches of Brazil and India diverging from the EU and the United States. Given the role of China in the world economy, there needs to be a subsequent move to a "Quintet" (Brazil, China, the EU, India and the United States) in which China plays a role. This change will be quite difficult.

As we have seen, much of the recent stress to the multilateral trading system has stemmed from tensions between the United States and China. The US–China relationship has been extensively analyzed by Petros Mavroidis and André Sapir in their book *China and the WTO: Why Multilateralism Still Matters*. Mavroidis and Sapir describe the US Trump administration's approach to trade policy as "blithe, ignorant unilateralism," noting that "China has not kowtowed to U.S. pressure and is quite unlikely to do so going forward."[64] It is worth recalling that the Trump administration was willing to sacrifice the WTO for its misconstrued ends, and that its unilateralism was applied across the spectrum of international affairs. Mavroidis and Sapir state:[65]

> The Trump administration's attitude toward global grade is mirrored by their alarmingly dismissive attitude toward the Paris Agreement to combat climate change, an existential issue worldwide. They exhibited the same dismissiveness when abolishing President Obama's initiatives with respect to an eventual agreement to forestall Iran's nuclear weapons program. For President Trump, it is better to have no deal at all than a "bad" deal. [...] In this logic, it is better to have no WTO than a "bad" WTO.

The world trading community can do better than this, and it is worth noting a few things in this regard. First, as previously mentioned, it is widely recognized among trade policy professionals that, when it suffers a loss in the WTO dispute settlement process, China has mended its ways *in each instance.* While this is not a full solution to the problems and concerns that have arisen, it does suggest that the WTO's dispute settlement system can function to good effect. It needs to be re-embraced and applied to China wherever appropriate. Abandoning the system altogether is not a solution. Rather, the system needs to be utilized to its full extent. The US Biden administration's decision not to let it function was self-defeating.

Second, as previously mentioned, China's Protocol of Accession is "justiciable" so that China can be held to account for the commitments it made in these protocols above and beyond standard WTO agreements. This protocol can and should be used more intensively and, where violations of the protocol have taken place, the dispute settlement process should be invoked.[66] Rather than bemoan the accession of China in 2001, leading WTO members should leverage the terms of this accession.

Third, it seems that continued accommodation of China within the WTO is going to require new agreements on SOEs and (forced) technology transfer. Mavroidis and Sapir have extensively analyzed these two issues. They suggest that one path forward is that of a plurilateral agreement among an important subset of the WTO membership. The issues here are legally complex (revolving around the meaning of the term "public body") but avoiding the SOE and technology transfer issues now seems impossible. It is better to confront the issue sooner rather than later and to do so within the WTO.

More generally, it will be difficult to address many important issues without the WTO. As we will discuss in Chapter 8, the COVID-19 pandemic has amply demonstrated that the world needs multilateralism, within and beyond trade, to adequately respond to global public health threats. Unilateral responses are ultimately self-defeating. Failure to reengage with the multilateral trading system, while politically tempting to economic nationalists, will have long-term, deleterious effects on global welfare.

Fish Again

Recall from Chapter 2 that Thomas Mun complained bitterly about the Dutch "fishing in His Majesty's Seas of England, Scotland, and Ireland."[67] As it turns out, fishing has been an issue ever since, and it is a pressing issue right now. This particular product illustrates the necessity of multilateral solutions to important problems, and the role of the WTO in such solutions. Let us see why.

Fish have proven to be a critical component in global food security. For example, the Food and Agriculture Organization (FAO) states:[68]

In 2017, fish consumption accounted for 17 percent of the global population's intake of animal proteins, and 7 percent of all proteins consumed. Globally, fish provided more than 3.3 billion people with 20 percent of their average per capital intake of animal proteins, reaching 50 percent or more in (some) countries.

Fish consumption also provides a number of essential micronutrients (calcium, iron, zinc and omega-3 fatty acids). Unfortunately, marine fish resources are being significantly depleted. For example, the FAO estimates that, for 2017, approximately 34 percent of marine fish stocks were fished at unsustainable levels, up from 10 percent in 1974.[69]

It is now widely recognized that the sustainability of fisheries is undermined by the fisheries subsidies of many WTO members, which totaled US$35 billion in 2018. Leading subsidizers include China, the EU, the United States, South Korea, Japan, Russia and Thailand. Further, US$22 billion or over 60 percent of the total are "capacity enhancing" with direct connection to overfishing that undermines global food security.[70] It is also widely recognized that multilateral solutions are critical to address the subsidy issue. As stated by one pair of researchers:[71]

Many fish stocks inhabit and move between multiple nations' waters and/or the high seas; due to changing distributions as a result of climate change, new transboundary stocks are expected to be present in 35% of nations by 2100. International cooperation is thus essential for fisheries management, particularly when both marine species and fishers move across regions and jurisdictions. Beyond fish catch itself, legal or violent conflicts [...] can be triggered by overfishing in neighboring regions.

The world thus confronts a problem that is inherently multilateral in nature, and the approach to solving the problem must also be multilateral. For many years now, it has been recognized that the WTO is relevant as a forum for negotiations on this issue.[72] Negotiations on fisheries subsidies at the WTO have a long history but restarted in earnest beginning in 2017. Fortunately, an agreement on this issue was reached at the June 2022 WTO Ministerial Meeting.[73] Global food security in part depends on the success of the multilateral trading system. Other important issues do as well.

Assessment

Overall, there is a widespread recognition among international economists and international relations researchers that the WTO and its multilateralism represents a *global public good* of great value. The relevant counterfactual to its effective functioning is not some idealized realm of economic nationalism bringing prosperity to national citizenries via under-described means. Rather it is a world of subsidy wars, tariff wars, unresolved disputes, significantly decreased transparency, dramatically increased commercial uncertainty and increased conflict.[74] This is an outcome that needs to be strenuously avoided.

Historically, the United States has played an important leadership role in maintaining the multilateral system. Of late, however, it has abandoned post. This has had several implications for global trade relations but also, as we will see in Chapter 8, global public health. The countries forming the "Quintet" (Brazil, China, the EU, India and the United States) have much to lose from these recent developments. It is past time that they recognize this and recommit themselves to multilateralism.

Chapter 6

THE ETHNICITY TRAP

In February 2020, US president Donald Trump paid a state visit to India. Indian prime minister Narendra Modi organized a welcome for him at the world's largest cricket stadium with a crowd of 100,000. As President Trump entered the stadium to be greeted by Modi, the crowd was treated to the Village People's 1978 hit song Macho Man. The two macho men hugged at center stage, and two versions of ethnonationalism met in an expert piece of performance art. President Trump led a long-standing ethnonationalist project in the United States, while Prime Minister Modi led a similar project in India.[1] Both emphatically embraced political performance, intuitively knowing that they were leading projects in political psychology. This is a rather widespread practice, both historically and geographically. With its close relationship to stochastic violence, it is also a potentially dangerous one.[2]

Economic nationalism is a form of nationalism, and nationalism is about the "nation." Nations, however, are not states or governments. They are something different. Nations are most often conceived of in terms of an in-group and an out-group. As one researcher put it many years ago, "the concept of 'us' requires 'them.'"[3] More recently, a team of business researchers put it this way:[4]

> Prejudice and discrimination are [...] generated within an in-group by the perceived or actual threat of a distinct out-group to the physical, social, or economic health of the in-group. In attempting to reduce this threat, the opportunities of the out-group are restricted, and negative stereotypes of the out-group are developed to justify discrimination. (p. 763)

It would be nice to claim that economic nationalists are free of such discrimination, but this is often not the case. These authors also note that "hostility toward the out-group may be augmented during conditions of instability in the relative economic fortunes of nations" and that, during such episodes, pressure increases to maintain in-group solidarity.[5] Such hostility is usually combined with a sense of crisis to strengthen its political psychology impacts.

As noted by *The Economist*, "nearly all drawbridge-up parties argue that their country is in crisis and explain it with a simple frightening story involving outsiders."[6] This can be a volatile and sometimes lethal formula of political mobilization.[7]

What Is a Nation?

Before delving too far into the subject of ethnonationalism, it is important to mention and to keep in mind that it is primarily cultural, linguistic and psychological. The idea of "nation" has little basis in scientific fact. Nations have no real genetic substance, nor are they closed systems maintaining themselves. Therefore, in the words of an encyclopedia entry, "the popularly held conviction that one's nation is ethnically pure and distinct is intuitive rather than rational and, as such, is capable of defying scientific and historic evidence to the contrary."[8] Economic nationalists often leverage this irrationality.

Take the case of Japan, whose supposed ethnic purity has been a long-lived touchstone for Japanese nationalists. As stated by one researcher, traditionally, "racial unity is equated with racial superiority."[9] However, researcher Stephen Murphy-Shigematsu calls the notion of a single ethnic origin of the Japanese a "myth."[10] This "ethnicity" has ancient origins from many parts of Asia, with immigrations of Chinese and Koreans being important through the ninth century. Added to these are various indigenous groups. Similar types of analysis (and myth-busting) apply to most countries and nations of the world.

Or consider the political theorist Yael Tamir, a general supporter of the concepts of the nation and nationalism. She states:[11]

> The concept of a nation is defined by a list of criteria, none of which are either necessary or sufficient. A "nation" emerges as a result of the interplay between many variables including culture, religion, language, law, geographical conditions, bureaucratic decisions, and international policies. Yet, its paramount common denominator is *cognitive rather than factual*: The existence of a national consciousness fosters feelings of belonging and national fraternity. [...] It thus seems that there is little or no correlation between the clarity of a concept and its power to motivate action. In fact, the opposite may be true; the vagueness of a concept allows individuals to pour their feelings and thought into it, giving it the ability to appeal to very different people in very different ways.

In sum, the "nation" is largely a psychological phenomenon that rests on the shifting sands of many potential factors. Consequently, ethnonationalism can be inherently resistant to reason, with nationality of various types being developed and claimed, rather than being factually identified. As such, it is ripe for manipulation by political entrepreneurs, and these entrepreneurs know this.

There is also a practical issue. While there are many ways to measure the number of ethnicities in the world, there are *many more of them* than there are countries. Therefore, to base nationalism on ethnicity is inherently to discriminate against fellow citizens of different ethnicities. Add in migration (an ancient and continuing phenomenon) and forcibly displaced people (currently approximately on out of every hundred individuals globally), and both the practicality and desirability of ethnonationalism diminish. As stated by former United Nations secretary general Boutros Boutros-Ghali in the landmark *Agenda for Peace* document, "if every ethnic, religious or linguistic group claimed statehood, there would be no limit to fragmentation, and peace, security and economic well-being for all would become ever more difficult to achieve."[12]

Take the example of Ethiopia. It is a single country or state, albeit of an internally contested nature. One study identified 27 national identities within Ethiopia based on language, genealogy and culture.[13] Should Ethiopia be partitioned into 27 separate nations? What would that process look like? Who would oversee it, and could it be done peacefully? Most certainly, it could not, as the bitter 2020–22 conflict in Ethiopia's Tigray province suggests.[14] And in the case of Nigeria, ethnic groups number in the hundreds. This would be potentially even more complex and fraught. These are just two examples among many.

There is a tendency to view economic nationalism as a purely economic phenomenon. In times of economic uncertainty, "nations" circle the wagons to symbolically support economic welfare. There is truth to this, but economic nationalism itself is in part a psychological phenomenon, a project in ethnopsychology. Indeed, even mainstream economists have interpreted economic nationalism as a kind of social psychology. For economists, economic nationalism is conceived of as a "taste" that provides psychic income from both tangible benefits (e.g., employment in prized sectors) and intangible benefits (e.g., pride in certain ideologies or national accomplishments).[15] Given the partly intangible benefits of satisfying the "taste for nationalism," fulfillment of these tastes by nationalistic politics often becomes symbolic. As expressed some time ago by international economist Harry Johnson:[16]

Nationalistic economic policy will tend to foster activities selected for their symbolic value in terms of concepts of "national identity" and the economic concept of nationhood; in particular, emphasis will be placed on manufacturing, and within manufacturing, on certain industries possessing special symbolic value of industrial competence.

It is for this reason that nationalistic governments promote the production of steel, automobiles and weaponry. It does, however, somewhat depend on context. For example, in contemporary France, nationalistic allure surrounds Danone yogurt.[17] Relevant economic symbolism is not universal but somewhat variable.

The problem is that the symbolism of economic nationalism can involve "tastes" for *discrimination* against other sorts of people. Indeed, the economics theory behind a taste for nationalism was inspired by economist Gary Becker's idea of a taste for discrimination in the United States against African Americans.[18] For example, let us remember Thomas Mun from Chapter 2 and his complaints about the Dutch fishing in "His Majesty's Seas." In the end, Mun needed to play the ethnicity card, stating: "We may truly say of the Dutch, that although they are among us, yet certainly they are not of us, no not they who are born and bred here in our own Country, for still they will be Dutch, not having so much as a drop of English blood in their hearts."[19] This sort of language is familiar in current times.

In the modern context of the United States, political conservatives call for the "affinitive power of shared national identity and group allegiance" and trace this back to British immigrants.[20] The call is often one of "inclusive nationalism" but is usually accompanied by exclusive policies and ideologies, an explicitly "Anglo-American conservatism," which clearly does not include everyone. As Philip Gorski and Samuel Perry extensively document in their book *The Flag and the Cross*, this morphs into a "white Christian nationalism."[21]

For example, in 2019, the US-based organization National Conservatism held a conference in Washington, DC, on the theme of nationalism.[22] One keynote speaker at this conference was television news personality Tucker Carlson. At the conference Mr. Carlson addressed racism and stated: "It's such a boring subject. It's such a dead end. It can't be fixed; it can't be changed."[23] Within a very short time, Mr. Carlson's long-term top writer was found to have posted many explicitly racist statements on internet sites. Similarly, a website cofounded by Mr. Carlson featured contributions from a writer who also contributed to a white supremacist publication, and Mr. Carlson subsequently endorsed the white nationalist "replacement theory."[24] It can indeed be quite difficult to keep nationalism inclusive.[25]

This is not just the concern of the political left. It has been a constant worry, for example, expressed in the pro-market *Economist*, which has identified ethnonationalism and its economic disintegrative tendencies as a defining feature of the current era.[26] The number of countries who have set down this path is increasing, and the lure of this framework seems to be strong with ethnonationalist governments doing well at the polls. Ethnonationalism, it seems, is here to stay.

The Cult of Personality

Ethnonationalism is usually coalesced around particular political leaders. These ethnonationalist leaders (including "macho men" Donald Trump and Narendra Modi) tap into a narrow conception of shared social identity "where the leader constructs him- or herself as the embodiment of the ingroup."[27] In the case of the United States in the 2020 presidential election, for example, the Republican Party did not have the traditional election platform or even any platform at all. They were simply running on Donald Trump himself, nothing more. The person was the party. Indeed, for the white Christian nationalist community in the United States, Trump is often considered the "savior," the "chosen one," and the "anointed one."[28]

In the case of India's Modi, the cricket stadium where he hosted Trump was renamed after Modi himself, and a satellite bearing his image was launched into space. He was promoted as "God's divine gift to India." As stated by one observer, "the glorification of Modi originated in service of a cause larger than the man. Its purpose [...] was to ennoble Hindu nationalism by elaborately showcasing its most successful proponent."[29] Hagiographic films and Modi's sense for photographic images contributed to the cause.

The danger of ethnonationalist projects embodied in singular persons is recognized by political psychologists who point to outcomes in which:[30]

> Anything the leader says or does by definition encapsulates the group identity and anyone who opposes the leader by definition becomes an opponent of the group. Where, on top of that, a sense of pervasive threat is created such that the ingroup appears to be in danger of destruction by imagined enemies, the extreme measures to quell dissent can be justified in the interests of self-defense.

In the case of US president Donald Trump, this justification led to a violent attempt to overturn national election results in the so-called Capitol insurrection of 6 January 2020. Beyond violence, the danger embodied in cults of personality is that they leave little room for policy analysis and deliberation. The practical matters of governance take second place to the personality embodying ethnonationalism. As we will see in Chapter 8, this tendency took a very deadly turn during the COVID-19 pandemic, contributing to millions of deaths.

Hindutva

In the case of Modi's India, ethnonationalism is embodied in the Hindutva movement with roots stretching back to the founding of India and its partition from Pakistan.[31] At the outset, it is important to note that this movement is not primarily religious, but ethnonationalist. As stated by one researcher on this subject, the goal of this movement was to create "a singular Hindu identity whose primary affiliation or loyalty was not to religious deities or other kinship, familial or cast ties but to the nation."[32] Hence its slogan "one nation, one people, and one culture."

The centerpiece of the Hindutva movement is the Rashtriya Swayamsevak Sangh, the RSS (National Volunteer Organization). Modi's political party, the Bharatiya Janata Party (BJP), is affiliated with the RSS.[33] The intellectual founder of the RSS was Vinayak Damodar Savarkar who in 1928 wrote *Hindutva: Who Is a Hindu?* The front-piece of this pamphlet includes the quotation: "Who delivers this our nation […], who endows us with wealth, do […] hurl thy mighty thunderbolt to destroy our enemies."[34] Increasingly, however, those enemies have become fellow Indian citizens.

Savarkar rejects the notion of *ahimsa* or nonviolence that had been a central element of M. K. Gandhi's nationalist movement during the anticolonial era, stating that "everything that is common in us with our enemies, weakens our power of opposing them."[35] He states that "we are not only a nation […] but a born brotherhood. *Nothing else counts.*"[36] At the conclusion of the pamphlet, Savarkar makes a statement that could have come from the 2019 US-based National Conservatism Conference:[37]

> A nation requires a foundation to stand upon and the essence of the life of a nation is the life of that portion of its citizens whose interests and history and aspirations are most closely bound up with the land and who thus provide the real foundation to the structure of their national state.

While it is uncomfortable to recognize it, despite being a modern political movement, the RSS and BJP both have *explicitly racist* roots. Indeed, Hindutva for Savarkar is defined in terms of "race," the "bond of common blood."[38] Hindutva's racial conception of national identity is central to the contemporary project of the BJP and, as social scientists have warned, contains genocidal elements.[39] As stated by one set of researchers, it is attempting to "maximize the mobilization capacity of the Hindu nationalist project, as it makes no critical distinction between the many peoples and faiths indigenous to the Indian subcontinent."[40] Indeed, Savarkar was a supporter of Naziism, and his speeches were included in Nazi publications.[41]

Despite the central role of race in Hindutva, its current expression is one of *religious bigotry* directed at Muslim fellow citizens. Savarkar's vision was "an all or nothing criteria for inclusion in the Hindu nation; either one was or had to become a Hindu, or otherwise be excluded from the Hindu—an effectively Indian—nation."[42] This ideology found its most virulently symbolic expression in the destruction of the sixteenth-century Babri mosque by the BJP and its followers in 1992 and in the Citizenship Amendment Act of 2019 that inserted an implicit religious criterion for India citizenship.

Narendra Modi is part of this bigoted history. Before he was prime minister, Modi was chief minister of Gujarat. He is credited with a set of pro-market economic policies that became known as the Gujarat model, favored among many international and development economists, potentially for good reasons. More darkly, however, under his watch there were anti-Muslim riots in 2002 that resulted in over one thousand deaths. While the courts cleared him of responsibility, questions remain. Also, during this time, the Gujarat State Board of Textbooks began to include positive statements about Naziism, one of Savarkar's touchstones.[43]

Under Modi's Hindutva-inspired government, many developments have taken place. These include increased levels of hate speech against Muslims, violent acts against Muslims and atheists, Hindutva-inspired textbook revisions, the politicization of vegetarianism and a "beef ban" (despite India's position among the largest beef exporters in the world even under the BJP), increased pressure to engage in "patriotic" activities, attacks on higher education in the name of Hindutva, persecution of interfaith couples, shutting down thousands of nongovernmental organizations (NGOs) including Amnesty International, attacks on press freedom (including against the British Broadcasting Corporation), extrajudicial destruction of houses and the new citizenship law that discriminates against Muslims.[44] In late 2021, these discriminatory measures morphed into explicit calls for the mass murder of Muslims (in the name of "cleanliness") at an event attended by BJP officials while Modi remained silent.[45] As a consequence of these policies, the climate of fear for Muslim Indian citizens significantly increased. Actual violence began in April 2022, and Modi again remained silent despite being petitioned by 13 political parties to appeal for calm.[46]

It has long been recognized that economic nationalism can be economically deleterious because there is a tendency to substitute such nationalism for clearly thought-out policy considerations.[47] Perhaps it is a recognition of this fact, as well as an aversion to bigotry, that resulted in an agreement between two Indian economists, Amartya Sen and Jagdish Bhagwati, who vehemently disagree on economic policy, that the Modi-Hindutva movement is a step back for India.[48] And indeed, Modi has had a difficult time putting a foot right in the policy realm. While initially hailed as a pro-market beacon, he presided over a poorly handled demonetization, revised GDP and employment figures, quickly burned through a series of economic advisers and rushed through a (necessary) agricultural reform with too little consultation that led to one of the most prolonged protests against the Modi government until the proposed reforms were cancelled. Most, importantly, as we will see in Chapter 8, he bungled India's response to the COVID-19 pandemic, contributing to an estimated four million excess deaths.[49]

Hungary

One country that has caught the attention of ethnonationalists is Hungary. After he became prime minister in 2010 (for a second time) as head of the Fidesz party, Viktor Orbán began to rewrite the Hungarian constitution as a nationalist project much to the consternation of many and with an aim to entrench his power.[50] This constitution helped to support the Fidesz government and provided it with a particular identity based on an evolving ethnonationalism. Most recently, Orbán won another reelection in 2022.

In 2014, Orbán introduced the idea of "illiberal democracy" with "liberals" or "elites" playing the role of an antinationalist enemy.[51] In this conception, "liberals" were no longer able to legitimately represent the "Hungarian nation." This nation was identified as Christian, with repeated claims that Hungary had played an important role in defending Europe from Islam.[52] Consequently, when the Syrian refugee crisis began in 2015, Orbán quickly announced that he was building a fence to keep what he called the "enemy" out. The enemy was now multidimensional, namely liberal, foreign and Islamic, and posed an existential threat to the "real" Hungary. In the subsequent frictions with the EU, Orbán was able to brand himself as a defender of the "nation" against outside influence, the protector of what he referred to as "we, the millions with national feelings."[53] He stated that the EU should "rely on the ancient source of European democracy: the will of the people" as if representative democracy represented something different from that.[54] Since liberal democracy was more or less enshrined in the 2007 Treaty on European Union (TEU) via numerous provisions (e.g., nondiscrimination, rule of law, representative democracy), this put him at odds with the EU. Consequently, Orbán became, in the words of EU scholar Desmond Dinan, "the personification of illiberal democracy in the EU."[55]

As a result of this recent history, Budapest has become the go-to city for aspiring ethnonationalists. In 2018, it was the site of the "Future of Europe Conference," and Orbán met with some choice participants of that conference, including the US ethnonationalist Steve Bannon who had recently been forced out of the US Trump administration, and the conservative, pro-Brexit British author Douglas Murray. Murray is the author of the book *The Strange Death of Europe: Immigration, Identity, Islam*, which expresses views very much in line with those of Orbán.[56] Both Bannon and Murray use the term "Islamofascism," but it is not clear how refugees fleeing for their lives and livelihoods fit into that idea.

But rhetorically, Orbán is not against all refugees. In a 2017 national address, he stated: "We shall let in true refugees: Germans, Dutch, French, and Italians, terrified politicians and journalists who here in Hungary want to find the Europe they have lost in their homelands."[57] This was a call to all European ethnonationalists, and some notable entities heeded such calls. For example, the publisher Arktos Media relocated to Budapest.[58] Arktos is a "traditionalist" publisher, but one of its original founders, John Morgan, changed his affiliation to the "white nationalist" Counter-Currents.[59] The CEO of Arktos, Daniel Friberg, is a Swedish former neo-Nazi and current intellectual leader of the "new right" in Europe. Arktos notably published the first English translations of the works of the Russian "neo-Eurasian" writer Alexander Dugin. Dugin's writings have had a significant influence on multiple "new-right" movements in Europe. One researcher referred to Dugin's ideas as "the lynchpin of innumerous irregular networks of anti-liberal political resistance and sabotage."[60] But he also serves as an informal intellectual adviser to new-right political parties, including Britain's National Party, France's National Front, Greece's Golden Dawn and Hungary's Jobbik party. Given this connection to Russian ethnonationalism, it is perhaps not surprising that Orbán supported Vladimir Putin's 2015 visit to Budapest where he expressed his Dugin-inspired views regarding Ukraine.[61]

Another "true refugee" who appeared in Orbán's Hungary was the previously mentioned ethnonationalist Tucker Carlson. In his comments from Budapest in 2021, Carlson invoked "Western civilization" as the value upheld by Orbán's government. Carlson's affinity with Orbán was perhaps no surprise given that, in 2018, Carlson had said that low-skilled immigrants into the United States make it "dirtier," a racially tinged sentiment that Orbán would no doubt approve of. Indeed, in a speech he made during his visit, he praised Orbán's response to the Syrian refugee crisis and characterized Hungary as freer and more democratic than the United States, which had become an "authoritarian" government under the Democratic (but not Republican) Party. Ironically, he accused the Democratic (but not Republican) Party of "illiberalism," the very centerpiece of Orbán's political party.

With anti-immigrant policies in place, Hungary began to experience labor shortages. The president of Hungary's Chamber of Commerce lamented the lack of "white-skinned workers with Christian roots." The government had to turn to a "slave law" that allowed employers to require workers to work for an additional 400 hours of overtime annually, leaving German multinationals operating in Hungary to distance themselves from the law and tens of thousands of Hungarians to seek their fortunes outside of the country.[62] Allowing targeted, skills-based immigration would have been much more effective but would have undermined Orbán's ethnonationalist project.

It is worth recalling that Hungary had been a case of a successful transition to representative government, joining the EU in 2004. And despite praise for Orbán's government from "true refugees" like Carlson, the EU has had its own concerns about Hungary's evolving "illiberal democracy." Indeed, in 2018, the European Parliament voted to trigger Article 7(1) of the TEU in the case of Hungary. This means that there was a "clear risk" of the Hungarian government violating the EU's "fundamental values," defined in Article 2 of the TEU as "human dignity, freedom, democracy, equality, the rule of law and respect for human rights, including the rights of persons belonging to minorities."[63] As a result of this vote, the Hungarian government received a formal warning, and sanctions could eventually be imposed, although Poland has blocked this in solidarity with Hungary. In 2022, the European Court of Justice (ECJ) planned to also take up the issue of EU values, and this could eventually lead to financial ramifications.

The April 2022 election victory of Orbán and Fidesz brought new attention to his ethnonationalist project. The EU appeared to be more ready to apply measures in support of its stated values and had more leverage based on a July 2020 COVID-19 stimulus package. With the support of both the ECJ and the European Parliament, it appeared to be poised to invoke a rule of law conditionality mechanism that would begin to withhold COVID-19 recovery funds from the Hungarian government.[64] It is worth noting that, despite his anti-EU rhetoric, Orbán defends Hungary's place as one of the largest per-capita recipients of EU funds from other programs such as economic and social cohesion, so this funding conflict could prove to be an important one.[65]

Another set of "true refugees" visited Hungary in the wake of Orbán's 2022 election victory, namely the US-based Conservative Political Action Committee (CPAC), which held a special meeting outside of the United States to celebrate Orbán's victory and ideology. The meeting featured as speaker the Hungarian racist and anti-Semitic Zsolt Bayer who Orbán had bestowed the 2016 Hungarian Order of Merit.[66] Former US president Donald Trump and Tucker Carlson put in virtual appearances. In the case of Carlson, his appearance supported a theme he and Orbán have espoused, namely *le grand remplacement* or great replacement theory. The timing was a bit awkward because, in the United States, a gunman had just killed 10 Black individuals under that ideological banner. Once again, the stochastic violence of ethnonationalism, now with an international coalition behind it, proved deadly.

In July 2022, Orbán explicitly condemned "race mixing," namely of Europeans with non-Europeans, invoking the condemnation of Jewish rights groups.[67] That did not prevent CPAC featuring Orbán at its own conference in the United States two weeks later where he called on ethnonationalist forces to "take back the institutions in Washington and in Brussels" in defense of "Western values." With this speech and the standing ovation given to Orbán by CPAC attendees, the alliance between two branches of ethnonationalism was set in motion.

Performance and Policy

In the end, the ethnicity trap and its discrimination prove to be self-defeating because discrimination holds back economic growth and development. Consider the case of the United States. One prominent group of economic researchers estimated that between 20 and 40 percent of the growth that took place in the United States between 1960 and 2010 can be explained by the *removal* of racial and gender discrimination in human capital development. Enhancing discrimination has the opposite, growth-suppressing effect.[68]

Ethnonationalism also requires *performance*, as "macho men" Trump and Modi intuitively knew. In the case of American ethnonationalism, the columnist Jamelle Bouie recognizes this, stating that "It is a performance of nationalism, one that triangulates between open chauvinism in favor of the dominant ethnic group and narrow appeals to inclusion, with the promise of material gain from anyone who joins (the) coalition."[69] The problem with performative policy is that it is often *bad policy* for the simple reason that "thinking with blood is not conducive to thinking with mind."[70] For example, Prime Minister Modi had a penchant for replacing heads of the Reserve Bank of India, and President Trump felt the need to fire a competent chairwoman of the US Federal Reserve. As we will see in Chapter 8, both macho men dramatically failed when faced with the challenge of the COVID-19 pandemic. Countries that rely on performative nationalism as a source for policies in alleged support of economic growth and welfare are apt to be disappointed. We will return to this issue in Chapter 8 on pandemic nationalism.

Assessing Ethnonationalism

In a noted review of economic nationalism, Andreas Pickel stated that it "is not so much about the economy as it is about the nation—the economic dimensions of specific nationalisms only make sense in the context of a particular national discourse."[71] This is indeed the case. However, as we have seen, the concept of the "nation" is often cast in primarily ethnic terms and can consequently be problematic. Nonetheless, there is a tradition that states that ethnonationalism is inevitable. For example, the historian Jerry Muller makes this point in his well-known article "Us and Them." He states:[72]

> There are two major ways of thinking about national identity. One is that all people who live within a county's borders are part of the nation, regardless of their ethnic, racial, or religious origins. This liberal or civic nationalism [...] has competed with and often lost out to a different view, that of ethnonationalism. The core of the ethnonationalist idea is that nations are defined by a shared heritage, which usually includes a common language, a common faith, and a common ethnic ancestry.

This is the conceptual tension that arises in economic nationalism as a larger expression of nationalism. In many instances, the tilt is toward ethnonationalism. For example, Muller describes what he calls the "balance sheet" of ethnonationalism. In the negative column are the human suffering of violence and forced dislocation, the reduction of market size and therefore of economic efficiency, the reduction of cultural vitality and the potential loss of human capital in emerging ethno-states that expel others. But in the case of Europe, Muller suggests that, despite the horrors of World War II, the positive column is paramount. He states:[73]

> One could argue that Europe has been so harmonious since World War II not because of the failure of ethnic nationalism but because of its success, which removed some of the greatest sources of conflict both within and between countries. The fact that ethnic and state boundaries now largely coincide has meant that there are fewer disputes over borders or expatriate communities, leading to the most stable territorial configuration in European history.

This is certainly plausible, but another possibility is that Europe was helped along by the postwar effort to develop regional institutions to prevent the repeat of the two world wars. This is the overall conclusion, for example, of the historian Desmond Dinan in his book *Europe Recast*. In Dinan's view, the postwar political principle of European political development was "tempering the nationalist ethos [...] in favor of collective peace, economic integration, and supranational governance" motivated by "the miserable legacy of heroic European nationalism." Rather than a paragraph, Dinan provides an entire, well-researched book making this point.[74]

Muller's policy prescription for the communal conflict that inevitable arises from ethnonationalism, particularly in LMICs, is simple: partition. But as we have previously stated, the number of nationalities vastly exceeds the number of states, so presumably this partition would have a very long way to go. There is also the problem of whether we want to risk the violence of finely grained partition for a conception of nationalism that is shaky at best. These shaky foundations have been summarized by political philosopher Bernard Yack who himself is not entirely opposed to the idea:[75]

> Ethnonationalists rid themselves of their discomfort by picking out one source of identity in our ever-changing communal heritage and turning it into a norm against which we should measure our political communities. [...] They [...] insist [...] that we can each trace our cultural identities back to some discrete ethnic community; that these communities maintain their original character through time; and that even where there seems little evidence of ethnic consciousness, these communities persist in their original character. [...] In truth, ethnic identities are part of a contingent and ever-changing legacy of shared memories and communal identification. Portraying them as the norm against which to measure the pre-political sense of community associated with modern states requires a gross misrepresentation of the historical record.

This long quotation points to the factual limitations of ethnonationalism. However, there is a deeper problem lurking in it. Ethnonationalism is based on identity, but there is an important distinction made by organizational scholar Gelaye Debebe between *avowed* identity and *ascribed* identity.[76] Whereas avowed identity has to do with personal qualities embraced by an individual, ascribed identity is socially imposed. Ascribed identity is the way society conceives of an individual and may be inconsistent with that individual's self-conception. Ascribed identities can be negative and singular in dimension wherein complex and positive avowed identities are reduced to unidimensional and negative connotations that become the basis of discrimination and even violence. For example, in his book *Identity and Violence*, the Nobel Laureate economist Amartya Sen refers to this process as *miniaturization*.[77] Miniaturization of individuals through negative, ascribed identities can become the basis of discrimination and violence, and Muller's partition solution is often the spark for such violence.

These considerations have ethical consequences as well. In particular, there are implications for the sets of individuals to whom we have ethical duties. In a famous article, the ethicist Peter Singer claims that ethical responsibilities must transcend geographic distance.[78] However, social distances created by ethnonationalism can be just as potent and therefore relevant. Indeed, ethnonationalism can become the basis of pervasive *partialism* that relegates individuals to not-so-benign neglect instead of being the beneficiaries of universal rights and relational responsibilities. Indeed, individuals often feel more ethical responsibility to other individuals of the same ethnic or racial group abroad than to fellow citizens of different ethnicities and races. Countries in which ethical responsibilities evolve along purely ethical lines are countries that find it difficult to function effectively and ethically.

"Western Civilization"

Ethnonationalists of the "Western" variety have a fascination with "Western civilization," although they might not always have a well-developed and accurate idea of what the concept refers to. For example, in his 2017 speech in Warsaw's Krasiński Square, US president Trump invoked "the West," stating that "We write symphonies. We celebrate our ancient heroes and embrace our timeless traditions and customs. We cherish inspiring works of art that honor God." He stated that the "fight for the West begins with our minds, our wills, and our souls" and that "our civilization and our survival depends on the bonds of history, culture, and memory." He concluded by stating: "I declare today for the world to hear that the West will never, ever be broken. Our values will prevail. And our civilization will triumph."[79]

Most proponents of "Western civilization" point to traditions inherited from ancient Greek civilization. For example, the classicist Bruce Thornton has credited the Greeks with "the ideas that have created Western civilization."[80] There is a further temptation in that the ancient Greeks gave us the term ethnos from which "ethnicity" derived. However, looking closer, most researchers on ancient Greek ethnicity come away from the subject with a conclusion that even there and then, it was less than straightforward. One researcher characterizes ancient Greek ethnicity as "an extremely complex and fluid construction, or rather system of constructions."[81] Another researcher suggests that ancient Greek ethnicity was partly based on "*a shared myth of descent.*"[82] To the extent that such researchers identify a single ancient Greek "ethnicity," it is one of shared territory rather than what we would identify as ethnicity in the modern era.

Regarding the oft-mentioned ancient Greek polis, to the extent that Athenians can be considered a single "ethnicity," it was more of an "imagined community" than anything ethnically homogenous, one based on an evolving shared culture.[83] Some classicists stress that this imagined community was developed in opposition to another imagined community, namely the "barbarians," a predisposition that can be recognized even today, for example, in the nearly constant invocation of "the enemy." In this line of research, for example, classicist Edith Hall concludes that "the conceptual boundaries which estrange different peoples, as they divided Greeks from non-Greeks, are socially produced rather than inherent in nature."[84] This ultimately resulted in the "institutionalized xenophobia" of Athenian law.

While we cannot be entirely sure of these matters, the touchstone of modern, "Western" ethnonationalists was most likely not ethnically homogenous but rather based on the "social imaginary" of that long-past era.[85] Indeed, the "ethnicity" of "Western civilization" is another social imaginary of "whiteness." If we avoid claims about the moral superiority of a particular "race" (a concept not invoked in ancient Greece and also morally repugnant) interpretations of "Western civilization" must be cast in cultural terms. Here proponents of "Western civilization" are on safer grounds, but then they must cast aside the notion of ethnicity.

This is not to suggest that there is nothing valuable in what might be perceived as "Western" culture. Equality before the law, human rights, gender equality, formal ideas about market systems, scientific inquiry, freedom of religious practice are the stuff of human progress while not being exclusively "Western."[86] And indeed, these very valuable contributions are often the ideas that are implicitly attacked and undermined by ethnonationalists supporting "Western civilization." This is one of the many ironies of modern, "Western" ethnonationalism.

Refugees

Nothing, it seems, inflames ethnonationalism like refugees. As we saw, in 2015, Hungary's Viktor Orbán began to build a fence to keep out the "enemy" in the form of Syrian refugees but later accepted Ukrainian refugees because they were more ethnically similar to Hungarians. Refugees have become essentially unwelcome in the United States as well. Unfortunately, the number of refugees has been increasing significantly and is set to rise even further. Even under the very narrow definition of refugees of the UNHCR mandate (which excludes all internally displaced individuals), there are over twenty-five million refugees. This is shown in Figure 6.1 where the current era is noticeably different than most of the post–World War II era. Further, climate change and conflicts are going to increase the number of displaced people and therefore the number of refugees.

The UNHCR estimates that climate change displaces over twenty million people per year.[87] Most of these individuals never become official refugees but rather internally displaced people or what are sometimes called "environmentally displaced persons" or EDPs. For this reason, the UNHCR rejects

Figure 6.1 Number of refugees under UNHCR mandate. Source: unhcr.org.

the use of the term "climate refugees." Nonetheless, people displaced within their countries due to climate change are more likely to seek to go abroad than those who have not been displaced, particularly when the internal displacement feeds into existing conflicts. This has led to an increased discussion of the appropriateness of the climate refugee term, one proposed definition being "one who has been forced to leave their home or country due to the effects of severe climate events which [...] force them to seek asylum in other [...] countries."[88] This is an issue that will not go away.

Syria is a good example of this. While the headlines surrounding the Syrian uprising and subsequent civil war emphasized the political angle of the Arab Spring, an important precipitating event was a drought in the northeastern Jezira region during the years 2006–10.[89] The difficulties surrounding the drought led to a migration of hundreds of thousands of individuals out of the Jezira region to southern cities in the search for better conditions. Many of these migrants ended up in what were in effect refugee camps around the cities of Damascus and Aleppo. This humanitarian crisis was one significant cause of the political crisis that began in 2011 and eventually caused nearly six million Syrians to become officially recognized refugees. As even the UNHCR acknowledges, climate change played a part in this.

It is important to recognize that countries do have *responsibilities* to official UNHCR refugees. The 1948 Universal Declaration of Human Rights includes the right to seek asylum from persecution. Further, the 1951 Convention Relating to the Status of Refugees grants refugee status to any person with a "well-founded fear of being persecuted for reasons of race, religion, national-ity, membership of a particular social group or political opinion." While this 1951 convention originally applied to European refugees, a 1967 protocol extended the convention to all such defined refugees. Further, although it is nonbinding, the 2018 Global Compact on Refugees commits countries to cooperate in providing the global public good of refugee resettlement.

It is important to keep in mind that the bulk of refugees (approximately 85 percent) reside in LMICs and, in some cases such as South Africa, sen-timents are turning against these individuals.[90] However, as noted by *The Economist*, "even the relatively few asylum-seekers who make it to the rich world can up-end their politics" and that, in particular, "some nationalist politicians have no interest in meeting the duties imposed by the (UN refu-gee) convention."[91] In particular, ethnonationalists are often hostile to their country governments meeting obligations with regard to refugees. Hence the refrain in the United States, Hungary and other countries to "build a wall."

In the case of the United States, legal scholar Robert Tsai comments on the Trump administration's posture to refugees as follows:[92]

A first-time presidential candidate, who had never held elective office, rode a wave of grassroots dissatisfaction with demographic changes all the way to the White House, despite losing the popular vote. Trump campaigned on ethno-nationalist themes shared by other right-wing candidates throughout Europe. [...] By outflanking his opponents to their right on such issues, he bet his presidency on taking a hardline view on [...] refugee policy. [...] What we are seeing is an ethno-nation-alist movement that has been fused with a more traditional conservative movement. [...] Trumpism relies heavily upon demographic control as a means to restore a sense of cultural integrity and prevent the loss of political power for a white majority.

In the case of the United Kingdom, as we will see in Chapter 7, the refugee issue was implicated in the 2016 Brexit vote, having bled over into the general concern regarding free movement within the EU, despite the fact that very few refugees were allowed to enter. As stated by one migration researcher, "the British public, with its very limited knowledge of the EU [...], did not differentiate between free movement and other migration, nor seemingly between a Polish doctor and a Syrian refugee (who might of course also be a doctor)."[93]

One lone voice on the refugee issue was former German chancellor Angela Merkel. In 2015, she made the decision to let one million Syrian refugees into Germany. Many predicted that this would be a disaster of large proportions, and Henry Kissinger, a former refugee himself, advised her that it would compromise "German civilization." But nonetheless, she persisted, stating that "If Europe fails on the question of refugees, then it won't be the Europe we wished for" and that "I don't want to get into a competition in Europe of who can treat these people the worst."[94] In an age of conflict and climate change, as well as decline in workforces in high-income countries, Merkel's brave and humane posture toward refugees will become ever more relevant.

As with many other aspects of nationalism, opposition to refugees is supported by zero-sum thinking, and this tends to hold true for opposition to immigration as a whole. The mediating factor seems to be the association of zero-sum mindsets with hostility to out-groups.[95] In this way, a mindset behind the larger phenomena of economic nationalism and ethnonationalism is behind the failure to meet international requirements to address the refugee issue.

Civic Nationalism

Civic nationalism provides an alternative to the problems inherent in ethnonationalism. This idea was introduced by the American philosopher and historian Hans Kohn in his 1944 book *The Idea of Nationalism*. This is the origin of what has been called "Kohn's dichotomy" between Western/civic/high/liberal nationalism and Eastern/ethnic/low/authoritarian nationalism.[96] We will consider here Kohn's dichotomy in the simple and more relevant distinction between civic nationalism and ethnonationalism.

With civic nationalism, the allegiance is not to race or ethnicity but to a multiethnic state, its history, culture(s) and most importantly, its civic institutions.[97] It was, for example, defined by the Canadian writer Michael Ignatieff as follows:[98]

> Civic nationalism maintains that the nation should be composed of all those—regardless of race, color, creed, gender, language, or ethnicity— who subscribe to the nation's political creed. This nationalism is called civic because it envisages the nation as community of equals, rights-bearing citizens, united in patriotic attachment to a shared set of political practices and principles. [...] According to the civic nationalist creed, what holds a society together is not common roots but *law*. By subscribing to a set of democratic procedures and values, individuals can reconcile their right to shape their own lives with their need to belong to a community.

Civic nationalism provides space for African American citizens in the United States despite not being descendent from "English settlers," as well as to Muslim citizens of India whose presence dates back many centuries. It helps to avoid the deadly impracticalities of ethnonationalism in the form of stochastic and sometimes organized violence. For example, there were perhaps 75 million casualties in World War II in response to the ethnonationalism of Germany and Japan, and in the partition of India, both the forced migration of more than ten million individuals and one million casualties.

Civic nationalism as a concept has been widely criticized. The political philosopher Bernard Yack calls it a "myth," stating that "it misrepresents political reality as surely as the ethnonationalist myths it is designed to combat" and that "wishing won't make it so."[99] Political scientist Nicholas Xenos refers to it at an "oxymoron" and a "contradiction."[100] These are valid criticisms, but as we have seen, ethnonationalism is also a myth and beset with contradictions. It, too, has oxymoronic qualities but is nevertheless strongly defended.

Political theorist Yael Tamir argues that "the civic/ethnic distinction encourages the view that in civic nations the roles of culture, language, religion, ethnicity, and race are minimal and can therefore be ignored."[101] This is not the case. The argument is not that such differences should be ignored but that, to avoid conflict and violence, they should *not be inflamed* for short-term political advantage. Further, defending the civic nationalism concept is not a case of rejecting what Yack calls "inherited culture" in favor of an abstract notion of citizenship. It is a case of rejecting *bigoted* culture in favor of *inclusive* citizenship. Further, civic *institutions* are part of culture and have a history and are therefore part of inherited culture. Indeed, given the critical role that institutions play in modern social science (including economics), it is striking how little attention is given to them in the debate over civic nationalism.

Institutions require involvement. In the ancient Greek context, for example, Yack noted that they "appear to have had a passion for political activity, rather than an overwhelming identification with their polis."[102] As stated by political scientist Emilia Palonen in an analysis of the Hungarian case discussed above, "society does not pre-exist articulation, and must be somehow articulated through practices as the basis of democracy."[103] These sorts of considerations hint at a nationalism based on *shared civic practices* that become traditions.

Nevertheless, Yael Tamir does not mince words in her criticism of civic nationalism. She states:[104]

We have been deluded into believing that modern societies can move from the desire to rely on particular cultural or national ties to a sphere of political maturity and reliance on abstract principles. We now find that the seemingly childish desire for stability and continuity is coming back to haunt us. For those who understand personal and social

psychology, this should come as no surprise. [...] Compelling individuals to continually act in accordance with axioms that contradict their
instinctual inclinations is asking them to live—psychologically speaking—beyond their means. As the purely civic vision of nationalism is
based on this type of quest, its repeated failures should be anticipated.

But as just emphasized, it is not a question of abstract principles but of
shared civic practices: from registering children for school and planning for
a neighborhood park to registering to vote and exercising that right. These
sorts of practices are what contribute to stability and continuity in a more
durable way than ethnic inclinations. Indeed, researchers are beginning to
appreciate the role of civic activities in both preventing and deescalating
conflict. For example, researcher Roger Mac Ginty introduces the notion of
"everyday peace" as "the practices and norms deployed by individuals and
groups in deeply divided societies to avoid and minimize conflict [...] at both
inter- and intra-group levels." He mentions "the banality of civility or the
everyday and familiar social practices that constitute life in the workplace,
the neighborhood, the park, the shop and the bar." The practices of civic
nationalism constitute everyday peace.[105]

Regarding civic nationalism's alleged "repeated failures," the question
of relevant comparison arises. While civic nationalism might represent an
incomplete and limited idea, ethnonationalism has a great deal to account
for. World War II was an example of "successful" ethnonationalism. So was
the South African apartheid system, the Rwandan genocide of 1994, and the
Yugoslav wars of the 1990s. Perhaps the "banality of civility" is being held
to too high a standard, and ethnonationalism is not sufficiently held to task.
Indeed, there is the question of how much room we should allow Tamir's
"instinctual inclinations" that caused these tragedies.

These sorts of limitations of ethnonationalism are recognized by Michael
Ignatieff when he states that "the only reliable antidote to ethnic nationalism turns out to be civic nationalism, because the only guarantee that ethnic
groups will live side by side in peace is shared loyalty to a state strong enough,
fair enough, equitable enough to command their obedience."[106] Despite the
limits of civic nationalism, Ignatieff is correct. It is not a matter of finding an
ideal version of nationalism, but of *avoiding violent catastrophes* small and large
in order to support peace and prosperity.

More recently, in response to the revival of ethnonationalism, one writer
stated that "when it comes to divisions of race, ethnicity and religious belief,
the unforgotten is the destroyer of nations."[107] Further, however, as Ignatieff
states, the "unforgotten" is really a "language of fantasy and escape," "a form

of speech which shouts, not merely so that it will be heard, but so that it will be believed."[108] Belief in a fantasy is always attractive, but the dire consequences that tend to tear communities apart are not worth the psychic "high" it allows. Most important, fantasy is a poor basis for policy, something we will find in the next two chapters on Brexit and the COVID-19 pandemic.

Ethnonationalism and Economic Nationalism

We need to be clear here: economic nationalism and ethnonationalism are, in principle, two distinct things. Economic nationalism need not be ethnonationalist, but in practice, it often is. When Viktor Orbán met with Steve Bannon, they both recognize this. Steve Bannon is a self-described economic nationalist, but he is also an ethnonationalist, and Orbán wants to promote this melding of nationalisms in Hungary. When "macho men" Modi and Trump met in the cricket stadium, they also both recognize this. Trump was a self-identified economic nationalist who took policy advice from Steve Bannon, and he was also an ethnonationalist as is Modi. These ideological and emotive affinities are real and must be recognized, and they are both based on zero-sum views of the world: "they" are going to take something from "us."

This frequent melding of economic nationalism with ethnonationalism is potentially dangerous. It promotes conflict and stochastic violence. It can undermine social cohesion and the rule of law without which market economies do not function well. For example, in the case of Trump, his ethnonationalism led to the violent storming of the United States Capitol building after a lost election.[109] Conservative business groups in the United States such as the (protectionist) National Association of Manufacturers, the Business Roundtable and the US Chamber of Commerce all quickly condemned the violent attempt to overturn an election because they recognized it as a threat to the institutional underpinnings of the economic system that supports them.

The much-criticized idea of civic nationalism is more aligned with the functioning of the market system than is ethnic nationalism. It imperfectly supports the "everyday peace" on which market systems rely. It allows for ethical duties to extend to all citizens so that the institutional underpinnings of the market system, including social safety nets, can have the political support necessary to address the vagaries of markets, both domestic and international. It also recognizes that ethnicities are, to some degree, a mirage and that, given the vastly larger number of ethnicities than countries, civic nationalism is the only practical way forward. For these reasons, we should heed its call.

Chapter 7

THE BREXIT BLUNDER

In January 2013, responding to a perceived rising tide of British opinion, Conservative UK prime minister David Cameron proposed a referendum on British membership in the EU. He said at that time: "It is time for the British people to have their say. It is time to settle this European question in British politics. I say to the British people: this will be your decision."[1] In doing so, he was attempting to mimic Labour's Harold Wilson who had successfully done the same thing in 1974 regarding membership in the European Economic Community (EEC). Cameron launched a years-long campaign that culminated in a June 2016 Brexit vote in which the British people "had their say." In what has been called Cameron's "great miscalculation," they voted to *leave* the EU or at least to try.[2] Prime Minister Cameron resigned with his political career in tatters.

The Brexit campaign had deep roots in what is known as Euroscepticism, a mix of nationalist, ethnonationalist and populist ideas about the state of Britain in the world. Its rise is often linked to the signing of the 1992 Maastricht Treaty forming the EU, as well as to perceived economic decline in the UK. It is primarily but not exclusively linked to the political right in Britain and has some parallels with similar development in the United States.[3] The vote was a close call, with majorities in Scotland, Northern Ireland and London voting to stay in the EU. It was a signature event.

Populism has been described as an antiestablishment movement that pits "the people" against "the elites." The fact that populists are themselves often members of the elite does not seem to matter. Populism engages in myth-making and the gross simplification of complex issues (heuristic substitution from Chapter 4).[4] In the current era, these complex issues include economic globalization and multilateral relations. Mythmaking and the us/them cleavage work together in populist rhetoric, conjuring up "enemies of the people." Further, as discussed in the previous chapter, "the people" can be defined in ethnonationalist terms (the "English"), and the results can be dramatic.

For example, Nigel Farage is a descendant of Huguenot refugees who fled from France to England in the seventeenth century to escape religious persecution. He became the face of the populist UK Independence Party (UKIP) that took up the pro-Brexit cause. As the Brexit referendum drew close, he posed in front of an anti-immigration poster with an image of a long queue of Syrian refugees. On the poster it stated: "Breaking Point: The EU Has Failed Us All." Farage, the (elite) descendant of refugees, was on the offensive against refugees. That same day, Labor MP Jo Cox was shot dead for her support of Syrian refugees by a gunman who shouted, "Britain first!"[5] These are common features of populist movements that have been leveraged by political entrepreneurs and result in stochastic violence.

To be fair, we can conceive of populist mythmaking by the UKIP as a partial response to another type of mythmaking within the EU, that of "governance without government" where all issues become merely technocratic.[6] While the word "technocratic" has become the go-to term for some social scientists who apply it to many things they do not like, it does still have meaning. The EU has been criticized for deploying a language that inevitably alienates less educated citizens of EU member countries who quickly tire of "directives," "regulations," and "subsidiarity," what has come to be known as "Euro-speak." In addressing the consequent "democratic deficit," political scientist Thomas Diez states:[7]

> Its citizens claim that the EU is far too bureaucratic, technical, distant, and its decision-making procedures too intransparent. This might be the case or not. [...] But the institutional language [...] has prevailed until today, and provides the ground to continuously reconstruct the EU as a monster bureaucracy concerned with technical matters that increasingly affect the everyday life of its citizens without their formal consent, while the nation state carries with it the ideals of self-determination and democracy.

The role of this technocratic distance is important. However, there is a larger nationalistic component to the Euroscepticism movement that resulted in Brexit. Indeed, political scientist Ben Wellings has argued that British nationalism is, at its center, an opposition to Europe and that, when British nationalists invoke British sovereignty, it is sovereignty vis-à-vis European integration.[8] From this perspective, the Brexit vote was a repeat of the 1975 referendum on membership in the EEC in which the "Yes" vote prevailed. At that time, the political right in the UK was pro-membership (Thatcher campaigned for Yes), but many of the same issues of sovereignty were rehearsed.

The Brexit vote was even more astonishing given the fact that the UK chose to use an opt-out provision of the Maastricht Treaty to remain outside of the European Monetary Union (EMU). For economists, the EMU has been the most controversial part of the European integration project, the one that has caused the most policy difficulties. It is important to recall that the EMU's intellectual history goes back to the 1970s and has therefore paralleled the entire European integration project.[9] The UK's opt-out choice was a privileged one, and the fact that it was not sufficient to stem the tide of British Euroscepticism is a testament to the deep political roots of that movement.

The road from the Leave vote in 2016 to an actual Brexit was a long one and is still in progress at the time of this writing. Nigel Farage famously stated in 2016 that: "To me, Brexit's easy. We have back British passports, we have control of our fishing waters, and our companies are not subject to EU law through the single market." In the same year Boris Johnson (then mayor of London) stated that: "Actually, there are plenty of people who now think the cost of getting out would be virtually nil and the cost of staying in would be very high." In the real world of economics, the UK Office of Budget Responsibility subsequently put the cost of Brexit at 4 or more percent of GDP, while the Bank of England suggested that it would cost more in lost output than the COVID-19 pandemic.[10] If slightly exaggerated, these estimates were not entirely off the mark.

Enter Boris Johnson

Boris Johnson was mayor of London from 2008 to 2016 before moving into Parliament. As of 2013, Johnson was not necessarily pro-Brexit and wrote an article saying so. In particular, he stated that "the question of EU membership is no longer of key importance to the destiny of this country." Part of his reasoning was the previously mentioned factor of the UK not being part of the EMU. Further, he stated that "most of our problems are not caused by 'Brussels,' but by chronic British short-termism, inadequate management, sloth, low skills, a culture of easy gratification and under-investment in both human and physical capital and infrastructure."[11]

Here he sounds a bit like Thomas Mun in Chapter 2 bemoaning "the general leprosy of our Piping, Potting, Feasting, Fashions and mis-spending of our time in Idleness and Pleasure."[12] Only the relevant comparison was not to the Dutch as with Mun but to the Germans. Indeed, Johnson asked: "Why are we still, person for person, so much less productive than the Germans? That is now a question more than a century old, and the answer has nothing to do with the EU."[13] That seems clear enough, but after some prevarication, and not for the first time, he subsequently changed his mind in order to advance his political career.

The entry of Johnson into the Leave campaign mattered. As one observer put it, "polling certainly persistently suggested that voters were more inclined to believe what Mr. Johnson said about Brexit than they were the utterances of any other politician."[14] His celebrity status, fuzzy nostalgia and antielite (but nonetheless elite) character all helped significantly in the cause. So did his "Englishness" and nationalistic leanings. More ominously, during the Brexit campaign, Johnson went so far as to compare the EU to the Nazis. He stated that: "Napoleon, Hitler, various people tried this out, and it ends tragically. The EU is an attempt to do this by different methods." By voting Leave, Johnson hoped that the British people would once again be the "heroes of Europe" as they were when fighting the Nazis.[15] Given the EU's commitment to the rule of law, one undermined by many Eurosceptics, this comparison was inaccurate, childish and even dangerous. But politically, it worked, and he quickly became foreign secretary under Theresa May in 2016 after David Cameron's resignation over the Brexit vote.

Meanwhile, these strong political winds in favor of Brexit did not encounter any stiff resistance from the Labour Party. While the bulk of the Labour membership was pro-Remain, the leadership under Jeremy Corbin did not effectively communicate this nor campaign effectively for the Remain cause. Indeed, public opinion did not even recognize Labour's position on the issue, and more than one-third of Labour voters in the referendum voted in favor of Leave.[16] In the end, these currents overpowered careful thinking, and the Labour leadership was complicit in the Leave vote.

Sovereignty and Immigration

As mentioned, the notion of "sovereignty" quickly emerged as a key theme in the Leave campaign, particularly as it related to immigration. At a general level, the EU was portrayed as a *constitutional* threat to UK sovereignty. Of course, the UK famously does not have a formal constitution, but absent that, the standard argument is that constitutional authority rests with the notion of Monarch-in-Parliament and, therefore, any supranational authority that impinges on this idea is to be rejected.[17] Consequently, a popular slogan of the Leave campaign was "Take Back Control," and this slogan was applied most vociferously to the issue of immigration. In his original 2013 speech calling for a referendum, David Cameron did not mention immigration at all. But he quickly had to pivot in response to the ethnonationalist UKIP and introduce the issue, calling for an order-of-magnitude reduction in immigration from the EU.

As noted above, the Eurosceptic movement had been focused on immigration and refugee resettlement as key issues. These were at the center of the British tabloid campaign for Brexit that took place, for example, in the pages of the *Daily Express* in an implicit alliance with the UKIP. In their words, Britain was "full and fed up" with no room for migrants from other EU countries.[18] Notions of British sovereignty were couched in terms of the EU forcing unwanted immigrants on the disenfranchised English.

It was indeed the case that UK had given up control of immigration as part of the Schengen Agreement allowing free movement of people within the EU. The EU also set the agenda in the realm of human rights, something that seems reasonable given their universal nature. But it is worth recalling that the UK retained its own policies in the areas of defense, health, education, social security, welfare, fiscal policy and monetary policy. Therefore, it still maintained a great deal of policy sovereignty outside of immigration.

While the Leave campaign often claimed that net migration into the UK was at levels of 500,000 annually, the actual figure peaked in 2015 at slightly above 300,000. In that year, net migration from the EU itself also peaked at slightly over two hundred thousand.[19] Nonetheless, migrants originating from the EU became a central issue in the Leave campaign, with the "Polish plumber" taking center stage. This culminated in the 2016 post-referendum murder of Polish factory worker Arkadiusz Jóźwik in Essex. There were also allegations that EU migration could expose the UK to terrorist threats, as well as the potential for health and welfare benefits tourism.[20]

The immigration issues also became mixed up with the issue of Syrian refugees despite the fact that the UK had taken in only approximately eight thousand of them. Further, even though Turkey had only closed on one of 35 EU accession chapters, the potential for Turkish immigration to the UK in some far-off, imagined future also came into the political mix. The resulting role of migration in the Leave campaign was summarized by one researcher as follows:[21]

> Deliberately mixing EU migration and the refugee crisis, with Turkey operating as the link between the two, allowed Leave campaigners to [...] play on the idea of the existential future of Europe. [...] Europe [...] is portrayed as surrounded by hotbeds of population growth, poverty, and fanaticism; as being under siege or even under assault by the rest of the world.

Indeed, in 2015, George Osborne, chancellor of the Exchequer, stated that "we are looking for substantive changes to our relationship with the European Union [...] that reflect our concerns about migration and people coming into our country just to claim our welfare payments."[22] He offered no credible evidence that the "claiming of welfare payments" was in fact a serious issue. As it happened, in February 2016, David Cameron had been able to persuade the European Council to relax the requirements for welfare payments to EU immigrants, but this appeared to have little effect. Further, there was evidence that EU migrants actually had a *positive* fiscal effect for the UK.[23] But none of this seemed to have mattered as myths took over from facts.[24]

Because we tend to bury past truths in the sands of history, even recent history, it is worth recalling that the primary refugee flows were from the Middle East, particularly Syria. While the Syrian conflict can be traced to the Arab Spring and drought, the UK did play a role in the general destabilization of the Middle East by joining the "Coalition of the Willing" in the 2003 invasion of Iraq. The echoes of this destabilization can be heard to this day.[25] With all the focus on British sovereignty, the sovereignty of other countries was ignored.

But what of immigration? As can be seen in Figure 7.1, the UK has a relatively high fertility rate compared to some other countries (1.56 births per woman in 2020). This might make the country less reliant on immigration in the long run relative to some of its high-income peers. But the fertility rate is below the rule-of-thumb replacement level of 2.1 births per woman, and by 2035, nearly one-quarter of the population will be over sixty-five.[26] For this reason, *immigration will necessarily be part of the UK's future.* Missing from the Brexit debate was how to best construct policies to shape immigration to best economic effect. Indeed, as we will see, it eventually turned out that the British economy was quite dependent on EU workers and that their absence was sorely missed in some sectors.

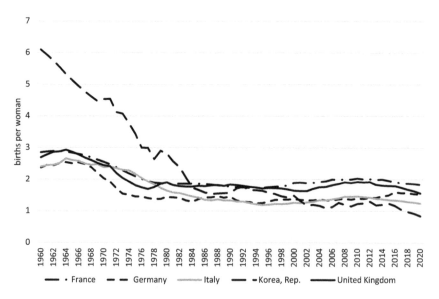

Figure 7.1 Fertility rates. Source: databank.worldbank.org.

Putting aside questions of evidence however, as previously mentioned, issues of sovereignty and immigration played a significant role in the Brexit vote.[27] In this and other respects, it was an exercise in performative economic nationalism and was widely recognized as such. But what did Brexit actually mean? Let's start with the economics of it.

The Economics of EU Membership

There is indeed reason to believe that membership in the EU (but not necessarily the EMU) confers economic benefits on its members, including the pre-Brexit UK. It had the effect of increasing trade in both goods and services, facilitated the liberalization of foreign direct investment (FDI) among member countries and allowed for the relatively free movement of labor. Each of these effects tends to increase the level of economic activity, which tends to increase incomes. There are technical issues about the relative roles of trade creation versus trade diversion, but there is also some empirical support that the EU has had positive impacts on trade.[28]

The early days of European integration in the form of the European Community (EC) coincided with a revolution in growth theory. As a result of this confluence of events, there was a tendency among economists to suggest that EC membership would raise the *growth rates* of member countries.[29] At the time, trade economists made growth rate claims about much of the trade liberalization being proposed, but such hopes often proved to be elusive. Nevertheless, there was the distinct possibility that EC membership would increase *levels* of per-capita GDP, and this is still important.[30]

While the studies are not conclusive, the evidence suggests that EU membership did indeed have a positive effect on member countries' level of GDP per capita.[31] In the case of the UK, some of these effects seem to be related to the role of inward FDI on firm performance.[32] Even the migration bugbear seems to have had positive impacts on both labor productivity and, as mentioned above, fiscal contributions.[33] In the run-up to the vote, the Bank of England did emphasize these points, but to little effect.

Much was made during the campaign about the fiscal transfer effects of EU membership, with allegations on the part of the Leave campaign that EU membership cost the UK £350 million per week. This was a gross exaggeration. Indeed, the "membership fee" paid by the UK to the EU needs to be weighed against the economic benefits of membership. This benefit–cost analysis was undertaken by British economist Nicholas Crafts on the eve of the Brexit vote. His conclusion was that "EU membership has raised trade and income levels in the UK in the past through increasing economic integration. It seems quite clear that these gains have outweighed the 'membership fee' which has primarily consisted of budget transfers and costly regulation."[34]

There was also the matter of the EU's preferential trade agreements. As was reported in the financial press at that time, the EU had negotiated over one hundred of these and, in leaving the EU, the UK would lose access to them. To restore the status quo ante, along with negotiating a trade agreement with the EU itself, it would need to conduct over one hundred more of these as well, an impossibility. Therefore, there was no feasible Brexit path to ensuring that the UK's export markets would remain intact.

For these reasons, the preponderance of the evidence going into the Brexit vote was that Brexit would be an economic blunder. The Remain campaign, however, did not effectively leverage this fact. In one assessment, "even though the Remain side's main strapline was 'Britain Stronger in Europe,' rather less was said about how the UK economy might be strengthened further by continued EU membership."[35] Actual economics was sidelined by the politics of economic nationalism. One reason for this might have been something we mentioned in Chapter 5, namely socioeconomic nostalgia.

Nostalgic Deprivation?

One assessment of the Leave campaign suggested that, despite its focus on Brussels, globalization and the like, "in the end it was about gut-wrenching issues like borders, culture, and the homeland."[36] This sounds a lot like the ethnonationalist Trump movement in the United States, and indeed, there appear to be several overlaps to be found in these two national contexts, overlaps having a lot to do with the themes taken up in previous chapters. Consider, for example, the following summary from political scientists Justin Gest, Tyler Reny and Jeremy Mayer:[37]

> White working-class communities in the United States and the United Kingdom [...] share a similar sense of social and economic decline. Socially, the two countries have experienced great demographic change since the middle of the 20th century, owing the to the admission of immigrants from Latin America and East Asia in the United States, and immigrants from South Asia, the West Indies, and Eastern Europe in the United Kingdom. [...] Economically, the two countries have shed much of their manufacturing sectors in favor of a more global, service- and high technology-driven economy. There has been little refuge for those trained in manufacturing trades, in which wages have stagnated and work has become scarce. [...] Many White working-class people in the United States and United Kingdom associate this loss in economic status with coinciding losses in social and political status.

These authors associate these (and other) developments with what they term "nostalgic deprivation," which they define as "the discrepancy between individuals' understanding of their current status and their *perceptions* about the past."[38] As we saw in the previous chapter, the past indeed looms large in economic nationalism, but sometimes it is an imagined past rather than an actual past. Nonetheless, Gest, Reny and Mayer suggest that nostalgic deprivation helps to explain what they call the "Radical Right" in Western Europe and the United States. Drawing on the work of political scientist Elisabeth Ivarsflaten, they focus on economic, political and social grievances.[39] This grievance model suggests that each of these sources of grievance can help to explain the rise of the populist right in Europe and the United States.

Gest, Reny and Mayer do not discount the role of economic and political grievances, but they emphasize social grievances in the form of demographic change and immigration. This is in line with the empirical results of Ivarsflaten suggesting that immigration grievances are the primary driver of successful right-wing parties in Europe. Gest, Reny and Mayer suggest that "for many individuals, immigration and demographic change pose a visible and direct threat to established concepts of nation, identity, and their constitutive social hierarchies."[40] We are back to ethnonationalism again.

These researchers note that British identity is "grounded in a sense of heritage, blood, and territory" and is supplemented by an "ossified social structure."[41] Their empirical evidence suggests that their measured nostalgic deprivation helps to explain support for the UKIP among Conservative voters, and thereby, implicit support for Brexit. These results verify what most observers already know intuitively, namely, that support for the UKIP and Brexit is a psychological phenomenon.

What can we make of results such as these? The idea of nostalgic deprivation depends on perceptions about the past and perhaps even racial resentments. And as the authors note, it is not clear how to address this type of deprivation (as opposed to, say, real economic deprivation). Since "whiteness" is implicit in their construct, do we want to promote it to the exclusion of nonwhite British citizens? Do we embrace British ethnonationalism in an attempt to diminish it? Or do we hope for a revived British civic nationalism and a renewed focus on material deprivations? The latter would be a more positive way forward.

Getting Brexit Done

The Brexit vote took place in 2016, but Brexit itself only came into effect in 2021. The intervening years were filled with posturing, first under Theresa May through mid-2019 and then under Boris Johnson. Many of the issues that the Brexiters claimed would be resolved in their favor were not. These included fishing, labor standards and the Northern Ireland border. As *Guardian* columnist Polly Toynbee put it, "Those who shout betrayal will be dead right." Toynbee refers to the "forever unattainable sovereignty phantasm" at the heart of the Brexit idea. This phantasm implied that the Johnson government did not want to "kill off the car industry, manufacturing, farming, finance and fishing."[42] Such concerns limited the UK's scope for action.

In December 2020, as the Brexit deadline neared without an agreement, Boris Johnson was forced to call Ursula von der Leyen, president of the European Commission, to secure an invitation to Brussels. The issues to be addressed were fishing rights, rules for fair trade and an enforcement mechanism for Britain's regulatory standards. Johnson continued to claim that Britain would "prosper mightily" even if there was no agreement with the EU. This, of course, was completely false.

What emerged from this episode was the Trade and Cooperation Agreement (TCA), consisting of more than 1,200 pages of text, whose purpose was to get the less specific Withdrawal Agreement "done." The TCA attempted to address the usual border issues, as well as the possibility of the UK tilting the playing field via regulatory rollback vis-à-vis the EU. The Johnson government's overall objectives were in keeping with its symbolic, economic nationalist governing philosophy. In the words of one observer:[43]

> The overall pattern […] is one of the UK being driven to secure symbolically significant concessions, even at the price of economic efficiency. The TCA avoided the worst-case effects of a non-agreement, without obviously compromising the […] rhetoric of "Brexit means Brexit."

Brexit was thus performative from beginning to end, and the TCA negotiations process compromised the relationship between the UK and the EU, particularly on the EU side. Nonetheless, the TCA was ratified in April 2021, and Brexit began to go into effect.

Impacts

In October 2016, Brexit minister David Davis stated that there would be "no downside" to Brexit and "many upsides."[44] The assumption of the Leave supporters is that, somehow, Brexit would not alter its trading relationship with the EU. Nonetheless, border checks began on 1 January 2021. These included everything one would expect at, well, a *border*: import/export declarations, security documentation, and sanitary and phytosanitary checks for agricultural goods. In short, trade compliance requirements appeared as they would for any normal trade transaction. As a result, British exports to the EU fell significantly in early 2021. British firms did eventually adjust, but they absorbed the trade compliance costs in the process.

By October 2021, five years after Davis' "no downside" claim and with Brexit "done," the UK began to experience significant shortages of foodstuffs and petrol.[45] The fuel crisis involved fights among panicked customers, a third of the country's petrol stations being closed, panic buying and the military being put on standby to distribute petrol. The cause was a shortage of approximately a hundred thousand lorry drivers. Of course, not all this shortage was due to Brexit, but an estimated loss of approximately ten thousand EU lorry drivers certainly did not help.[46] The food shortage was also attributable to a worker shortage, including meat packers, poultry workers and farm workers, and the situation was serious enough that some meat producers petitioned the government to be allowed to hire prisoners. Some of these missing food sector workers had previously been EU migrants.

Most careful assessments of the fuel and food crises point to the loss of over one million EU workers. The Conservative Party presented this as a potential boon to domestic UK workers who would receive higher wages, but the severity of the shortages suggested that this mechanism was not working. As stated by *The Economist*, "migrant flows used to respond to the state of the economy, but under the post-Brexit immigration regime they have responded to ministerial diktat."[47] In fact, the pro-Brexit Johnson's government was forced to begin offering temporary visas for EU truck drivers and poultry workers with the president of the British Chambers of Commerce suggesting that this was far from adequate.

Who knew that EU workers were so important to the functioning of the British economy? Anyone that had carefully studied the issue. Indeed, by October 2021, YouGov polls were indicating that half of British citizens felt that Brexit was going badly. Critically, less than 20 percent felt it was going well. By January 2023, 60 percent of British citizens thought that Brexit was a mistake.[48] The negative predictions of economists have proven to be relevant, and at least in the short run, the experiment seems to have failed.

On the trade front, a paper from the Centre for Economic Performance at the London School of Economics suggests significant TCA impacts. These included a 25 percent reduction in UK imports from the EU and a 30 percent reduction in what trade economists call the "extensive margin" of exports to the EU. That is, small UK exports are exiting small EU markets because they had to absorb the fixed costs of market entry. These effects are part of what the authors term "an unprecedented unravelling of deep integration" between the UK and the EU.[49] Meanwhile, the advertised free trade agreement with the United States has not transpired. UK businesses have been left in the lurch.

Fish over Finance

In the endgame of "Getting Brexit Done," Thomas Mun's "Fishing in Her Majesty's Seas" loomed large. Indeed, the fishing sector negotiations nearly scuppered the deal altogether. Interestingly, the fishing sector counts for less than 0.1 percent of the UK's GDP, while estimates for financial services range as high as 11 percent. Once again, economic nationalists downplayed the role of services, with only about five of the more than 1,200 pages of the TCA being dedicated to financial services. Nonetheless, a 2017 study by the European Parliament had concluded that "the most significant economic implications of a withdrawal of the UK from the EU can be found in relation to financial services."[50] That assessment was on the mark.

Pre-Brexit, London was the largest financial services cluster in the world, providing a dizzying array of products. The 2017 European Parliament study found that the UK supplied approximately one-quarter of the financial services consumed by the rest of the EU. One big client, in fact, was the European Central Bank. Just under 70 percent of EU over-the-counter exchange turnover took place in the UK, and approximately one-half of all global financial firms had their headquarters in the City.

In the advent of a "hard-Brexit," the UK's access to the EU market would revert to WTO rules in financial services as established by the GATS and its protocols. This would take away the UK's "regulatory equivalence" in the EU market and, consequently, the "passport" of its financial firms. But it is even more complex than that because financial services are complex. In fact, there would need to be nearly sixty types of equivalences granted.

The financial industry was aware of these issues once the 2016 Brexit vote took place. *The Economist* reports that, between 2016 and the advent of Brexit itself in 2021, US$1.6 trillion in assets and more than 7,500 financial service jobs were moved from the UK to the EU.[51] This trend continued once Brexit began in 2021. In January 2021, the Johnson government admitted that they had essentially excluded the sector from Brexit negotiations. Then chancellor of the Exchequer Rishi Sunak was still talking up the promise of Brexit as a force that would invigorate the sector, but others in the government admitted that equivalence was unlikely. Even Boris Johnson stated that the TCA trade deal did "not go as far as we would like" on financial services.[52] That is to say, it did not go anywhere. In a word, they botched it.

There are of course arguments that the City represents an overly expanded cluster, not all of which has a positive impact on the UK. There are further concerns about the role of the City in nefarious financial deals, namely hiding ill-gotten gains.[53] These concerns need to be taken seriously, but they do not provide justification for the focus on fish over finance. This is why, in early

2021 after the TCA had been negotiated, one observer stated: "It is a cry-ing shame that financial services have waited so long and that planning is so clearly in its infancy."[54] Again, performative economic nationalism prevailed over careful thinking.

There was some breathing room. Equivalence was granted on a tempo-rary basis through 2022. Originally, Chancellor Sunak hoped for an agree-ment on financial services by March 2021. This did not happen. Scrambling, Chancellor Sunak proposed a new system of financial regulation for the UK in November 2021. While cast in terms of enhancing growth prospects in the sector, it was really an attempt to stem the flow of financial firms to Frankfurt, Paris and Amsterdam. Having had since 2016 to work out these details, the Brexit forces left themselves six months to put something in place to protect the City. At the time of this writing, the issue remains unresolved.

On finance and the City, *The Economist* got it right when it stated:[55]

> As with so much of the Brexit process, Britain now faces a choice between divergence and market access. Some in government believe that Britain could benefit from financial deregulation and become a centre for new types of innovative global finance. But many in the City would prefer to hold on to markets they already have.

The impact on financial services as of the end of 2021 was significant, with financial services exports to the EU falling by approximately 30 percent. London-based euro-swaps fell significantly, and Amsterdam became the center for equity trading.[56] But the impacts of Brexit will be felt far outside of London and in ways that could call into questions the United Kingdom itself.

Disunited Kingdom

In Chapter 6, we noted that there are many more nations than countries. The United Kingdom is made up of the "nations" of England, Wales, Scotland and Northern Ireland. England looms largest in the bunch, accounting for more than 80 percent of total British population. As noted above, to a significant extent, Brexit was an outgrowth of a resurgent English nation-alism. As *The Economist* put it, "English nationalism is the most disruptive force in British politics. Brexit would have been impossible without it."[57] The Conservative Party has embraced this resurgent English nationalism and has "used this powerful identity to grab power."[58] But like the Republican Party in the United States in the thrall of the ethnonationalist Trump movement, the British Conservatives risk losing control of the nationalist dynamic and being forced to follow where it leads them. The outcomes have not been productive.

One uncomfortable truth that confronts English nationalists is the devolution of 1999 in which Scotland and Wales each gained their own legislatures and the right to set policies not reserved for the center (foreign and macroeconomic policies). But there is a great deal of ambiguity in these arrangements, and the Northern Ireland case is more complex than Scotland and Wales in that Northern Ireland has had its own Parliament since 1921. Moreover, British citizens in Northern Ireland can identify as Irish and therefore European and can even hold Irish passports.[59] This is a multinational context in which ethnonationalism falls dramatically short.

Scotland has seen a long-active independence movement under the Scottish National Party (SNP) and a referendum on independence in 2014. A second referendum is firmly on the agenda, especially when the SNP fares well at the polls as it did in 2021. Awkwardly, in 2016, more than 60 percent of Scottish voters voted in favor of Remain. In response, Scottish first minister Nicola Sturgeon suggested that Scotland would try to "secure" its place in the EU and threatened another referendum. She requested such a referendum in 2019, but Boris Johnson refused this request. While Sturgeon's resignation in early 2023 has made the prospect of independence less likely, the issue still simmers.

In the case of Wales, a majority of the electorate voted in favor of Leave. Nonetheless, the Brexit vote, and the tortuous process of "getting Brexit done," has improved the prospects of the Welsh independence (Cymru) movement with an increased percentage of the population of Wales in favor of it.[60] Although Welsh independence does not seem to be a future prospect, Brexit has strengthened the hand of those in favor of it and complicated the relationship between the Welsh government and the UK government.

The Northern Ireland issue is perhaps the most complicated. As long as Ireland and the UK were both part of the EU, there were no tariff or nontariff barriers between the Republic of Ireland and Northern Ireland. With the departure of the UK from the EU, this trading relationship was thrown into disarray. As part of "Getting Brexit Done," the Johnson government negotiated the Northern Ireland Protocol in order to avoid a hard border between it and the Irish Republic, which retains its EU membership. The protocol states that, while Northern Ireland is part of the UK's customs territory, it will apply the EU's customs rules, essentially leaving Northern Ireland in the EU with regard to trade.

The protocol, however, left unaddressed significant differences between the UK and the EU. The fly in the ointment is that the protocol essentially creates the Irish Sea "border" between the UK and Northern Ireland into a border between the UK and the EU. As stated by one set of writers, "While the border in the Irish Sea is not meant to divide the UK into Great Britain and Northern Ireland, it is de facto, an international customs boarder (the EU's external border) running through the UK's territory."[61] This is quite awkward and a cause of grave concern for Northern Ireland's Unionist (pro-British) population.

The protocol protects against the potential for transshipment from Great Britain to the EU via Northern Ireland by applying EU duties to any goods where there is such a risk as they enter Northern Ireland. Assessing transshipment risk is therefore one area of potential disagreement between the UK and the EU. There is also the matter that, as part of the EU's single market for goods, Northern Ireland must comply with any relevant EU regulations on goods, so there is a need to harmonize EU and UK regulations in this area. The UK government's position on these issues was set out in a 2020 "Command Paper," but the remaining differences in interpretation show just how important an effective TCA is for even intra-UK trade, particularly since the Command Paper differs from the Northern Ireland Protocol in some significant ways.[62]

After the conclusion of the TCA and the Northern Ireland Protocol, the anti-EU Brexit negotiator David Frost began to suggest that the protocol itself might be abrogated. In September 2020, government lawyer Sir Jonathan Jones, having advised Mr. Frost of the illegality of any abrogation, decided to resign.[63] About a year later, in October 2021, Frost again suggested that the Northern Ireland Protocol could be scrapped, and Boris Johnson later reiterated the threat despite having signed it himself. This was in response to the fact that the EU's proposal to scrap border checks on 80 percent of goods entering Northern Ireland fell short of these political actors' demands. The Johnson government went so far as to demand a "total rewrite" of the protocol and a removal of the ECJ from the process.[64] Both Frost and Johnson threatened to invoke Article 16 of the protocol, an emergency safeguard measure, but Frost himself resigned in December 2021.

In response, the EU began to consider the termination of the entire TCA, allowable with 12 months' notice. Most observers agreed that the Northern Ireland issue had the potential to turn into a trade war between the parties, as well as increased conflict in Northern Ireland.[65] To inflame the situation further, in May 2022, the Johnson government went so far as to propose a bill giving it the power to override the protocol, earning it the rebuke of the Confederation of British Industry. Once again, foreseeable issues were ignored by the Brexiters. Given that all EU governments had to ratify the TCA and the Northern Ireland Protocol, and that the matter is thereby one of international law, the EU was reluctant to concede the issue.[66] At the time of this writing, a breakthrough does seem possible with the Windsor Framework, a document that will supplement the Northern Ireland Protocol.[67]

Get Back to Rwanda

In Chapter 6, we discussed the role of refugees in ethnonationalist movements, and in this chapter, we previously mentioned that the refugee issue loomed large in the Brexit Leave campaign. Perhaps then it was no surprise that it would return, and indeed in April 2022, the Johnson government announced that it was going to begin to send some asylum seekers to Rwanda. The UK home secretary, Priti Patel, travelled to Rwanda to make the announcement. The UK Home Office stated that the agreement would "overhaul our broken asylum system" and that "there is nothing in the UN Refugee Convention which prevents removal to a safe country."[68] Awkwardly, the UNHCR disagreed, and condemned the policy, as did many human rights experts and Amnesty International. The UNHCR response was clear: "UNHCR remains firmly opposed to arrangements that seek to transfer refugees and asylum seekers to third countries in the absence of sufficient safeguards and standards. Such arrangements simply shift asylum responsibilities, evade international obligations and are contrary to the letter and spirit of the Refugee Convention."[69] Strong opposition was also voiced by Secretary Patel's own Home Office staff as well as by Prince Charles.[70]

The measure was meant to apply to those who "come to the UK illegally, or by dangerous or unnecessary means." Ironically, those refugees coming by dangerous means are most likely to be those whose situations are the most desperate. And given the number of scandals that were plaguing Boris Johnson at the time (including a police fine for breaking pandemic lockdown rules), there was the suspicion that this was a means for Johnson to divert attention toward the safer themes of the Leave campaign. There was also the awkward fact that, as the Johnson government was negotiating the 120-million-pound deal, it had agreed to take in over fifty-five thousand Ukrainian refugees fleeing the Russian invasion. This raised the question of why the Ukrainian refugees were more deserving than those from Iraq, Sudan and Syria fleeing equally devastating conflicts.

Assessing the Blunder

The Brexit process has reflected a mix of economic nationalism, ethnonationalism and populism. Parallels have been drawn between the politics of Brexit and the Trump movement in the United States, with both having been initiated in 2016, as well as between the political figures of Boris Johnson and Donald Trump. The latter comparison is perhaps unfair to Mr. Johnson who has not advocated violence. Nonetheless, Brexit is emblematic of an economic nationalistic movement that has taken root in an increasing number of countries.

Being largely an exercise in political psychology, Brexit was a *blunder*. There were no credible economic analyses that suggest anything but negative economic impacts. The only issue was how large these would be. Cameron's "great miscalculation" led to significant economic costs that are still playing out. Many years after the vote, it is still not fully clear what the Brexit arrangements are or even if they are really settled. Persistent uncertainty abounds. As an exercise in political psychology, Brexit also lacked a *strategic* purpose. One observer called it a "decision without a rationale." Incredibly, there is a parallel with the Viktor Orbán government in Hungary in that the EU has been cast as an "other" for which all ills are blamed.[71] Despite the rhetoric of "Global Britain," through the Brexit process, the UK has surrendered any global role that involves the EU and its grounding in international law.

The relative meaninglessness of Brexit was on display at a March 2022 Tory conference where Boris Johnson compared the Brexit vote to the bravery of Ukrainians in fighting against the ongoing Russian invasion. Lost to Johnson was the irony here that Ukraine had been invaded precisely because they wanted to more closely associate with the EU and its rules-based system of economic governance. There was also the small matter that voting in a referendum is not quite the same as risking your life to confront an invading army. Johnson gave every appearance of a man casting about for a rationale and grabbing the nearest one no matter how ill chosen. In June 2022, he barely survived a no confidence vote of his own party. The next month, he was forced to resign after scores of his own ministers resigned.[72]

Despite Johnson's resignation, adherence to the Brexit ideology remained central in the Conservative Party leadership contest. In 2022, the Conservatives *selected* former foreign secretary Liz Truss who was a vocal supporter of Brexit but awkwardly campaigned for Remain. This process involved approximately eighty thousand Tory Party members out of an electorate of approximately fifty million. Truss and her chancellor of the Exchequer, Kwasi Kwarteng, proposed a budget without any oversight from the UK's Office of Budget Responsibility that the financial markets found to be fanciful due to its unfunded tax cut. Interest rates surged, the pound collapsed and even the International Monetary Fund issued a warning. Truss ended up being the shortest-lived prime minister in history, being replaced by Rishi Sunak.[73]

In one pro-Remain speech, Truss had stated that "I think the British people are sensible people. They understand, fundamentally, that economically Britain would be better off staying in a reformed EU."[74] She was right then but changed her posture to keep up with Boris Johnson. Ironically, she was known as a pro-growth politician.[75] What she did not recognize was that EU membership itself was the best pro-growth strategy available to the UK.

Recall from the beginning of the chapter that Boris Johnson had asked: "Why are we still, person for person, so much less productive than the Germans?" He also stated that "the answer has nothing to do with the EU." He was correct, and Brexit has made productively addressing this issue even more difficult and less likely than before. As with much of economic nationalism, the difficult questions took a back seat to the political performance. On current trajectory, British citizens will be the worse for it.[76]

Chapter 8

PANDEMIC NATIONALISM

On 5 October 2020, US president Donald Trump appeared on the Truman Balcony of the White House. Days before, he had tested positive for COVID-19 as had many other individuals who had attended recent White House functions. On the balcony, he extoled his own leadership and strength. Many likened this event to Evita Peron's similar appearance on a balcony of the Casa Rosada in Buenos Aires on another October day in 1951 when she gave her final speech to supporters in the Plaza de Mayo. Given President Trump's COVID-19 status, and his checkered approach to combating the pandemic, critics dubbed this his Covita moment, and it was indeed emblematic of his administration and its approach to the pandemic.

The COVID-19 pandemic changed the world in many ways. For starters, it impacted growth, employment, investment and trade. The World Bank suggested that the pandemic-induced recession was the worst since World War II. It was more pronounced than the recessions of 1975, 1982 and 1991. In some respects, it even overshadowed even the global financial crisis of 2009. What is more, because the pandemic undermined several important growth factors, the recessionary effects were likely to be long term, particularly given the continued emergence of new variants, including Delta and Omicron.[1]

In 2020, Carmen Reinhart and Vincent Reinhart put it this way:[2]

> The shared nature of this shock—the novel coronavirus does not respect national borders—has put a larger proportion of the global community in recession than at any other time since the Great Depression. As a result, the recovery will not be as robust or rapid as the downturn. And ultimately, the fiscal and monetary policies used to combat the contraction will mitigate, rather than eliminate, the economic losses, leaving an extended stretch of time before the global economy claws back to where it was at the start of 2020.

Despite these dire economic conditions, some economic nationalists saw the pandemic as an occasion to further their cause. For example, as the deaths from COVID-19 reached 100,000 in the United States, US trade representative Robert Lighthizer referred to the pandemic as an opportunity to reshape trade relations and had the audacity to refer to these trade relations (and not the pandemic) as a "disease."[3] Senior Trump administration adviser Peter Navarro (with no real background in trade policy) echoed Robert Lighthizer, stating:[4]

> This is a wake-up call for an issue that has been latent for many years but is critical to US economic and national security. [...] If we have learned anything from the coronavirus and swine flu H1N1 epidemic of 2009, it is that we cannot necessarily depend on other countries, even close allies, to supply us with needed items, from face masks to vaccines.

In the end, deaths in the United States reached one million, with Peter Navarro playing a part in the initial non-strategy, which, with its herd immunity default and culture war against mask wearing and vaccines, proved to be catastrophic.[5] These failures were mirrored the world over by other nationalist politicians.

There are two important things to understand about the relationship between economic nationalism and pandemics. The first is that economic nationalism makes the health and medical policy response *worse*, not better. Given the global nature of pandemics, international cooperation among countries, firms and NGOs is critical. Second, successfully emerging from pandemic-induced economic downturns requires multilateralism rather than unilateralism. Open but managed economic relationships among countries are critical for sustained recovery.

Consider, for example, the issue of vaccine development. In late 2020, the drug company Pfizer announced significant progress on a COVID-19 vaccine. Nationalistic US president Trump immediately announced that this breakthrough was part of its Operation Warp Speed vaccine development program. In reality, it was not. It was the product of a corporate partnership between the US-based multinational Pfizer and the German-based biotechnology firm BioNTech. BioNTech, in turn, was owned by two German citizens of Turkish origin. Pfizer itself was headed up by a Greek citizen.[6] The production of the vaccine requires approximately two hundred and eighty inputs from 19 countries.[7] Rather than economic nationalism, this was more like globalization in action.

The pandemic serves as a natural experiment to test the effectiveness of economic nationalism. As we will see, it has proved economic nationalism to have failed in multiple country contexts and pointed out the importance of multilateral alternatives in both health and trade. We will set the context by first considering multilateralism in health.

Multilateralism in Health

This book has argued in favor of the multilateral alternative to economic nationalism, and this multilateral alternative extends to the realm of health. As it turns out, there is a long history of multilateralism in health going back to the nineteenth century. For example, a series of European International Sanitary Conferences began in 1851 to address cholera outbreaks, and these continued through the 1930s. As stated by the medical historian Howard Markel, "it was (the) cholera pandemics, as well as [...] threats of yellow fever, bubonic plague, smallpox, and typhus, that inspired the development of the modern, international health regulations."[8]

These international conferences continued into the early twentieth century, and Markel describes how they began to set in place global public health principles that proved to be enduring. These included "modern disease surveillance and reporting, rapid dissemination of new scientific information and therapeutic agents between investigators and nations, the development of universal quarantine and isolation regulations, and environmental approaches to cleaning up unsanitary or deleterious influences associated with various diseases."[9] This proved to be a lasting, positive legacy.

The Pan-American Health Organization (PAHO) was founded in 1902 when it was known as the Pan-American Sanitary Bureau, and the Office International d'Hygiène Publique (OIHP) was founded in 1907. Both of these were signature events that furthered the global public health infrastructure. Next, the League of Nations, founded in 1919, had a Health Committee with broad aspirations, but it proved to lack the necessary support. As with the realm of international economic relations, it took the ravages of World War II to spur further institutional development in global public health.

In July 1946, the emerging United Nations endorsed the idea of a World Health Organization (WHO), and this organization came into existence two years later. As with much of the multilateral architecture that emerged after World War II, the United States was at the forefront of this effort. The WHO held its first meeting in Geneva in 1948. A year later, PAHO became a part of the WHO, and similar entities were created in five other regions as well. This new structure had successes in addressing infectious diseases, most notably in the case of smallpox but also in the cases of polio, measles, tuberculosis, malaria, HIV and influenza.

To anticipate the discussion of this chapter, it is important to acknowledge that the WHO has come under a good deal of criticism for any number of failings in its response to particular crises. That said, Howard Markel states that "given its lack of international policing power, relatively small staff and inadequate budget, it is clear that there is plenty of blame to be attributed to many other sources." He continues to say:[10]

What is urgently needed from the United Nations, and the individual nations it comprises, is an effective and universal system of global health governance that has the authority and power to harmonize objectives, establish priorities, coordinate activities, set budgets, execute programs, and monitor progress. All of these functions require enormous fiscal support and is incumbent upon the wealthier nations of the world meeting their moral, social and ethical responsibilities.

It has long been recognized that the limitations of the WHO are by design, with an annual budget of only US$2.5 billion.[11] Further, the WHO had often sounded the warning about what it termed "Disease X" and set up a program to address that likely outcome. In this and other actions over the years, it has demonstrated an imperfect but sustained commitment to its mission. Its failures are often that of its membership and do not take away from its institutional importance. In the case of COVID-19, its degree of failure is a matter of ongoing debate.

COVID-19 Origins and Tensions

As part of its public health preparedness, Taiwan's Center for Disease Control monitors health-related chatter on the Chinese internet. In December 2019, as a result of this practice, it alerted the WHO of an "atypical pneumonia" in Wuhan, China. This warning was ignored, including by the United States, whose own Center for Disease Control and Prevention had trained much of Taiwan's public health staff.[12] For its part, China began a propaganda campaign against Taiwan, and the incomplete responses of the WHO, the United States and China set the stage for a global disaster.

Like the SARS epidemic of 2002–3, COVID-19 emerged in China. China's response to the SARS pandemic was widely considered to be secretive and insufficient. Foreign policy analysts Colin Kahl and Thomas Wright refer to it as "a textbook example of how *not* to respond to a pandemic."[13] But things were supposed to be better. After SARS, China established a Contagious Disease National Direct Reporting System whose purpose was to provide independent early alerts if another outbreak occurred. Unfortunately, this system was not allowed to perform when it mattered most with COVID-19, the pandemic response being quickly centralized within the upper echelons of the Chinese Communist Party (CCP).

As discussed in Chapter 5, the Trump administration touted a "phase-one" trade deal with China, and this was signed in January 2020. Unbeknownst to the Trump administration, Chinese president Xi had begun chairing emergency meetings on COVID-19 a week earlier, and neither President Trump nor President Xi had any interest in letting COVID-19 upstage the "deal." There was a complicity on both sides to initially ignore the emergent pandemic in order to give President Trump a political "win." However, given the trade war initiated by the Trump administration, the bilateral relationship was at an all-time low. At the same time, and as discussed in the next chapter, the United States had also precipitated an attack on the Chinese technology firm Huawei, and this was an additional source of tension. Consequently, there was little room for cooperation between the two powers to address the emerging pandemic.[14]

President Xi immediately took the reins of China's pandemic response, applying a political lens and engaging in what political scientist Dali Yang referred to as "discourse power."[15] This response included outright propaganda designed to deflect responsibility. On the US side, in January 2020, Larry Kudlow, President Trump's director of the US National Economic Council, claimed that the emerging coronavirus would have "no material impact" on the US economy.[16] If this was not propaganda, it was at least gross ignorance.

While a February 2020 telephone call between Xi and Trump found the relationship between the two countries on relatively solid ground, that soon dissipated. Shortly after this call, both countries would be expelling the other's journalists in a tit-for-tat retaliation episode, and China's Foreign Affairs Information Department spokesman Zhao Lijian would be claiming that the "political virus" was worse than the actual one. Again, gross ignorance if not propaganda. Zhao went a step further, expressing various conspiracy theories that the COVID-19 virus had actually emerged in the United States. True to form, President Trump retaliated, labeling the COVID-19 virus the "Wuhan virus" and the "Kung flu." Political scientist Dali Yang summed up the situation in 2021 as follows:[17]

> Prior to the COVID-19 pandemic, US-China relations already had come under heavy strains as a result of the intensely contested trade war between the two countries. The trade war generated much bitterness, mistrust, and animosity. [...] The flexing of Chinese power during the COVID-19 pandemic [...] aggravated already strained US-China relations in ways that would be hard to repair. There (was) simply no returning to the pre-pandemic status quo, let alone the pre-trade war status quo.

But that was not all. In April 2020, the Australian government, along with other countries, reasonably suggested that an independent inquiry be held into the origins of COVID-19. In May 2020, China retaliated by applying heavy antidumping and countervailing duties on Australia's barley exports that priced Australia out of the Chinese market and suspended beef imports from specific Australian exporters. Further trade coercion measures were taken against Australia's exports of wine, wheat, wool, lobsters, sugar, copper, timber, coal and cotton. Only iron, it seems, escaped China's ire.[18] While China had a history of other episodes of politically motivated trade coercion, this battle with a major trading partner across a wide scope of products was a dramatic departure from the multilateral norms of the WTO. Pandemic nationalism had spilled over into trade nationalism.

Trump's Failure

At a political rally in October 2018, US president Trump explicitly embraced the nationalist label. He said to his audience: "You know what I am? I'm a nationalist, OK? I'm a nationalist. Nationalist! Use that word! Use that word!" He contrasted the "nationalist" label with that of "globalism" with its anti-Semitic overtones. He told his audience "Now you have a president who is standing up for America."[19] His pandemic record strongly suggested, however, that he was not interested in "standing up for America" but rather engaging in the performative aspects of nationalism for his own satisfaction and that of his political "base."

To cite some examples, in July 2020, President Trump announced that the United States would withdraw from the WHO in the middle of the pandemic. In November 2020, attending the Group of 7 (G7) meeting, President Trump skipped the session on pandemic response to play golf.[20] This choice was not surprising given that he spent over three hundred days of his four-year presidency engaged in this activity. In December 2020, with the number of US deaths surpassing its combat deaths in World War II and intensive care beds in critically short supply, President Trump referred to the US infection rate as "terrific." Terrifying would have been a more accurate description. Indeed, beyond the scope of Trump's understanding, in 2020, the death *rate* in the United States was 500 times that in South Korea.[21]

The US-based national security analysts Colin Kahl and Thomas Wright spent a great deal of effort tracking President Trump's response to the COVID-19 pandemic on nearly a week-by-week basis. Their assessment was that "from the time Trump heard of the dangers posed by the virus, his instinct was to minimize it." They also concluded that he was "the world's top purveyor of misinformation about the virus and public health." For Trump, the pandemic "was not a public health crisis so much as a political one."[22] This approach to health policy had deadly consequences. One study published in October 2020 by Colombia University's Earth Institute estimated excess deaths at that time relative to other high-income democracies at a minimum of 100,000.[23] Another study published and sponsored by *The Lancet* in 2021 estimated these to be closer to two hundred thousand.[24] In this regard, it is worth noting that in October 2014, when there was a single death of a US citizen during the Ebola crisis, Donald Trump called upon then President Barack Obama to resign.[25] He did not apply this standard (or even a much lower standard) to himself.

Modi's Failure

As we discussed in Chapter 6, Indian prime minister Narendra Modi's preoccupation was with ethnonationalism in the form of Hindutva. In January 2021, regarding his government's response to COVID-19, Modi boasted that "we not only solved our problems but also helped the world fight the pandemic" based on India's capacity to manufacture vaccines. If only. In April 2021, to better develop his Hindu political base, Modi allowed the Kumbh Mela festival to take place. This involved approximately one million people congregating near the Ganges River, perhaps the world's largest superspreader event. Modi and his ministers also spent April 2021 campaigning in four Indian states where elections were being held, convening large crowds without masks and social distancing. Members of Modi's government were also advocating cow urine as a COVID-19 cure. Meanwhile, his COVID-19 task force had not met for two months.[26]

By the end of April 2021, 400,000 Indians were testing positive for COVID-19 each day (a figure widely regarded as an underestimate), the country's hospital system was collapsing under COVID-19 cases, oxygen and other medicines were in short supply, and both formal and informal crematoria were working around the clock to keep up with the number of the dead. It became clear that, distracted by what *The Economist* called his "unrelenting quest for partisan advantage," Modi failed to respond to the COVID-19 challenge.[27]

While the daily death rate eventually began to decline, estimates of total deaths that subsequently emerged indicate a public health catastrophe. As of June 2021, the official estimate was at approximately 350,000 deaths, but most reliable estimates put the figure somewhere near two million, a disaster on the order of magnitude as the 1943 Bengal Famine.[28] As of the end of 2022, the WHO's own cumulative excess death estimates for India were at 4 million, but the Modi government tried to suppress these estimates.[29] Modi's continued identification of India's Muslim population as the main threat (discussed in Chapter 6) to the country was entirely misplaced. The real threat came from a virus that Modi ignored.

Ironically, India is home to one of the world's largest vaccine makers, the Serum Institute of India. The original plan was for the Serum Institute to help supply the world with the AstraZeneca vaccine. Instead of fulfilling contracts for this vaccine, the Serum Institute began to default on them, and domestic vaccination efforts faltered, failing to keep up with new infections. India's noted pharmaceutical capacity initially failed to respond to the crisis.

Modi's ethnonationalist posturing was not just a threat to his own citizens but to the entire world, providing a breeding ground for new viral variants, particularly the Delta variant, which appeared in December 2020 and went on to become significant in countries such as the United States and United Kingdom. The Delta variant was far more transmissible than even the Alpha variant that appeared in the United Kingdom, making it a particular threat to the unvaccinated of the world. When Modi's Hindutva confronted COVID-19, the virus prevailed.

Bolsonaro's Failure

Beginning with his election in 2018, Brazilian president Jair Bolsonaro never stopped criticizing "globalism" and defending his country's "sovereignty." Regarding COVID-19, he stated that it was just the common cold and that those sounding the alarm were "sissies." By April 2021, with more than four hundred thousand Brazilian citizens having perished from the disease, however, his government began to turn to the rest of the world for aid to combat the pandemic. At that time, Oliver Stuenkel of the Getulio Vargas Foundation commented that: "America could get away with having a Trump because it doesn't need the world that much. It can produce its own vaccines. But in Brazil, that behavior has been particularly reckless because it's a country that depends on the international community. We need multilateralism."[30]

The initial turning point in Bolsonaro's thinking might have been a March 2020 meeting with US president Donald Trump at the latter's Florida resort Mar-a-Lago. Bolsonaro's health minister Luiz Henrique Mandetta, who he fired over disputes on how to handle the pandemic, stated that "from that time on, it was very hard to get him to take the science seriously."[31] Upon return, 22 members of Bolsonaro's delegation tested positive for COVID-19. Nonetheless, as reported in one source, "the Mar-a-Lago dinner [...] cemented a partnership between Mr. Trump and Mr. Bolsonaro rooted in a shared disregard for the virus." In concert, the two leaders turned on the PAHO, and Trump withheld funding from the organization.[32] Bolsonaro was in league with Trump to kneecap PAHO at exactly the time when it was most needed.

Part of the bond between Bolsonaro and Trump was nationalism. As stated in this same source, "the two most powerful leaders in the Americas, Mr.

Trump and Mr. Bolsonaro are both ardent nationalists defiant of mainstream science." Bolsonaro kept holding mass rallies of supporters, and "Brazil soon emerged as a regional pandemic epicenter."[33] Inspired by the Trump model, an antiscience pandemic nationalism had taken a foothold in Latin America. Another part of the bond is that both Bolsonaro and Trump embraced a populist approach to politics that involved both antipathy to "elites" and what some observers have called a "politics of cruelty" that involves the deliberate disregard of the welfare of citizens.[34]

By May 2021, Bolsonaro's handling of COVID-19 became the subject of a parliamentary commission of inquiry (CPI). During the CPI, two former health ministers testified that Bolsonaro's initial strategy was composed of herd immunity and hydroxychloroquine, the latter being a discredited strategy at the time, but one that was supported by US president Trump. It was also revealed that the Bolsonaro government failed to respond to six offers of vaccines from Pfizer.[35] By June 2021, the death toll had increased to 500,000.

In October 2021, the Brazilian senate issue a thousand-page report accusing Bolsonaro of "crimes against public health," characterizing his approach to the pandemic as "macabre." By that time, *The Economist* had estimated that excess deaths due to COVID-19 were at nearly seven hundred thousand and characterized the report as "far more damning than expected."[36] Like Trump and Modi, Bolsonaro put his performative nationalism before public health.

There was one area where the Bolsonaro government was effective, however. This was in using the COVID-19 pandemic as an excuse to further expand its consolidated database of Brazilian citizens. Concerns about public health implications of the virus might be for "sissies," but leveraging the crisis to what has been called Brazil's "techno-authoritarianism" was just fine.[37] As is sometimes the case, the line between nationalism and authoritarianism becomes blurry. Indeed, to cement his authoritarian reputation, on the eve of Russia's invasion of Ukraine in February 2022, Bolsonaro made a special trip to Moscow to offer his "solidarity" to Vladimir Putin. For someone who famously stated that "I am an army captain. My specialty is killing," this probably made complete sense, but such political theater did little to help with Brazil's pandemic response.

Nationalism and Populist Leadership

In the eyes of their admirers, performative nationalists exercise "leadership" and "strength." Indeed, Trump, Modi and Bolsonaro are held up as models of robust "masculine" leadership. The notion of masculine leadership has a long history in early leadership studies but has proven to be of limited value.[38]

It appears to have been particularly ill suited to the COVID-19 pandemic, which required a very different skill set. Indeed, we can begin to get a sense of this using a performative nationalist checklist adapted from *The Economist* and presented in Table 8.1. This checklist has five elements:

- Claims to represent the "will of the people"
- Promotion of hatred of ethnic or religious minorities
- Undermining institutions
- Failing to respect the rule of law
- Ignoring science

As seen in Table 8.1, Trump, Modi and Bolsonaro met all five of these elements and, in adhering to them, failed in their responses to the pandemic. Viktor Orbán of Hungary, discussed in Chapter 6, met four of the five and is consequently known more for his ethnonationalism and illiberal tendencies rather than for a deliberate pandemic failure. Orbán did, however, use the pandemic to cement his illiberalism by pushing for and obtaining emergency powers, earning Hungary the "coronavirus autocracy" moniker.[39] Nonetheless, the COVID-19 pandemic laid bare the limits of performative nationalism as a substitute for real leadership, and this failure can be seen in the total deaths presented in Figure 8.1. The United States, Brazil and India were at the lead here. Of course, these are all relatively large countries by population size, and what really matters are the death rates, which we will also consider.

Given these shortcomings, there has been a suggestion that the masculine leadership style of performative nationalism is ill suited to public health challenges. Political scientists Carol Johnson and Blair Williams suggest that the

Table 8.1 The performative nationalist checklist.

Quality	Donald Trump	Narendra Modi	Jair Bolsonaro	Viktor Orbán
Claims to represent the "will of the people"	✓	✓	✓	✓
Promotion of hatred of ethnic or religious minorities	✓	✓	✓	✓
Undermining institutions	✓	✓	✓	✓
Failing to respect the rule of law	✓	✓	✓	✓
Ignoring science	✓	✓	✓	

Source: Adapted from *The Economist* (2021d).

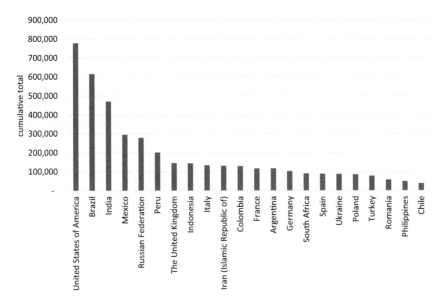

Figure 8.1 Cumulative COVID-19 deaths through December 2021. Source: https://covid19.who.int/info/.

traditional "protective masculinity" leadership style has had a "masculinity fail" during the COVID-19 pandemic, and that certain women leaders (e.g., Jacinda Ardern in New Zealand and Angela Merkel in Germany) were better positioned to address the public health challenge.[40] This is a possibility worth considering.

Take the case of the past German chancellor Angela Merkel and her relationship with US president Trump. As reported by Kahl and Wright, in 2019, Merkel concluded that "she simply embodied everything that Trump opposed: science, humility, intelligence, and multilateralism." Consequently, "any form of personal engagement with the American president brought out his absolute worst qualities. [...] When they spoke, he went off the rails" because, apparently, he could not abide her PhD in quantum chemistry and, more generally, her long-standing reputation for competence.[41]

Nonetheless, this is about more than gender alone. Another counterexample to performative nationalism can be found in Japan, which has to date largely rejected populism, illiberalism and unilateralism. There have been no recent Japanese Trumps, Modis, Bolsonaros or Orbáns, and Japan's response to the COVID-19 pandemic has been relatively successful. While by Western Pacific standards (Australia, New Zealand, South Korea and Taiwan), Japan's response was somewhat lackluster, comparing it to the G7 group of countries, it did quite well. At the end of 2021, its cumulative death rate was 14.5 per 100,000 compared to 235 in the United States.

An assessment based on COVID-19 death rates through 2021 is presented in Figure 8.2 for a select set of countries that includes the G7. It is important in looking at Figure 8.2 to keep in mind that the official death rate in India is probably a significant underestimate. Indeed, it is likely that the actual death rate is at the very least twice the official rate.[42] The cases of Hungary, Brazil, the United States and India suggest that the performative nationalism and "masculine" leadership styles in place at the beginning of the pandemic were not up to effectively addressing the public health task.

In the case of the United States, it might seem unfair to hold Trump accountable for deaths through the end of 2021, a year after the end of his term. But the evidence suggests that the disinformation campaign he launched for political reasons had lasting effect. Indeed, this disinformation effect was so significant that the COVID-19 death rate in US counties that voted for him was nearly three times higher than in counties that voted for his opponent.[43] For this reason, he bears responsibility. A very relevant comparison here is between the United States and Canada, which have very similar economic and social conditions. The US rate was approximately three times that of Canada.

The overall conclusion here is that, for global public health challenges, performative nationalism fails, sometimes spectacularly. Other models of governance offer better responses. However, this is just the national-level

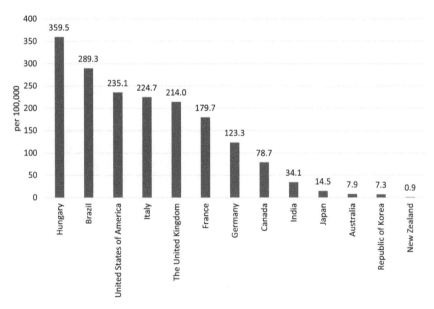

Figure 8.2 Cumulative COVID-19 deaths rate through December 2021 (per 100,000). Source: https://covid19.who.int/info/.

responses, and we also need to consider international cooperation and even the nationalist bugbear: multilateralism.

Personal Protective Equipment (PPE) and Medical Supplies

Early in the pandemic, trade economists stressed the importance of open borders in maintaining access to PPE and medical supplies. In the case of the EU, at the beginning of the COVID-19 pandemic, 90 percent of its PPE was imported, and this caused initial panic.[44] For example, in late March 2019, the French government seized six million masks at the Swedish medical company Mölnlycke's European distribution facility in Lyon. Such blatantly nationalistic moves exacerbated an already delicate situation.

Beyond seizures of questionable legality, early in the COVID-19 pandemic there was also the application of export controls on PPE and other types of medical supplies in a form of *medical nationalism* with more than seventy counties applying export controls and more than a hundred restrictions on these products. Some of these even took place within the EU single market with Germany and France initially leading the way and then the EU Commission itself issuing a string of continuously modified directives throughout early 2020. In doing so, the commission gave no regard to the impacts on counties dependent on the EU for PPE supplies.[45] The self-defeating nature of these sorts of actions can be seen in the case of the United States and China. As explained by trade economists Richard Baldwin and Simon Evenett:[46]

> The US is heavily dependent on imports of PPE while simultaneously being a major exporter of PPE. And the same is true of China. Indeed, the US is China's number one customer and China is the US's number four. Plainly, a tit-for-tat retaliation between the US and China in PPE would hinder the supply of PPE in both nations.

Further, there is a consensus among trade policy analysts that export restrictions result in prices that are both higher and more volatile than they otherwise would be, and this also contributes to their self-defeating nature. In the case of PPE export restrictions, these price effects proved to be real, with consequent negative impacts on frontline health workers that undermined pandemic response.[47] Misreading this reality, early in the pandemic, US president Trump's adviser Peter Navarro proposed rules to force the US health care system to only purchase US-produced PPE and medicines, even though the United States did not have the necessary capacity.[48] The Trump administration also began to put export restrictions in place under the US Defense Production Act (DPA), restricting access to PPE in many Latin American countries.

Trade restricting directives such as those of the EU and United States ignore the complexities of suppliers, assume that the imposing countries will not be affected by tit-for-tat actions in other countries (including on key PPE manufacturing inputs), ignore the fact that the imposed lack of export opportunities can reduce the incentives for new market entrants in medical sectors with large, fixed costs and significantly increase overall market uncertainties. Consequently, during 2020, the global PPE market was described by one trade economist as being in "chaos."[49] This is how pandemic nationalism becomes self-defeating.

The truth is that there are perhaps one million medical technologies, and not even technologically advanced countries can produce them all.[50] Perhaps equally important, the GVCs for these products can be very complex and are spread out over many countries. Further, the structure of the GVCs can vary from one medical product to another. While prudential diversification of these GVCs is always wise for those firms involved, complete "reshoring" as often called for by economic nationalists is simply not viable.[51]

Baldwin and Evenett state that "a liberal world trading system gives health ministries, hospitals, and other medical service providers a wider range of suppliers to choose from. [...] This facet of globalisation should be seen as a massive risk minimization device."[52] They are correct in this assertion. By all knowledgeable accounts, the multilateral trading system can help the world effectively source necessary medical equipment in the current and future pandemics. Nonetheless, economic nationalists used the episode to further their cause. As summed up by trade economist Simon Evenett:[53]

Economic nationalists [...] exploited [...] shortages of medical supplies to argue that sourcing from abroad cannot be relied upon in extremis. In this view, greater self-reliance is needed in the future and medical supply chains should be shortened or even repatriated entirely. [...] The debate over how to source medical kit has become the latest battleground over competing visions of the world economy.

Fortunately, as the pandemic proceeded into 2020, corrections were made with a number of countries beginning to liberalize trade in PPE and medical supplies. And China, the world's largest supplier of masks, increased production by multiples. Going forward, attempts should be made to ensure that a more cooperative posture is locked into the multilateral trading system. Because full-blown WTO negotiations are now cumbersome and, indeed, often fraught, a second-best solution would be a plurilateral agreement among a (hopefully large) subset of WTO members.[54] Plurilateral solutions need to ensure access for LMICs since many of these countries have little or no domestic manufacturing capability in medical supplies and are mostly or even wholly reliant on imports.[55]

Vaccines

As was clear from the beginning, the COVID-19 pandemic was going to be a race between the ability of the virus to mutate and the ability of humankind to develop, produce and distribute vaccines. Given that viruses mutate fairly quickly, it is a race that is difficult to win, and this was shown by the emergence of the Delta and Omicron variants. The emergence of these variants also showed that *vaccine nationalism* made winning more difficult.

Vaccine nationalism involves high-income countries producing, buying and hoarding vaccines for their own domestic use to the detriment of poorer countries. Because the virus knows no borders, this is ultimately self-defeating because it provides the virus more opportunity to mutate in ways that make the early vaccines less effective.[56] On this conundrum, WHO director general Tedros Adhanom Ghebreyesus stated that "vaccine nationalism is not just morally indefensible. It is epidemiologically self-defeating and clinically counterproductive." He also stated that "the pandemic will not be over anywhere until it is over everywhere. This is the reality of an interconnected world, and that reality can be met only by a reaffirmation of solidarity and an inclusive public-health order that distributes vaccines globally, quickly, and equitably."[57]

Similar sentiments were echoed by WTO director general Ngozi Okonjo-Iweala who called for increased equity in access to vaccines, stating that "we cannot accept that in a world where the technology exists to save lives, we let people die because they live in poor countries that have neither the resources, nor the access to vaccines and other medical countermeasures needed to save their populations."[58] Again, nationalist approaches to vaccination are both ethically unsound and medically incorrect.

From the very beginning of the pandemic, trade policy analysts recognized these realities. For example, Thomas Bollyky and Chad Bown stated:[59]

Absent an international, enforceable commitment to distribute vaccines in an equitable and rational way, leaders will instead prioritize taking care of their own populations over slowing the spread of COVID-19 elsewhere or helping to protect essential health-care workers and highly vulnerable populations in other countries.

Indeed, vaccines are one area where the trap of zero-sum thinking can emerge:[60]

Without global coordination, countries may bid against one another, driving up the price of vaccines and related materials. [...] In the interim, health-care workers and billions of elderly and other high-risk inhabitants in poorer countries will go unprotected, which will *extend the pandemic*, increase its death toll, and imperil already fragile health-care systems and economies.

There is a concept in economics of a *global public good*. A public good is one that is "non-excludable" and "non-rival." There is no effective way to prevent someone from consuming the good, and everyone can consume it at the same time. The classic case at the country level is national defense. A *global* public good is non-excludable and non-rival at the global level, and in their contribution to pandemic response, vaccines have global public good characteristics.[61] In the face of the need to provide a global public good, nationalistic policies will simply be less effective. They might be politically satisfying, but they do not change the nature of the global public good. We will return to this concept in Chapter 10.

Despite these realities, vaccine nationalism was the default posture of most country governments. This became apparent when considering the data from Duke University's COVID Global Accountability Platform (COVID GAP).[62] The low-bar, global public good target was to have 40 percent of the population of all countries vaccinated. COVID GAP assessed progress on this target at the end of 2021. Their data showed that only one high-income country failed to meet that target. Nineteen upper-middle income countries also failed to do so, but a total of 57 lower-middle income and low-income countries did not meet the target. As is apparent, there was a strong, inverse relationship between income levels and vaccination rates.

The failure to meet the 40 percent target was not an issue of global supply. By the end of 2021, vaccine manufacturers had produced 11 billion doses with a production capacity of over one billion per month. There were more than enough vaccines to exceed the target and soon reach the higher-bar 70 percent target. The issue was one of allocation with millions of doses of vaccines being discarded in high-income countries like the United States.

Given the temperature requirements of COVID-19 vaccines, allocation was always going to be a problem. These challenges were to be addressed by the COVID-19 Vaccines Advance Market Commitment (COVAX AMC), an entity related to the more general COVAX Facility but funded separately.[63] The stated aim of COVAX was to use advanced purchase agreements to deliver two billion vaccine doses by the end of 2021 in an equitable manner, but it achieved only slightly above six hundred million. This failure was the result of funding shortfalls, the difficulties of building out vaccine cold chains, failure to join (China and Russia), joining later (the United States) and competition from other facilities (the EU).

A mid-2021 assessment of COVAX by public health researchers Mark Eccleston-Turner and Harry Upton concluded the following:[64]

> The prevalence of vaccine nationalism appears to be limiting the participation of some of the world's wealthiest countries in COVAX. These countries have pursued bilateral advanced purchase agreements with the vaccine manufacturers, placing those countries in direct competition with the COVAX Facility for doses when they become available. This act of countries hedging their bets represents an existential threat to the facility and puts its mission in peril.

Some arguments against vaccine nationalism have focused on IP issues. There were calls for the waiver of these rights for COVID-19 vaccines within the WTO's TRIPS.[65] This waiver was originally proposed by India and South Africa and had the support of the US Biden administration.[66] The EU was characterized as being recalcitrant on this issue. The reality, however, was that the EU was broadly in line with the concern for equity and called for a declaration on TRIPS and Public Health in the case of the COVID-19 pandemic.[67] This action would have triggered a set of existing mechanisms for the production of off-patent, generic versions of vaccines via "compulsory licensing." These mechanisms were the important legacy of the HIV-AIDS pandemic and the activism that took place in that context. They could have helped a desperate situation.

The good news regarding COVAX was that, in December 2021, it had increased its vaccine delivery rate substantially with supplies from India finally materializing and increased attention to delivery. At the time of this writing, it was very unlikely that it would meet the 70 percent target in 2022, but any forward progress would help in meeting new variants. Perhaps more importantly in the long run, the patent-free CORBEVAX was announced at the very beginning of 2022 and was immediately licensed to an Indian pharmaceutical manufacturer. Developed specifically with global public health in mind, with fewer storage requirements, and a focus on delivery in LMICs, CORBEVAX promised to have an immediate, positive impact.[68]

China's Vaccine Nationalism

In the case of China, vaccine nationalism took the form of a stubborn refusal to embrace any vaccine other than Sinopharm and Sinovac despite their not being based on mRNA technology and consequent poorer performance.

As the highly transmissible Omicron variant arose in 2022, this nationalistic posture painted China into a corner. The county's zero-COVID goal and its commitment to Chinese vaccines began to work at odds with each other. How this would ultimately play out was clear in early 2022 when it became apparent that the Chinese vaccines were relatively ineffective against Omicron. Consequently, in March 2022, China was forced to put the entire city of Shanghai with its 26 million residents in lockdown. As of April 2022, a total of more than 350 million Chinese citizens were in lockdown, and such lockdowns continued through 2022.[69] China was holding up approval of tried and tested mRNA vaccines so that it could ultimately develop its own no matter the consequences.[70]

As of November 2022, approximately one-fifth of China's GDP was under lockdown, and riots broke out in Zhengzhou at the world's largest iPhone factory employing 200,000 workers.[71] Meanwhile, only 40 percent of China's population over eighty years old had received a third COVID-19 shot and there was no campaign for a fourth shot.[72] For a government with dictatorial powers, this was not a good record, and still it refused to approve the use of "foreign" vaccines.

By December 2022, the Chinese government reversed its "zero-Covid" policy and ended all lockdowns. Although information has been sparse at the time of this writing, the death toll increased substantially.[73] In January 2023, the annual New Year travel took place without any restrictions, further spreading the virus. While at the time of this writing the official death toll is under hundred thousand, most sober assessments put it at approximately one million.[74] China's vaccine nationalism had largely been a failure.

Back to Multilateralism

Beyond the issue of medical equipment and vaccines, any pandemic makes open trading relations more rather than less important. This is purely economic in that trade restrictions tend to be recessionary, offering fewer pathways into recovery. Consequently, expanded import protection and export subsidies that could launch a set of countervailing actions need to be avoided. Further, there are many ways that an open trading system can support pandemic response.[75] This is not an argument against the prudential diversification of GVCs to promote resilience, which is simply a part of global corporate strategy and has empirical support. However, as stated by one researcher, "it is a mistake to equate self-sufficiency with robustness."[76] GVC diversification is not isolation but engagement.

Multilateralism also needs to extend beyond trade to the realm of global public health itself, including a continued commitment to the WHO and to equitable vaccine access. In September 2021, WTO director general Ngozi Okonjo-Iweala stated that "We have a choice. Either we converge downwards by allowing the virus to drag us all back down, or we converge upwards by vaccinating the world." In her speech, she also stated:[77]

The WTO has been working with every leading COVID-19 vaccine manufacturer from around the world to better understand the challenges preventing greater production. [...] Supply chain problems, for example export restrictions and prohibitions, red tape and input shortages are real barriers to production. In that respect, vaccine policy is trade policy. [...] The WTO is working with its members to keep critical products moving by facilitating trade and reducing export restrictions, addressing supply bottlenecks and regulatory obstacles. [...] Eighty percent of the world's vaccine exports come from 10 countries and pandemic politics has shown us that this may be problematic. When push comes to shove, politics trumps global priorities. So production must be more decentralized to emerging markets and developing countries.

As of September 2021, when this speech was made, there was indeed cause for concern. In response to this speech, trade policy analysts Chad Bown and Thomas Bollykyl proposed a new COVID-19 Trade and Investment Agreement. They make an interesting and important point regarding the WTO and COVID-19:[78]

The unglamorous, day-to-day import and export of raw materials, equipment, and vaccines taking place under the rules of the multilateral trading system have already helped save millions of lives and livelihoods. The WTO should be celebrated for creating an environment to facilitate this progress, however limited.

It is facts like this that get misconstrued by economic nationalist and other critics of the WTO who take the day-to-day operation of the WTO trade regime for granted. That said, Bown and Bollykyl criticize the WTO for not doing more. In particular, and as mentioned above, they called for the use of a plurilateral mechanism within the WTO to help further the COVID-19 response and to prepare for future pandemics. This would involve a commitment to work with COVAX, a commitment not to use export restrictions and transparency requirements. Ideas such as this can be very helpful.

As part of potential multilateralism in response to COVID-19, in March 2021, there was also a proposal for a Pandemic Treaty.[79] The locus of this treaty would be the WHO. This proposal was considered at the World Health

Assembly (WHA) in May 2021, but no consensus was reached. The same was the case in December 2021 at a WHA special session. While this avenue should be pursued to prepare for the inevitable pandemics of the future, the use of the plurilateral mechanism within the WTO might be a more realistic avenue.

Economic nationalism failed the pandemic test, and the threat of future pandemics makes multilateralism more rather than less relevant. The global public good nature of pandemic preparedness and response requires a well-functioning multilateral system. This is the reality of global public health ignored by economic nationalists.

Chapter 9

TECHNO-NATIONALISM

In August 2021, Lee Jae-yong was released on parole from prison in South Korea where he had been held on a bribery conviction. The Korean government cited overcrowded prison conditions when announcing his release, but Lee was no ordinary prisoner. He was the vice-chairman of Samsung Electronics and the son of Samsung's founder, Lee Kun-hee. Despite an official five-year ban on employment, as soon as he was released, Lee went directly to the Samsung's headquarters for a briefing, and deploying an interesting ambiguity, Samsung considered him to have resumed work despite not being employed.

At the time, the world was experiencing a shortage of semiconductor chips. Perhaps not coincidentally, Samsung was one of the three largest chipmakers, the other two being the US-based Intel and the Taiwan Semiconductor Manufacturing Company (TSMC). Indeed, the South Korean president justified Mr. Lee's release as a matter of national interest. Half of the world's chipmaking or "foundry" capacity resided with TSMC, and Taiwan was experiencing what could politely be called "political risk" given China's stated goal of reintegrating it back into the Communist fold. Indeed, almost exactly a year later, Chinese forces surrounded Taiwan in a four-day military exercise that interrupted trade.

Samsung's potential to offset this kind of risk was a topic of discussion in the business world, and firms relying on TSMC chips were looking for ways to diversify their chip sourcing. More generally, Samsung and Mr. Lee were caught in the crosswinds of evolving techno-nationalism. China is one of the world's biggest demanders of chips, and Samsung operates in China to help to satisfy this demand. At the same time, the US government is keen to ramp up semiconductor manufacturing capacity in the United States, and Samsung has agreed to be part of that effort as well. We need to consider rival techno-nationalist regimes, as well as the very concept of techno-nationalism, to understand these dynamics.

The Emergence of Techno-Nationalism

As we saw in Chapter 3 on industry and war, techno-nationalism as a feature of economic nationalism is nothing new. It was part of List's "productive power" project that was embraced by Japan in the late nineteenth century. As for the contemporary use of the term, legal scholar Robert Reich played an important role in a 1987 article. This article took a US perspective on the technological threat of Japan (something that we don't hear much about anymore), and the focal point was semiconductors (something we still hear a lot about).[1] As Reich states, the overall goal of US techno-nationalism at that time was "to protect future American technological breakthroughs from exploitation at the hands of foreigners, especially the Japanese."[2] Using evocative language, Reich states that US techno-nationalism[3]

> presumes the possibility—indeed the necessity—of viewing American technology as a body of knowledge separate and distinct from that possessed by other nations. Technology is viewed as uniquely American—developed here, contained within the nation's borders, applied in America by Americans. It is like a precious commodity that we should save for ourselves rather than allow foreigners to carry off.

There are limitations to this view that Reich emphasizes. For example, in technology fields, it is sometimes difficult to strictly identify the nationality of workers and, even more importantly, firms. When the bulk of civilian R&D is conducted by multinational firms, the nationality of the resulting technology is not always clear. As Reich noted at that time, "most American high-tech companies are well along in the process of losing their uniquely American identities."[4] The same is true for present-day MNEs the world over.

Reich went a bit too far in his consideration of techno-nationalism, arguing that technology was not scarce but nevertheless needed to be subsidized. In truth, technology can be scarce (if not always), and its development should be subsidized only under certain circumstances. But he had hit on a real phenomenon and introduced a term to describe it. That term has stuck. For example, it is used throughout Richard Samuels' 1994 book *Rich Nation, Strong Army* on the technological development of Japan. Samuels defines the term as a "coherent and consistent view of technology as the source of national security."[5] That definition is still a useful one.

One issue that is often raised is the role of military technology in techno-nationalism, and Reich identified the military-focused nature of US techno-nationalism as a *hindrance*.[6] In his view, US military research is often classified with little regard for commercial applications, oriented instead to the military mission. He noted at that time that only 3 percent of Japanese government-funded R&D was defense related compared to 70 percent in the United States. In Reich's opinion, this held back the commercialization of new technology in the United States. This observation seems to have support in Samuels' much more thorough analysis that characterizes Japan as having gone through "a historical transition from a military-led to a commercial-led national system of innovation."[7]

Moving forward some decades, international business researcher Yadong Luo identifies what he terms the "conventional techno-nationalism" of Reich and others and describes it as follows:[8]

> Conventional techno-nationalism focused on the use of technology as a means to advance nationalist agendas, with a goal to promoting connectedness and a stronger national identity. This idea established the beliefs that the success of a nation can be determined by how well that nation innovates, diffuses, and harnesses technology, and that national R&D efforts and FDI inflows in technologies are key drivers of growth [...] and prosperity.

But something different is going on in the current era in that there has been an expanded use of technologically oriented sanctions against foreign entities as an explicit part of perceived geopolitical rivalries. It is an example of national security harnessing globalization for its own ends. Luo describes the "new techno-nationalism" as follows:[9]

> New techno-nationalism is a strain of systemic competition thinking that links cross-border technological exchanges directly to a nation's national security, advocating for strong interventions by the state against opportunistic or hostile states or non-state actors from other countries. Under new techno-nationalism, country leaders seek to attain geopolitical gains, building on the premise that the world has entered a new era of systemic rivalry between competing geopolitical powerhouses that differ remarkably in ideological values, political systems, and economic models.

This new techno-nationalism is emerging, for example, in calls for both the EU and the United States to push back against China in multiple technological realms. These include 5G networks, artificial intelligence (AI), quantum computing, robotics, bioscience and semiconductors. As part of this, there is a new trend toward regulatory restrictions such as export controls (including foreign direct product rules), blacklists and sanctions.[10] In some cases, the sanctions have been extraterritorial and, therefore, of questionable validity under international law. After its invasion of Ukraine, many of these measures were also applied against Russia.

Nonstate Actors: MNEs

The new techno-nationalism, as a variety of political realism, is nation based. As such, it does not have much conceptual and policy space for the role of nonstate actors, in particular, international business in the form of MNEs. While perhaps allowing for their important role as sources of political donations, politicians of the techno-nationalist bent want to limit the activities of MNEs, a new development. There is no small amount of irony here in that the collaborative research networks maintained by MNEs across national boundaries have been the source of much of the technology the new technonationalists purport to support.

As previously suggested, the new techno-nationalism is part of a larger trend toward "realism" in international affairs, one that attempts to harness not just trade policy but international business itself toward strategic ends. Here, "MNEs are a political tool for attaining power."[11] For this reason, the larger geopolitical contexts of techno-nationalism have pushed international business researchers to begin to consider issues of global political economy out of necessity rather than inclination.[12] MNEs find themselves in a relatively new world where they are less the masters of the global economy and more the chess pieces in a global strategic game. Some see this as an inevitable process of MNEs adapting to "deglobalization." Even if this turns out to be overblown, there is clearly pressure to a least begin to regionalize what was once global. The extent to which MNEs agree to play this new game or push back will be critical for how these processes play out over time. But it is clear that MNEs are entering into a new era and will be pushed to adjust their usual business decisions.

From Advanced Research Projects Agency (ARPA) to Defense Advanced Research Projects Agency (DARPA) in the United States

In discussions of techno-nationalism, one piece of US history is often a touchstone. In 1958, the US Eisenhower administration responded to the Soviet Union's launching of the Sputnik satellite by creating the ARPA with the task of "inventing the future" in technology. In 1972, ARPA became DARPA, with the D standing for Defense. DARPA has had a role to play in many technological innovations, including the internet, GPS, stealth planes, self-driving cars, voice recognition and mRNA vaccines. Although DARPA answers to the US Pentagon, it focuses on dual-use technologies and even broader technological needs. For example, in 2013, DARPA made an award to the firm Moderna to develop mRNA vaccines. Moderna had only been founded in 2010 with a corporate name based on "mRNA" or "mod-RNA." As we saw in Chapter 8, this mere US$25 million was later to play a dramatic role in addressing the COVID-19 pandemic, and this is certainly a feather in the DARPA cap. It is generally considered to be a success.

DARPA's model is to have a nonhierarchical structure with relatively few staff that are willing to place inherently risky bets on new technologies with potentially important applications. The staff are not just defense oriented but also include nondefense scientists. It is a high-risk, high-payoff endeavor that tolerates failures. In the realm of total R&D expenditures, its annual budget is very small, typically only a few billion US dollars. Participating researchers might not even be US citizens, and DARPA partners with entities outside of the United States. As one researcher put it, "the only guiding heuristic for DARPA is that the scientific program accomplishes the targeted technological advances in the shortest possible time with the best team possible."[13]

The DARPA model is also an *open* one. Multiple venues are used for brainstorming with scientists, and ideas are "pitched" both to and within the agency. The role of program managers has also been noted as both unique and important. These individuals serve in limited tenures, "on tour" with DARPA for three to four years. They are *scientists* with home bases in other universities and organizations. A theme in the DARPA process is one frequently found in the open innovation systems we will discuss below, namely "coopetition." Another theme is "de-conflicting" of the program managers. In many respects, then DARPA has got things right.[14]

DARPA has become something of a gold standard for budding techno-nationalist governments, but copying its success is not always easy. For example, Britain now has its Advanced Research and Innovation Agency (ARIA), and Germany now has its Federal Agency for Disruptive Innovation (SPRIN-D). Whether these new entities can effectively implement the "DARPA model" is a question on the minds of many techno-nationalists and will take some time to evaluate. In the case of the UK's ARIA, it is somewhat related to the Brexit blunder discussed in Chapter 7. One of the many consequences of Brexit is that the UK has potentially lost its role in the EU's Horizon Europe program for technological development. Consequently, the UK government launched the ARIA program to compensate for this. The first head of ARIA, Peter Highnam, was hired from none other than DARPA.[15] The purpose of ARIA according to the UK government is to "cement the UK's position as a science superpower," and the government explicitly cites DARPA as an inspiration.[16]

Indeed, the government tries to copy much of the DARPA model right down to the role and tenure of program managers.

Britain does have some real advantages in life sciences in its "Oxford-Cambridge arc" that rival what takes place in two US cities (Boston and San Francisco) and has significant aspirations in genomics and bioinformatics. This has been traditionally supported by the Research Councils UK (RCUK), and the UK appears to have a "head start" over many other countries in these realms. The question is whether, given the open nature of much innovation (to be discussed below), the Brexit-inspired techno-nationalism is in synch with innovation itself. Innovation within the context of the EU might have been a more realistic and fruitful path forward, but losing this context was another cost of Brexit that was not well thought through.

Target Huawei

In 2018, the US Trump administration banned exports of semiconductor chips to the Chinese telecommunications equipment manufacturer Huawei. The export ban, however, had an extraterritorial component in that the United States was also blocking non-US-made chips being sold to Huawei by firms based in other countries that use US technology. The United States went even one step further, instigating the arrest of Huawei's chief financial officer in Canada while she was changing planes in Vancouver. This followed the arrest of the chief financial officer of the ZTE Corporation at the Logan Airport in Boston. The stated reason for the Huawei arrest was a breach of US sanctions against Iran and North Korea, but its timing suggested otherwise: it seemed to be part of the US–China trade war discussed in Chapter 5.

Traditional US allies followed the US lead or at least appeared to. In relatively short order, Australia, Japan, New Zealand and the United Kingdom took measures to begin to exclude Huawei products from their 5G networks. These actions seemed to have had some real and deleterious effects on Huawei. As reported by *The Economist*, Huawei's revenues declined by almost one-third in 2021.[17] True to form, however, the Trump administration acted unilaterally without consulting allies beforehand. This shortsightedness led some of these allies to surreptitiously go their own way, shifting parts of their semiconductor GVC to places beyond the realm of US export regulations. Trade compliance law firms were happy to help in this process.

Along with assuming a zero-sum world, economic nationalists often mistakenly assume a world of single-stage games. But global games are almost always multistage. So of course, China retaliated by subjecting US companies working in China to an increasing number of "qualitative measures" and by banning foreign computers and software from all its public institutions. There is also evidence that the targeting of Huawei adversely affected US firms that acted as suppliers to Huawei, including Broadcom, Intel and Qualcomm.

As British intelligence analyst, Nigel Inkster, makes clear, the Huawei affair is part of the accelerating technological rivalry between the United States and China. He states:[18]

> The US now sees China's designs on becoming a peer competitor in advanced technologies as an existential threat to a presumption of American dominance in all aspects of technology. [...] Its priority is now to slow China's technology development to buy time for the US to take whatever steps may be necessary to ensure that it retains its technological edge. In the short term, this involves creating a more constrained environment for major Chinese technology firms, protecting US intellectual property and reducing exposure to Chinese ICT systems and products.

The US Biden administration continued to sail in the Trump administration's wake. In early 2023, it stopped issuing export licenses to US firms supplying Huawei below the 5G level at which export licenses had been previously blocked. This impacted Qualcomm and Intel that had been supplying these lower-level technology items.[19]

The problem with this approach is that US economic nationalists, often distracted by ethnonationalist aims and various "culture wars," have precious few ideas about how to support US technological development outside of retaliation. Regarding protecting IP, for example, the United States has cut itself off from enforcement via the WTO by sabotaging the WTO's dispute settlement procedures. There is also a lack of focus on broad-based educational attainment and achievement as well as infrastructure (both traditional and digital). Success in the technology realm over the long term will require more than arresting foreign business executives.

From Semiconductor Manufacturing Technology (SEMATECH) to Organisation of Semiconductor Exporting Countries (OSEC)

In 1988, worried about Japan's emerging technological trajectory and the fact that is supplied more than half of the world's semiconductors, the United States began to subsidize a project called SEMATECH. The subsidy came from the US government's DARPA and was initially at a level of US$100 million but would eventually total US$500 million. By some accounts, this initiative was a resounding success, and US government funding ended in

1996. Reflecting the global nature of semiconductor technology, and with US funding coming to an end, SEMATECH eventually became an international membership organization but ceased to exist in 2015.

After the US Trump administration, the less unilateral Biden administration helped to create the EU–US Trade and Technology Council (TTC). While this body had a general 'remit of export controls, semiconductors were an early area of focus and the council first met in September 2021.[20] Beyond the usual generic statements, the TCC called for FDI screening and export controls from national security points of view and identified targeted technologies such as AI and semiconductors. The TCC stated:[21]

> We recognise that the semiconductor supply chain, from raw materials, design and manufacturing to assembly, testing and incorporation into end products, is extremely complex and geographically dispersed. The development and production of semiconductors include multiple countries, with some very concentrated segments. The European Union and the United States have some important respective strengths as well as ongoing significant mutual dependencies, and common external dependencies.

This is an encouraging statement in its factual understanding of the complexity of semiconductor GVCs that goes beyond that of many nationalistic politicians. But behind the scenes, there were other activities. Many semiconductor GVCs depend on advanced machinery produced by the Dutch firm ASML. To use the word "advanced" hardly does it justice. At a price tag of US$150 million, the *New York Times* reports that exporting it "requires 40 shipping containers, 20 trucks and three Boeing 747s."[22] While ASML is Dutch, it draws on expertise and materials from the United States, Germany and Japan, and beginning in 2019, it stopped exporting its machine to China. In this way, what started as a US–China technological rivalry has become something larger. *The Economist* calls the evolving regime in semiconductors the OSEC with members from the United States, Japan and the Netherlands. Awkwardly, however, for US semiconductor machinery firms, China is still an important market.[23]

Because the semiconductor GVC is complex, assessing countries' role in the industry is not as straightforward as some would suggest. Figure 9.1 gives a sense of this based on data from the Boston Consulting Group and the US-based Semiconductor Industry Association. This figure divides the semiconductor GVC into stages.[24] "Upstream" in the GVC we find the most R&D intensive tasks, namely electronic design automation (EDA) and core IP. As can be seen in the figure, the United States is the largest player here. The

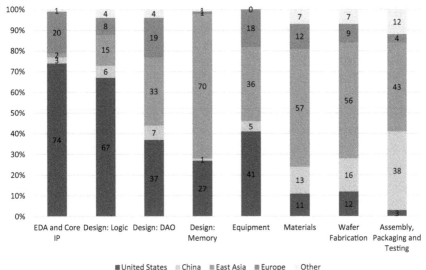

Figure 9.1 The geography of the semiconductor global value chain. Source: Varas et al. (2021). Note: EDA refers to electronic design automation, IP refers to intellectual property, and DAO refers to discrete analog and other.

authors of this report attribute this to "its world-class universities, vast pool of engineering talent and market-driven innovation ecosystem."[25] It is worth recalling in this regard Figure 3.3 in Chapter 3 on the "smile curve" indicating that these kinds of upstream activities are high in value added.

Next there are three aspects of design: logic, discrete analog and other (DAO), and memory. While the United States is prominent in logic, it is less so in DAO and memory, with East Asia accounting for increasing shares. Semiconductor manufacturing is also very intensive in equipment and materials, and while the United States and East Asia have similar shares in equipment, East Asia is more prominent in materials. Moving "downstream," wafer fabrication or "fab" is the actual construction of the semiconductor wafers that is most closely associated with "manufacturing." Here, East Asia has the largest share by far with the above-discussed Samsung and TSMC being the largest corporate players. China looms large along with East Asia in assembly and testing, the end of the semiconductor GVC. Overall, while the US–China rivalry in semiconductors is real, they currently dominate different parts of the GVC.

That fact does not make the rivalry any less potent, and as suggested above, there is emerging evidence that the rivalry is beginning to play out in the realm of equipment in Figure 9.1. Note the relatively strong role of the United States here vis-à-vis China. In particular, the role of machine tools in the semiconductor GVC is important. These tools are what etch the circuits onto silicon wafers in a mind-bogglingly numerous, detailed and perfect manner. The firms supplying these machine tools are Applied Materials, Tokyo Electron, ASML, KLA and Lam Research. Of these, Applied Materials, KLA and Lam Research are US-based firms, and they sell a large amount of their output to China.[26]

The US government responded in 2020 by requiring export licenses for firms supplying China's Semiconductor Manufacturing International Company (SMIC), but this only applied to US firms. As described by *The Economist*:[27]

> Any American company wishing to sell products to SMIC had to apply for a license. But tools have kept flowing to the Chinese firm, in part because America acted alone. The Chinese government's lavish subsidies have instead started finding their way to non-American companies. Applied Materials noted that this might help other firms as, in effect, shutting it out of China "could result in our losing technology leadership relative to our international competitors."

Indeed, the market for semiconductor machine tools in China shows no sign of slowing down, and indeed, SMIC's appetite for these tools is having a deleterious impact on other chipmakers who are having trouble getting their hands on them. The approach favored by US firms is to focus export controls on the high end of the technology spectrum, allowing exports at the low end. The trick will be to bring the Dutch firm ASML and the Japanese firm Tokyo Electron on board into a system of harmonized export controls. This appears to have taken place in early 2023.[28]

The Biden administration in the United States was also responsible for the 2022 CHIPS Act, which provided for approximately US$280 billion in spending to promote US-based semiconductor spending. A large amount of this money was to go into "reshoring" semiconductor manufacturing, such as the US$40 billion TSMC fabrication facility in Arizona. There was also money for the US-based Intel, which announced a US$20 billion investment in Ohio. Despite the magnitude of this spending, it is not clear whether it will alter the fundamentals of the global semiconductor economy. TSMC will not locate any R&D to the United States, and chip fabrication there will remain, in the words of *The Economist*, "cripplingly expansive."[29] The CHIPS Act, however, is a symbol of semiconductor nationalism on the part of the United States.

Not to be outdone, or maybe to signal their loyalty, South Korea passed the K-Chips Act, Taiwan passed the Taiwan Chips Act, and Japan subsidized a new TSMC fabrication plant in Kumamoto. These measures signaled what is being referred to as the Chip 4 Alliance of the United States, Japan, South Korea and Taiwan, but this leaves out the Netherlands, which, as we have seen, is a critical player.[30] All these policy moves are a far cry from a multilateral approach to "free trade." They are indicative of the extent to which techno-nationalism moves the world economy in new directions and puts new pressures on MNEs. Despite these developments, there are still benefits from what has been termed "open innovation," and these are worth examining.

Zero-Sum Global Technology versus Open Innovation

As pointed out by international business researcher Yadong Luo, the logic of techno-nationalism is fundamentally zero sum. But the zero-sum view is often at variance with reality. As stated by Luo, "in an interconnected world, in which technological components (or supply chains) are interdependent, technological complementarity widely occurs between countries and between cross-border companies, allowing for the coopetition logic to prevail." In particular, "global open resources foster innovation and speed, fostering positive-sum completion through complementary collaboration."[31] One example of this is the increasing complexity of GVCs and their technological inputs involved. Another is the equivalent complexity of MNE technology cross-licensing. Many political entrepreneurs fostering technonationalist policies have no understanding of these realities. Nonetheless, cooperation and coopetition are a widely observed means of technological development.[32]

By insisting on an alleged zero-sum nature of international business operations, the new techno-nationalists fundamentally distort reality. That is not to say that there are *no* zero-sum aspects to some international business transactions, but as an *overall view* of international business, the zero-sum lens is bound to fail. This is not a mere research or academic issue. The limitations of a zero-sum approach to technology directly affect MNEs themselves. Again, quoting Yadong Luo:[33]

Cross-border collaborative activities enhance the interoperability between networked products and services [...] and lower production and development costs. Yet, modern techno-nationalism may present obstacles to co-development and cause a breakdown of the global value chain. [...] MNEs can build competitive advantages through collaboration with global competitors [...] or with suppliers and distributors. [...] Unfortunately, new techno-nationalism is difficult to hedge and brings severe impact on maintaining global value chain operations.

Note here that, traditionally, the application of the need to "hedge" was most often applied in the international business realm to exchange rates and political risks. It is now being applied to techno-nationalism itself. Indeed, Luo points to the possibility that international business and its innovative processes might "fade" in the face of this new form of economic nationalism in which an increasing number of MNEs are forced to decouple their current GVCs that are embedded in particular technological relationships. Given that modern GVCs can span thousands of elements, this is not always a straightforward task.

As it turns out, collaboration among firms and research institutions of various kinds is an active area of international business research, and there is a good deal of evidence that it helps with innovation even among large firms. Indeed, technological issues are often cited as one of the reasons for coopetition. This can reflect multiple factors such as the need for standard setting; the large, fixed costs of some technologies; and shortening product lifecycles over which fixed costs can be spread.[34] One way or another, many international firms are embracing what has come to be known as *open innovation*.

The notion of open innovation came to the fore in the early 2000s. As stated by business researchers Henry Chesbrough and Marcel Bogers, open innovation refers to "an innovation model that emphasize purposive inflows and outflows of knowledge flows across the boundary of a firm in order to leverage external sources of knowledge and commercialization paths."[35] As stated by these researchers, open innovation can involve inbound leveraging of external knowledge, outbound leveraging of internal knowledge for better commercialization, and a combination of the two.

Of course, most open innovation concerns R&D. This usually involves other firms but can also take place with academic institutes and governments. These can include formal contractual agreements, non-equity alliances and strategic supplier agreements. But as stated by another set of researchers, informal open innovation is also important, and these can include "scouting relationships, conference participations, partnerships in standard-setting organizations, long-term relationships with key technology partners, such as prominent universities and research labs, or key market players" including customers and suppliers.[36]

To take one example, in 2004, archrivals Samsung Electronics and Sony began a collaborative relationship in the form of a joint venture to produce a new generation of liquid crystal display (LCD) panels. In short order, both firms were marketing their own brands of TVs based on the jointly developed LCD panels. This joint venture was responsible for several generations of LCD panels leveraged by both firms and increased both firms' shares of this market. As stated by one pair of researchers who studied this partnership, "each firm had resources and capabilities that the other one needed, which helped to prompt the firms to engage in coopetition."[37]

Regarding the licensing and cross-licensing of technology, all indications are that these activities significantly and positively influence the development and diffusion of technologies. One way that licensing does this is by allowing firms to combine different types of knowledge both in relationships with other firms but also relationships with research institutes and universities.[38] This and other aspects of open innovation are now under threat.

From Techno-Nationalism to Techno-Independence?

In the case of China, there has been a stated aspiration to move beyond techno-nationalism to techno-independence. The Chinese national government has established self-reliance in science and technology as a fundamental economic goal and has dedicated vast resources into making this a reality.[39] To this end, the Chinese government has funded the Made in China 2025 and China Standards 2035 initiatives. Given the nature of technology and GVCs, however, it is not clear that they will succeed.

We have already seen in Chapter 8 that China has pursued vaccine nationalism by denying Chinese citizens access to "Western" mRNA biotechnology. This appears to have been to support the Chinese firm Abogen Biosciences to develop a "Chinese" version in concert with the People's Liberation Army (PLA). Abogen Biosciences is led by Dr. Ying Bo, a member of the CCP. He received his PhD in bioengineering from Northeastern University in Boston, home of a US-based biosciences cluster, and went on to work at Moderna in that city. So once again, an economic nationalist project depends on multiple dimensions of economic globalization. Given this, it is not clear how sustainable such a strategy would be in the long run.[40]

In the realm of aircraft, too, China has goals for self-sufficiency and pursues this strategy via its state-owned aircraft company Commercial Aircraft Corporation of China (COMAC), which has received US$50–70 billion in subsidies to produce its C919 plane. Nonetheless, as reported in one study of COMAC, "it is misleading to call the C919 a Chinese plane because almost all of its components, including everything that keeps the plane aloft, are imported." Again, economic nationalism relies on economic globalization, in this case via GVCs, mostly to European firms.[41]

We discussed semiconductors above, and China's aspirations in this area rest on SMIC with the goal of self-sufficiency in Chinese chipmaking. In terms of the sophistication of its capabilities, it still lags both Taiwan's TSMC and South Korea's Samsung but is the beneficiary of the Chinese government's largesse. Self-sufficiency, if actually achievable, is still some way off.

As reported by *The Economist*, in January 2022, a research paper was posted by the Institute of International and Strategic Studies at Peking University, concluding that there would be substantial losses to the Chinese economy from the pursuit of techno-independence. A week later, it was gone, presumably a victim to Chinese government censorship.[42] This is reminder that economic nationalism backed up by authoritarianism can be an extraordinarily powerful force, but it does not obviate the conclusions of the research paper. The go-it-alone approach to technological development has real limits.

Digital Territory?

It is often noted that economic globalization has been spurred by improvements in information and communication technologies (ICT). These improvements have supported international trade via digitally enhanced transportation and logistics, increased virtual trade in services, increased international financial integration via online asset trading and increased international production via improved communication and coordination within MNEs and between MNEs and their suppliers. Most modern considerations of GVCs consider them to be supported by ICT from beginning to end and across their span of countries. Modern economic globalization and ICT have gone hand in hand.

Among trade economists, this view has been most strongly stated by Richard Baldwin in his book *The Great Convergence: Information Technology and the New Globalization*. Regarding production, for example, Baldwin states that "the contours of industrial competitiveness are now increasingly defined by the outlines of international production networks rather than the boundaries of nations."[43] He and other trade economists have called this process "unbundling," meaning that stages of production processes are moved outside of their original national location. This process has been a central part of the modern evolution of GVCs and its impact on economic globalization.

Baldwin is correct about this, but there are also recent movements in the other direction. As noted by the science and technology researcher Norma Möllers, there is a growing dissatisfaction among some national governments regarding ICT trends. In particular, there is increased concern about whether countries have the control they want over both the hardware behind ICT and the content stored on and communicated with ICT networks. Like other dimensions of globalization, ICT networks tend to be globally distributed and therefore at variance with techno-nationalism. In the view of Möllers, this is a new frontier in techno-nationalistic policies. In her assessment, an increasing number of countries are attempting to reshape their ICT networks in the form of "digital territory" over which to exert national sovereignty. In her words:[44]

"Digital territory" [...] is nationalized information infrastructure in a double sense: nationalized as in materially under state control and nationalized as in invested with normative ideas about nation and citizenship. Thus, territorialization projects have material and moral dimensions.

Trade economists have long celebrated trade in services, including many types of digital trade. They have also celebrated ICT-enabled international production.[45] What these economists seem unaware of is the possibility that the economic nationalism associated with manufacturing could eventually reach into virtual trade in services and ICT-enabled international production as national governments begin to recognize and attempt to establish digital territory as part of techno-nationalism or even attempts at techno-independence. The increased role of "realism" in international relations might not be confined to manufacturing trade but could extend to the increasingly important virtual trade in services.

Back to Basics

As we mentioned above, it was Robert Reich who introduced the contemporary use of the term techno-nationalism, and he did so in the context of the US–Japan technological rivalry of the 1980s. As part of what he calls the "quite path" to technological success, he includes the mundane issue of basic education, noting that "even if companies are willing to invest in the technological sophistication of their workers, the success of those investments depends fundamentally on workers' ability to learn, which depends in turn on the quality of their basic education."[46] He was, and is, absolutely correct on this matter, and this is a policy realm that is often overlooked by economic nationalists.

As stated, the techno-nationalism idea took hold in the context of Japan and its increasingly sophisticated exports, but it subsequently also responded to Taiwan and South Korea, which had their own extraordinary technological trajectories. It is difficult to imagine that these technological successes could have taken place without the careful and serious investments these three East Asian countries made in basic education after World War II.[47] There is also the broader historical pattern noted by development economists that advances in education universally *precede* periods of sustained growth and development.[48]

The link between education and technology has to do with what is known as *absorption capacity*, the fact that the ability of a country to engage with emerging technologies depends on the educational and skill capabilities of its citizens. There is a tendency to see technology as a freely available stock of knowledge, but this is not always the case. It can be a potentially restricted flow, and poorly educated citizens contribute to its potential restriction. For example, in a review of technology and development, the development economist Adam Szirmai concluded that the "acquisition of technology is neither easy nor costless" and that "technological capabilities include skills, experiences, attitudes and schooling."[49] In a list of critical capabilities, he included "levels of basic education."[50]

Jong-Wha Lee is a Korean economist with a stellar research record in both economic growth and education. In a lengthy article on education and technology, he focuses on LMICs, but the principles he illustrates apply to all countries. For example, he states:[51]

> The adaptation of new technologies requires human efforts and capabilities that cannot be just granted. New technologies often require new skills. As such, lack of human capacity to utilize advanced technologies has been one explanation for the failure of many [...] countries to fully exploit the existing global technologies. [...] That is, without the appropriate investment in human capital, advanced technologies cannot make [...] countries grow at a rapid pace.

Interestingly, Lee's empirical results suggest that both trade and FDI are part of this process. FDI can bring with it new technology, and new technology can also be imported in the form of machinery. But both positively interact with education levels. Lee also shows that education has been important in the diffusion of ICT among countries.

The reality of twenty-first-century technological development is that any country that hopes to approach the technological frontier needs an educated citizenry. And here we are not even talking about higher education. Rather, we are talking about *universal secondary education*, a much lower bar. As it turns out, most countries, including aspiring economic nationalist and techno-nationalist ones, fall short. For instance, Figure 9.2 plots secondary enrollment as a percent of the relevant age group for a handful of countries. While the United Kingdom and South Korea approach the mark, the others fall increasingly short. This is a key policy area that is often neglected.

Here we confront yet again the tendency of economic nationalists, including techno-nationalists, to downplay the role of basic policies that have both theoretical and empirical support across many national contexts in favor of a sort of knee-jerk "realism" that has zero-sum assumptions lurking behind it. In the process, important necessary conditions for technological and national

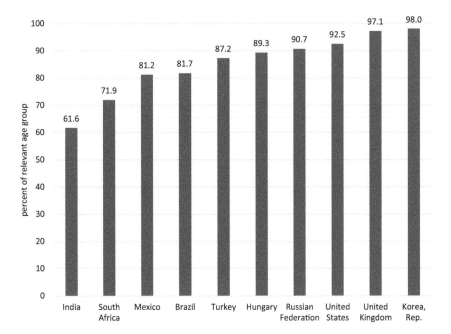

Figure 9.2 Secondary education enrollment (percent of relevant age group for most recent year available). Source: databank.worldank.org.

development are not given enough priority and can get lost in the rivalries among countries. Technological development and human development are set back in the process.

International Students and High-Skilled Immigrants

As we have discussed, basic education is a prerequisite for countries' techno-logical development, albeit one often overlooked by techno-nationalists. In addition, however, another means of pursuing technological development has been through higher educational service exports. By attracting some of the best students from the global market to study at its universities, a country can set in motion new research, particularly when these students are in science and engineering graduate schools. British- and US-based universities have relied on this strategy for many decades with overall successful results. But both countries are turning their backs on this strategy.

In the lead-up to the Brexit vote, and in keeping with the mood of the time, in 2015 the British home secretary (and future prime minister) Theresa May wrote a confidential (and then leaked) letter to UK ministers arguing that universities should "develop sustainable funding models that are not so dependent on international students."[52] This is an unusual argument for economic nationalists because they usually see exports in a positive light on zero-sum grounds, but the reason for this posture toward international students was the Brexit-inspired ethnonationalism discussed in Chapter 7. May did not want the students to stay in the United Kingdom, and indeed this followed on an effort in 2012 to make it more difficult for international students to do so via the scaling back of the post-schooling work visa program.

The limitation of this policy approach is that it puts a damper on potential high-skill migration that can benefit the host country, in this case, the United Kingdom. And interestingly, there were those in the Cameron government who opposed her policy on such grounds, including Chancellor George Osborne. So did industrial designer Sir James Dyson who wrote an open letter in *The Guardian* on this issue, characterizing the proposed May policy as "Train 'em up. Kick 'em out." He further stated:[53]

It's a bit shortsighted, isn't it? A short-term vote winner that leads to long-term economic decline. Of course the government needs to be seen to be "doing something." But postgraduate research in particular leads to exportable, patentable technology. Binning foreign postgraduates is, I suppose, a quick fix. But quick fixes don't build long-term futures.

Sir James adds a bit more insight. He notes that, absent the correct talent pool, UK firms would begin to move certain skill-intensive parts of their GVCs overseas where that skill or talent is to be found. Given the slow but nonetheless significant move on the part of MNEs to put greater amounts of R&D in new locations, that was not simply an empty threat on the part of one outraged businessman but rather a recognition of a relevant global trend.[54]

In the United States, somewhat similar issues are at play in that its role in scientific and engineering expertise has diminished relative to China and India whose output of natural science and engineering PhD graduates began to accelerate in the 2000s.[55] The noted labor economist Richard Freeman usefully identifies three ways in which the United States responded to these changes: hosting international students in science and engineering, employing immigrant scientists and engineers and collaborating with foreign scientists and engineers. The last two of these is a version of previously discussed open innovation model. The first involves the export of higher education services.

For a while, there was a complementary relationship between the United States and China in that the United States hosted an increasing number of Chinese graduate students in science engineering university programs. This subsequently changed as the antipathy between the United States and China increased.

Freeman also notes that:[56]

> Placing hurdles on international students working in the United States as permanent citizens or residents may have an economic cost for the United States. [...] In a world in which science and technology are critical in economic growth and comparative advantage, the United States (will) gain in those activities by keeping as many of the best and brightest from overseas who come to the country for education to continue their work in the United States if they so desire.

Beginning in 2018, the US Trump administration began to turn against not just Chinese graduate students wanting work visas, but against all the 350,000 Chinese students studying in the United States. While the stated aim was to address national security concerns, given the broad-brush nature of the proposal, the real aim seemed to be support of the ongoing trade war with China.[57] While this outright ban was not ultimately pursued, a policy of targeted visa delays and refusals went into effect with a 2020 proclamation stated in techno-nationalistic terms:[58]

> The People's Republic of China (PRC) is engaged in a wide-ranging and heavily resourced campaign to acquire sensitive United States technologies and intellectual property, in part to bolster the modernization and capability of its military, the People's Liberation Army (PLA). The PRC's acquisition of sensitive United States technologies and intellectual property to modernize its military is a threat to our Nation's long-term economic vitality and the safety and security of the American people. The PRC authorities use some Chinese students, mostly postgraduate students and post-doctorate researchers, to operate as nontraditional collectors of intellectual property.

In response, the Chinese government began to discourage its student from studying in the United States, and the US and Chinese responses began to divert US higher education service exports to other countries such as Canada and Australia.[59] Beginning in 2020, the COVID-19 pandemic discussed in Chapter 8 in effect did the work of economic nationalists opposed to student migration. Many of the paths to international education and subsequent work in other countries shut down. Given that at least 20 percent of US patent applications are the product of immigrants, this could have a long-term negative impact.

From Techno-Nationalism to Open Innovation

In May 2022, less than a year after he had been released from prison, Lee Jae-yong accompanied US president Joe Biden on a tour of a Samsung factory in Pyeongtaek, South Korea. Indeed, Biden appeared at this factory immediately after arriving in South Korea. Biden and Lee emphasized Samsung's plans to build a semiconductor facility in Texas and the role of the Texas facility in contributing to semiconductor GVC resiliency. This visit was a sign that business relations between the two countries had moved into the realm of international security. Indeed, South Korean president Yoon Suk-yeol stated that "I hope that Korea-U.S. relations can be born again as an economic-security alliance based on state-of-the-art technology and supply chain partnerships."[60]

This is an example of techno-nationalism spilling over into alliances between countries and is a testimony to techno-nationalism's current power. But this new phenomenon needs to be considered with some care going forward. At the beginning of this chapter, we quoted from international business researcher Yadong Luo on the new techno-nationalism. In the conclusion of his article, he states the following:[61]

Technological competition forms part of a larger strategic competition between states and firms. *But this competition does not have to be zero-sum.* In today's interconnected and interdependent business world, open innovation will continue regardless of intricate and sometimes despicable geopolitics. The dark side of technologies and certain digressed behaviors of certain economic powerhouses form a legitimate concern, but countering this concern does not have to cost economic openness, knowledge sharing, and technological connectivity. Global open innovation and cross-border knowledge flows should remain a cornerstone of international business while at the same time respecting security concerns.

Echoing the theme of this entire book, Luo emphasizes that strategic competition does not have to be zero sum. But as we have seen, there are many forces pressuring global economic relations to zero-sum views and practices, and at the current juncture, techno-nationalism is part of this zero-sum approach. The challenge will be to peel away the illegitimate techno-nationalism from legitimate security concerns. Historically, the potent "threat" of Japan to the United States and Europe has faded, while that of China has risen. Nonetheless, the Chinese, European and US economies are woven together in complex ways via trade and FDI, and innovation has moved to a new phase that is decidedly multinational. The new techno-nationalists have not effectively confronted this reality.

Chapter 10

BEYOND ZERO SUM

In the preceding chapters, we have seen how economic nationalism functions as a *lure* for both economic policy and political dynamics. Its associated zero-sum thinking is a default in many circumstances, even though the majority of relevant contexts are not actually zero sum. We have also seen that economic nationalism, including ethnonationalism, pandemic nationalism and techno-nationalism, can set back actual economic and human welfare in multiple ways. Overcoming these defaults represents a perennial, major challenge for human progress. Nonetheless, before we conclude this book, we need to give economic nationalism its due.

Giving Economic Nationalism Its Due

This book has been quite harsh on economic nationalism in its various forms, but there are elements of it that are worthwhile and contribute to our understanding of the world. Going back to mercantilism, for example, there was a serious attempt to explore how the economic world worked and to begin to engage in real economic analysis.[1] As stated in Chapter 2, the conception of the balance of payments possessed by some mercantilist writers was far superior to many present-day politicians. If their equation of power and plenty was too strong, they did at least identify two categories of concern that are relevant to this day.

There is less positive to say about Friedrich List and his vision of an imperial Germany. Nonetheless, his identification of both infant industry protection and the role of talented immigrants has relevance to this day. Unfortunately, his early followers also included imperial Japan, and his modern followers have both taken infant industry protection too seriously but not seriously enough. Retuning to this concept, modernizing it, and making it compatible with WTO law as a DFT remains a project surprisingly neglected. That said, we need to keep in mind that List and his followers wholeheartedly ignore the central role of services in modern economies, reducing the relevance of their ideas.

While economic nationalists often take zero-sum thinking for granted, their doing so has inspired researchers in other fields (political psychology, negotiations theory) to examine it in some detail. This examination reminds us that central concepts in economics can be difficult to understand and communicate and that, consequently, various forms of heuristic substitution are an inevitable default. This is part of the human condition and needs to be appreciated. However, when the heuristic substitution moves into the realm of discrimination against an "enemy other," a boundary has been crossed that can result in violence.[2] While not necessarily a component of economic nationalism, such descents into ethnonationalism are unfortunately quite common.

While the antipathy of economic nationalists toward the WTO and the EU is mostly misplaced, their (sometimes feigned) concern with those left behind by market forces is important. There *are* communities that have been devastated by these processes, whose members have been stranded in the evolution of national and international economies. This is a real and often tragic phenomenon. But by focusing on the pattern of countries' imports to the exclusion of exports; by ignoring the role of imported intermediate goods in domestic production and by downplaying the role of health, education and training, most economic nationalist policies fail to help the communities they claim to support. Renewed focus on those left behind, backed up by practical policies and long-range, non-zero-sum thinking is critical to the hoped-for improvement in well-being for all.

Finally, economic nationalists remind us that the world is a place of competition and potential conflict. The "community of nations" is wholly aspirational. However, to borrow a phrase from the open innovation field, the world is one of *potential coopetition*. Promoting this coopetition can make commercial relations more predictable in profoundly non-zero-sum ways. It can also better ensure agreements to address global challenges via global public goods provision. Given the estimated 15 million excess deaths from COVID-19, this is no small matter.[3] By escaping from zero-sum thinking and being open to cooperation and multilateralism, we can do better.

Back to Policy

At some point, we need to avoid excuses and return to careful policy analysis and formation. Importantly, despite emphasizing Ricardo's "difficult idea" of comparative advantage and the principle of multilateralism, most international economists are not "free traders" or "market fundamentalists." They widely acknowledge an important role of government in addressing externalities, providing public goods and mitigating the vagaries of economic globalization.[4] Despite this, for example, economic nationalist Michael Lind characterizes the profession as one where "there is no debate; the academic economists almost unanimously agree that free trade and investment benefit all sides. They instead postulate an ideal world where national borders would be insignificant and there would be free flows of goods, services, money and labor."[5] Such statements are *entirely off the mark*, perhaps purposively so.

In fact, most international economists repeatedly emphasize the need to provide social safety nets and retraining to address the impacts of international trade, as well as market-friendly measures to address volatile international capital flows. They do not envision a zero-tariff world of "free trade" but rather they advocate for a rules-based multilateral system of relatively low and predictable tariffs. In inflaming political passions regarding "globalization," economic nationalists often fail to address these policy issues adequately, preferring to engage in political performance. The limits to this were recognized by former Mexican president Ernesto Zedillo:[6]

Populist politicians have a marked tendency to blame others for their country's problems and failings. Foreigners who invest in, export or migrate to their country are the populist's favourite targets to explain almost every domestic problem. That is why restrictions on trade, investment and migration are an essential part of the populist's policy arsenal. [...] The "full package" of populism frequently includes anti-market economics, xenophobic and autarkic nationalism, and authoritarian politics. Populists display their protectionism and their xenophobia as proof of their "authentic patriotism" and excel at manipulating the public's nationalistic sentiments.

Zedillo refers to these tendencies as a "deflection of responsibility" and that is usually the case. Relatively mainstream (but not market fundamentalist) policies are available but often need some serious thinking through, tailoring to specific national context, and selling to the public. This in turn requires intelligent advisers, patience and recognizing that well-thought-out domestic policy still has an important role even in an era of globalization.[7] Indeed, globalization makes domestic policy even more important. While there is an unfortunate tendency to suggest that national policymaking is made impossible by economic globalization, that is not entirely the case. True, some policies such as fixed exchange rates might be much more difficult to pursue, but other important policies remain. These include appropriate types of infrastructure, education (including vocational) and training, progressive tax policies and social safety nets, public health investments, prudential regulation of financial sectors and market-friendly adjustment support.[8] Notably, these policy realms are largely ignored by economic nationalists.

There is the argument that globalization itself has made pursuing effective national policies more difficult and that this reality tends to support economic nationalist movements. The liberalization of markets in this view had diminished the ability of governments to raise the tax revenue necessary to compensate the "losers" from globalization because the "winners" become more effective at avoiding taxation.[9] It is true that it has become easier for individuals to hide income and wealth in offshore accounts, as well as for MNEs to engage in tax avoidance. But it is also true that market fundamentalist ideology (not mainstream economics) has pushed tax rates down as a political project, and that sometimes these tax reductions are pushed by economic nationalists themselves (e.g., the Trump movement in the United States). Dropping both market fundamentalism and economic nationalism for more mainstream economic policy would better allow governments to meet the challenges of globalization.

While zero-sum thinking is a notable and partially understandable default, this does not make it accurate or desirable in most circumstances. Recall from Chapter 2 that the historian of economic thought, Henry William Spiegel, referred to the mercantilist idea as "economic warfare for national gain."[10] While economic warfare leading to national gain might have been relevant centuries ago, it is hardly relevant in the modern era. Given current levels of international economic and commercial integration, the "economic warfare" of economic nationalism more often leads to national loss, and these losses are distributed among many countries.

A better way forward has four (often maligned) elements:

- Multilateralism
- Open innovation
- Global public goods provision to address global challenges
- Civic nationalism

Let's consider each one of these in turn.

Multilateralism

Recall from Chapter 2 that trade economist Jonathan Eaton states that: "Ricardo's message [...] took a universal rather than solely national perspective on welfare" and that "keeping this message alive poses a major challenge to trade economists."[11] As we have seen, modern economic nationalists often invoke List as their ideological beacon, but even List recognizes the potential role of multilateralism. Recall from Chapter 3 that List discusses the possibility of "all nations [...] united under one and the same system of law" and that the "decisions of law" should replace military force. He also suggests that ultimately "free trade" would replace "separate national commercial systems."[12] To a great degree, the multilateral system embedded in the WTO fulfills this particular aspect of List's vision but, ironically, not that of his followers.

Arguments for economic nationalism often suggest that it is a return to "normal" that the multilateral system developed after 1945 was an historical aberration. There is truth to this claim, but it is an incomplete truth. The postwar multilateral system was created by a world that had been laid low by the Great Depression and convulsed by war. Multilateralism was a precaution against repeated catastrophe. It was, in a sense, an answer to the mercantilist question about power and plenty. Power was to be circumscribed so that a minimal amount of plenty could be assured. The United States downplayed bilateral alliances with European countries and instead supported economic integration within Europe.[13] More broadly, it pursued a largely multilateral approach to the postwar order. As described by international relations scholar John Ruggie:[14]

> The American postwar multilateralist agenda consisted above all of a desire to restructure the international order along broadly multilateral lines. [...] The United States occasioned the creation of several major multilateral regimes, as in the fields of money and trade, and also helped establish numerous formal international organizations to provide technically competent or politically convenient services in support of those objectives. To be sure, the United States *hardly acted against its self-interests.*

Indeed, multilateralism at that time was perceived by the United States, and particularly the Roosevelt administration, to be what best served US interests. Further, in the economic issues that mattered most to its interests, it largely *got its way* at the 1944 Bretton Woods Conference, sidelining its British ally in the process. Its success in this matter appears to have reflected not just its international commitments, but also its domestic politics.[15] But the important historical reality is that it succeeded in building a multilateral regime.

The multilateral self-interests of most large players more or less remained intact for decades, but a few significant things began to change. First, the Reagan–Thatcher revolution of the 1980s ultimately led to an undermining of the public support required to provide sufficient adjustment to buffer citizens from the vicissitudes of an evolving global economy. It is important to again emphasize that, despite the popular opinion to the contrary, most international economists argue that basic public goods provision, social safety nets and adjustment assistance are *prerequisites* for effective engagement with economic globalization.[16] Without them, globalization cannot be managed, and a backlash will occur. That has proven to be the case.[17]

Second, China entered the world trading system. It is worth recalling that this was inevitable. Major players attempted to manage the event through the process of China's accession to the WTO. The WTO Working Party on this process was established in 1987 under the previous GATT, and the accession did not occur until 2001. The resulting 100-page accession document suggests that the institution did not jump blindly into Chinese membership.[18] Further, the ensuing export expansion of China was fueled by MNEs from high-income, "Western" countries who willingly participated in the process with the implicit encouragement of their home-country governments.

It is ironic that some of the most vociferous WTO members criticizing China's accession (e.g., the United States during the Trump administration) do not always make use of the available WTO remedies. For example, in a review of the foreign policy of the US Trump administration, *The Economist* takes up trade wars, noting that for President Trump, they "provide(d) a form of combat, brash and *performative*, which he positively relish(ed)" and that "America comes first, might is right, and saying so is *fun*."[19] But having fun is not the same thing as developing effective economic policy by engaging in the WTO dispute settlement process.

Third, economic nationalism, particularly ethnonationalism, began to strengthen. Regarding ethnonationalism, there is a tendency to see its development as somehow inevitable, but it is usually the result of the piecemeal chipping away of citizenship and governance norms until enough have been breached to give the *appearance* of inevitability. Rather than inevitable, rising ethnonationalism is usually the result of political entrepreneurs leveraging heuristics and bigotry for their own ends.

As we have emphasized, economic nationalism usually (not always) fails to enact good policy. It proceeds in a downward spiral of resentment, policy failure and further resentment, with political performance providing the requisite psychological fodder. Avoiding these failures will inevitably require a reengagement with multilateralism, in trade, finance, global health, climate and migration. Sometimes such reengagement necessarily follows catastrophe, such as after World War II, but it is more productive to make the effort before catastrophe strikes.

A major challenge to reengage with multilateralism was succinctly captured by the late British prince Philip who stated that "people still respond more easily to symbolism than to reason."[20] As we have seen, economic nationalism has many symbolic and performative aspects with palpable psychological appeal. However, particularly when politicians appeal to ethnically and racially charged "nostalgic deprivation," the serious policy agenda is often ignored. Indeed, the appeal to nostalgic deprivation can often exacerbate real deprivation by compromising the provision of basic goods and services, as well human security, with the implicit support of stochastic violence.[21]

Short of ethnonationalism, economic nationalism often revolves around call to "make things" in "Country X," and purportedly at least, abandoning multilateralism will make this possible. However, as we saw with the "smile curve" in Chapter 3, "making things" is where the least value added is often to be found. As stated by *The Economist*, "putting the components that make up a product together looks like the essence of the manufacturing process. But it often adds little to the finished product's value."[22] And manufacturing relies ever more on services as its stages or tasks are more finely defined and distributed around the world. Indeed, some of these services used to be part of the manufacturing sector and counted as such, so official statistics on manufacturing exaggerate its decline in many countries. To effectively address this new reality, education and training is where real economic nationalism should focus while maintaining a commitment to multilateralism.[23]

There were, of course, concerns that the US-created multilateral system was biased against LMICs. And it was. But the irony here is that, in recent years, this bias has been somewhat addressed with specific LMICs more fully engaged with the system and advocating effectively on their behalf.[24] This irony was noted by global political economy researcher J. P. Singh when he stated:[25]

The post-war multilateral system when created was deeply flawed but over time, through advocacy and continuing interactions, made way for inclusion and participation from the developing world. However, just when the multilateral system began to deliver a few positive results (to LMICS), it began to break down in the last two decades.

Recovering this progress for LMICs is another reason to reengage with multilateralism.

Open Innovation

While not universal, open innovation is a persistent feature of international business that has had substantial benefits both for the firms innovating and their customers. For example, recall from Chapter 8 that the Pfizer's COVID-19 vaccine was the product of a corporate partnership between the US-based multinational Pfizer and the German-based biotechnology firm BioNTech. BioNTech, in turn, was owned by two German scientists of Turkish origin, and Pfizer itself was headed up by a Greek citizen.[26] These forms of globalization are the realities of modern international business and help firms innovate.

Open innovation has been increasingly important in both manufacturing and services in an increasing number of firms of varied sizes and technological sophistication. In the words of one set of researchers, "rapid technological innovation in today's business world has made it nearly impossible for any firm to sustain technological supremacy without utilizing external knowledge and technologies," and this fact increasingly applies to MNEs.[27] Consequently, innovation has become increasingly global, something economic nationalists now want to thwart. This potentially threatens innovation itself.

As stated in Chapter 9, MNEs are now increasingly drawn into evolving systems of techno-nationalism and are becoming often-unwilling agents in international rivalries. This will limit the ability of MNEs to engage in the amount and quality of open innovation that they have been found to be critical to their business strategies. According to one set of researchers, "open innovation is crucial for a multinational enterprise to maintain its competitive advantage and become a leader in the market" and that "due to the challenges of market dynamism, MNEs have started to embrace the open innovation model, and reduce their reliance on inward-looking closed innovation."[28] Of course, MNEs are not always benign actors, but in closing off these avenues as they are just getting started, countries risk setting back processes that are now essential to MNEs' performance.

Open innovation also involves migration, particularly but not exclusively high-skilled migration. This avenue of innovation overlaps with entrepreneurship. For example, evidence suggests that approximately one-fourth of new firms in the United States are founded by first-generations immigrants, and immigrants generate more high-value patents.[29] The same seems to be true for the United Kingdom and other countries.[30] Consequently, the tendency of economic nationalists to oppose immigration, while politically useful, is shortsighted.

At the time of this writing, it appears that there is a trajectory toward separate techno-spheres, one centered on the United States and the EU, a second centered on China. Some countries such as Taiwan and South Korea are currently caught in the middle, but this might become the reality for an increasing number of countries. Having to choose between techno-spheres will limit the number of potential international collaborations for firms and will therefore limit future innovation and commercialization of new technologies.[31] The world will be poorer and more conflict prone as a result.

Global Public Goods Provision to Address Global Challenges

The rivalry between institutional multilateralism and economic nationalism is not helpful in confronting multiple global challenges. These include pandemic response, climate change, global food security and debt. Let's briefly consider each in turn.

No amount of economic nationalism will help in *pandemic response*. Indeed, our discussion in Chapter 8 suggests that it significantly inhibits such response since it ignores the necessary global public goods provisions, interrupts trade in health-related goods and services and promotes vaccine nationalism.[32] On the contrary, effective pandemic response will require a strengthened WHO, held to account but sufficiently resourced and supported to meet recurrent health threats with members supporting rather than undermining these efforts.

From a purely scientific point of view, addressing *climate change* must be a multilateral effort. While impacts are local and potentially strategic, the process of climate change demands a global public goods response. We tend to see multilateral efforts on climate change as a recent phenomenon, but these go back to the First World Climate Conference in 1979. The Intergovernmental Panel on Climate Change (IPCC), whose annual reports grow more dire each year, dates to the late 1980s as a joint effort of the World Meteorological Organization and the United Nations Environment Program. These scientific investigations and warnings therefore have a relatively long history.

Some economic nationalists maintain a side business in climate denialism. This allows them to burnish their antiscience and unilateralist bona fides. For example, former US president Donald Trump was famous for this. In November 2020, in an address to the G20 meetings, he stated that "the Paris accord was not designed to save the environment, it was designed to kill the American economy."[33] This was, of course, entirely false but accurately portrayed a point of view common to some economic nationalists.[34] Indeed, for some time now, it has been clear that climate change is a threat to most economies, including the United States. Nonetheless, in an act of performative nationalism, Trump withdrew the United States from the Paris Accord in 2017.

But the truth is that effectively addressing climate change will take an increased amount of multilateralism.[35] Such steps would follow on the 1997 Kyoto Protocol, which importantly included market-based mechanisms for achieving goals, and the 2015 Paris Accord, which was indeed designed to "save the environment" and to meet the demands of numerous country coalitions. The US Biden administration's reengagement with the Paris Accord was important. Nonetheless, even the Paris Accord is probably not enough to effectively address the problem, and multilateral efforts will need to go even further.[36] For example, there needs to be an agreement to end fossil fuel subsidies, a commitment to hard emissions targets and steps to put a price on carbon (either through national or multilateral taxes or tradable permits).[37] As with multilateral efforts in the trade realm, much will come down to the Quintet of Brazil, China, the EU, India and the United States and their ability to bridge competing national interests for the good of individuals and firms the world over, not least the citizens of "small island developing states" that are at risk of outright extinction.

At the time of this writing, there is also *global food security crisis.* In a 2018 book, the author addressed this issue, and at that time, the number of malnourished individuals was forecast to decline. The author noted, however, that "many things could interfere with this happy scenario" and pointed to climate change and conflict as likely contributing factors.[38] Unfortunately, he was correct in this assessment. Since then, the number of individuals experiencing food crisis requiring emergency action has doubled from approximately one hundred million to two hundred million. Some estimates put this "brink of famine" figure at 250 million.[39] Approximately 750,000 individuals are facing "catastrophic" hunger or, to put it less politely, are starving.[40]

Economic nationalism can do nothing to alleviate the food crisis, and if the past is any guide, will make it worse. As just discussed, climate change is beyond the reach of economic nationalists in any constructive sense. Further, the nationalistic Russian invasion of Ukraine dramatically contracted the supply of basic grains from these two countries, which together had supplied the world economy with nearly 30 percent of its wheat. The economic nationalist response is to impose agricultural export restraints (often outright bans) on grains and fertilizers, but trade economists have long warned that this exacerbates the problem. More specifically, analysis based on the 2007–8 food crisis shows that such export restraints increase the volatility of prices in ways that can harm poor households around the world.[41] As of 2020, at the beginning of the COVID-19 crisis, 13 countries had introduced export restrictions for food products. At the time of this writing, the number has increased to 23 countries covering 10 percent of globally traded calories.[42] Ensuring food security requires cooperation among countries not competition.

At the time of this writing, the world also confronts a growing *debt crisis.* An increasing number of LMICs find themselves with total debt levels at more than 200 percent of their exports, with a few exceeding 300 percent.[43] Unlike in the past, much of this debt is owed to commercial rather than official creditors, including at variable rates, and for low-income countries, the bulk of the debt is owed to China (the world's largest official lender). The Russian invasion of Ukraine, consequent increase in food import bills, higher oil prices and reduced tourist revenues in some countries have all exacerbated the debt situation. The recent crisis in Sri Lanka is just one example of these processes.

The G20 has a Common Framework for Debt Treatments established in 2020. Most sober assessments suggest that it is insufficient to address the current crisis. For example, at the time of this writing, only four countries have entered the Common Framework process (Chad, Ethiopia, Ghana and Zambia). It is inevitable that there will need to be substantial debt restructuring and forgiveness, and this will require cooperation within the G20 and with commercial creditors. Negotiations over debt owed to Chinese entities will be particularly difficult, although the presence of China in the G20, as well as its current participation in the Common Framework, will help.

On all these fronts (and others), adequate attention to global public goods is critical to prevent outright catastrophes. This is not hyperbole: the required policy responses are urgent and impossible to address with more economic nationalism. Instead, international cooperation, or at least coordination, will be necessary.

Civic Nationalism

As seen in Chapter 6, the idea of civic nationalism has many detractors. It is viewed as impractical, ill defined and unrealistic. Nonetheless, it is a concept and practice that deserves much more consideration and support. With communities currently under stress from climate change, food crises and economic crises, ethnonationalism is a combustible factor exploited to dangerous levels by political entrepreneurs many of whom are economic nationalists. Particularly where arms are plentiful, whether in Yemen or the United States, conflict is a potential result, leading to negative economic outcomes.[44]

To repeat what was stated in Chapter 6, there are many more "nations" than countries, and even more ethnicities. The partition solution offered by ethnonationalists will inevitably involve protracted conflicts that will spill across current national borders, setting back economic and human development in the affected countries. In most cases, it is not a solution at all. While civic nationalism is seen as a "fairy tale," it focuses attention on factors that can sustain economic and political life, namely institutional development and the broad-based participation in those institutions that sustain "everyday peace." It is widely acknowledged among development and growth economists that such structures and processes support market economies in fundamental ways. Armed conflict does not.

There is marked tendency to cast aside civic nationalism and to search for alternatives of one kind or another, but this process inevitably ends up at the ethnonationalist doorstep. It is time to fully reengage with an overly maligned concept to support economic development and deal more effectively with crises.

But What about Realism?

In today's intellectual climate, calls for multilateralism and non-zero-sum approaches to international policies (such as global public goods provision) run smack into a prominent school of thought in international relations, namely *realism*. Realism is difficult to pin down because there are so many varieties that have played out over time. In mercantilist terms, it focuses on power, with plenty taking a back seat if it is considered at all. The international relations scholar Jack Donnelly states that "realism emphasizes the constraints on politics imposed by human nature and the absence of international government. Together, they make international relations a realm of power and interest."[45] Realism is a recurrent touchstone in international relations and is currently experiencing a renewed prominence.

In its modern forms, realism poses a challenge to the views expressed in this book, particularly regarding the role of multilateral institutions. The self-described realist John Mearsheimer has referred to the "false promise" of this multilateral system and has criticized John Ruggie's promotion of it. Here is a taste of his own point of view:[46]

> Realism paints a rather grim picture of world politics. [...] International relations is not a constant state of war, but it is a state of relentless security competition, with the possibility of war always in the background. [...] Although it might seem counterintuitive, states do frequently cooperate in this competitive world. Nevertheless, cooperation among states has its limits because it is constrained by the dominating logic of security competition, which no amount of cooperation can eliminate. Genuine peace, or a world where states do not compete for power, is not likely according to realism.

A few points need to be made here. First, contrary to what Mearsheimer implies, institutional multilateralists do not see cooperation as unlimited. Indeed, negotiations theory explicitly accounts for alternatives to negotiated settlements that are always active (the best alternative to a negotiated agreement or BATNA). Second, cooperation is not just constrained by security competition but also by commercial competition, another reality recognized by institutional multilateralists. Third, and most fundamentally, institutional multilateralists do not claim that the rules-based system they espouse will in any way create "a world where states to not compete for power," and there is no presumption that "genuine peace" will be the outcome. As Jack Donnelly states, the failure to achieve "genuine peace" (whatever that is) "tells us nothing about the effects of international institutions on stability and security relations."[47] Rather, the goal has been simply to make commercial relations more stable and war less likely, nothing more.

We might take it even one step further. The efforts to create a set of multilateral institutions that took place after World War II were thoroughly informed by realist considerations less far reaching than those of Mearsheimer. The efforts were inspired by an episode in which "great power" rivalry led to catastrophic outcomes and were thoroughly infused with the hope to reduce the likelihood of repeated catastrophes. The substantial buy-in by countries (e.g., an increase in GATT/WTO membership from 23 to over 160 and including the accession of "great powers" Russia and China) suggests some real success in this matter. Why did countries put in all this effort it was not in their perceived interests?

Consider an article by the former chief economist of the WTO, Robert Koopman, and his colleagues. These individuals do emphasize the importance of cooperation over conflict, but the specifics they point to are the following: "more transparent and informed economic transactions, more secure and predictable economic relations, more cooperative or 'win-win' economic outcomes, and [...] more open exchanges of ideas, information and knowledge."[48] These are practical but essential components of relatively open commercial relations that are prerequisites for a global market system. Such defenses of multilateral institutions usually add on "promoting peace," but achieving an undefined "genuine peace" is seen as a step into fantasy.

Two further points are also worth mentioning. First, "great powers" are quite dependent on multilateral institutions. China's achievement of "great power" status was a result of a deep participation in the global trade and FDI system that facilitated its economic growth. Without that multilateral system in place, its trajectory would have been much different. Further, as can be seen in Figure 10.1, China has a dependency on high-income countries as export destinations (approximately 70 percent of merchandise exports in 2020) that has changed very little since 1960. That is, its exports are dependent on its rivals, namely the EU, the United States and Japan. In the realm of finance, ties are also strong with China holding over US$1 trillion in US government bonds.

Second, not all challenges fall into the realm of "great power" rivalry. For example, as just discussed, global health (pandemic response) and climate change mitigation cannot be effectively addressed within that framework.

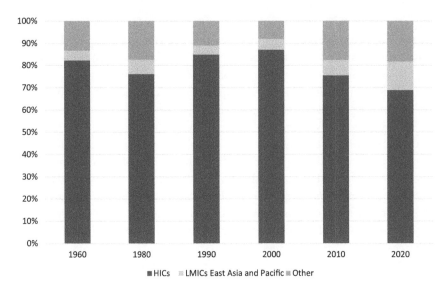

Figure 10.1 Destinations of China's merchandise exports (percent). Source: data-bank.worldank.org.

True, great power rivalry can and have made responses to those challenges worse than they could have been, but that would be an argument for mitigating these responses via multilateral cooperation rather than supporting them.

Realism can also lead us astray. For example, shortly after Russia's Ukraine war, the realist John Mearsheimer stated that Ukraine should be effectively ceded to Russia and that the United States should go so far as to *befriend* Russia.[49] One of the reasons for this posture (other than that we should let great powers be great powers because that is what they do) was a desired pivot to *confront China*. In Mearsheimer's view, the United States should befriend one great power to confront another greater power but without any institutional response because these are not recognized as effective by realists. But in truth, confronting China will require an institutional response. While this response will not be only multilateral, it will not be unilateral. It will involve an alliance of countries with agreed-upon aims. But such an alliance will also depend on multilateral institutions for backing. For example, as previously stated, there is no way to confront China on trade, including IP, without a fully functioning WTO.

Like economic nationalists, realists remind us of the role of power in international affairs, but they downplay the role of plenty and the role of multilateral institutions in enabling plenty. Consequently, realism is not a complete or final word on the matters discussed in this book. Avoiding catastrophes requires us to escape from its zero-sum mindset and think more creatively, indeed, more *realistically* in the full sense of that word.

And What about Sovereignty?

There is another popular criticism of the views expressed in this book, and it comes in the form of *sovereignty*. We began our consideration of economic nationalism in Chapter 1 with Albert Hirschman's book *National Power*, and we mentioned that he called for a reduction of *economic sovereignty* to promote peace and welfare. One quasi-realist concern with multilateralism and a focus on global public goods provision is that it can compromise sovereignty. For example, we encountered this in Chapter 7 on Brexit where the Leave campaign was explicitly set out in terms of British sovereignty vis-à-vis Brussels. But the distinction between sovereignty writ large and economic sovereignty is an important one.

At a basic level, there is the reality of public international law or the "law of nations." In a pure realist world, such a thing might not exist, and there are those who would suggest that it is really a fiction, but it would certainly be a much more chaotic world without it, as even a realist would acknowledge. Further, any international organization is bound by the 1969 Vienna Convention on the Law of Treaties ("treaty on treaties"), which circumscribes their activities.

The public international law of the WTO, as it turns out, is a set of non-self-executing agreements in most countries. That is, it cannot be invoked in domestic legal proceedings.[50] It is true that international economic agreements such as those of the WTO can put pressure on domestic legal systems to comply with those agreements, but noncompliance (with compensatory payments or allowed retaliation) is always an option. Further, the sovereignty issue is often raised by members such as the United States with dramatically outsized influence within the WTO, the IMF and the World Bank. It is not an exaggeration to state that these organizations (including the much-maligned WTO dispute settlement system) were largely tailored to US interests.

This is not to say there are no trade-offs between complete economic sovereignty and participation in international organizations, but that the net gains of a rules-based economic system are quite significant. Popular zero-sum, win–lose tallies of WTO dispute settlement processes, such as US president Trumps "we lose the lawsuits" statement, ignore this reality. All international agreements, and the organizations implementing them, are imperfect, but this is a call for careful amendments, not wholesale abandonment. Without these agreements and corresponding international organizations, the world would be more chaotic and much poorer.

Beyond Zero Sum

Paths diverge before us. The economic nationalist path involves continued commercial uncertainty and conflict, lower levels of innovation, the inability to adequately address global risks and inflamed ethnic conflict. These zero-sum tendencies can converge into a downward spiral that will reduce well-being across national boundaries. The non-zero-sum path involves smoother, if imperfect, commercial relations, higher levels of innovation, better responses to global risks and less ethnic conflict. The potential, imperfectly upward spiral of coopetition will prevent many needless deaths and stunted lives, but it involves leaving the psychological safety of zero-sum thinking to harness multilateralism, open innovation, global public goods provision and civic nationalism. The considerations of this book emphatically suggest that it is worth the effort.

AFTERWORD

As this book went into production in March 2023, Chinese president Xi Jinping met with Russian president Vladimir Putin in Moscow. The Chinese Ministry of Foreign Affairs announced that the two leaders "agreed to follow the principles of good-neighborliness, friendship and win-win cooperation," "to promote global governance in a direction that meets the expectations of the international community" and "to practice true multilateralism, oppose hegemonism and power politics." Ironically, these are the very values expressed in this book, ones undermined by China and Russia in practice. Are not the invasion of Ukraine and threatened invasion of Taiwan forms of hegemonism?

Unfortunately, China and Russia are not the only two countries undermining "win-win cooperation" and "true multilateralism." It is something of a trend. Indeed, defenders of multilateralism are commonly seen as idealistic, stuck in the past or wedded to a vague "Western" hegemony. In reality, the liberal principles of a rules-based international system, open economic relations and respect for human rights are universal and comprise the best approach to facilitating broad-based improvement in human welfare.

Also in March 2023, the United Nations issue its "synthesis" climate change report, and the results were described as a "final warning" on the issue, stating that the "pace and scale of climate action are insufficient to tackle climate change." No amount of further economic nationalism can help address this challenge. It would only exacerbate it. The imperative is for collective, multilateral action, most urgently in the elimination of fossil fuel subsidies and implementing carbon pricing.

As of the April 2023 annual IMF/World Bank meetings, more than twenty counties were either in debt default or seeking debt restructuring, with only Chad having been approved for the IMF's Common Framework discussed in Chapter 10. Further, China was refusing to either reduce the face value of debts or to increase payment periods, effectively refusing to seriously take part in the IMF's debt reduction process. The global public good of debt restructuring is proving to be elusive.

The United States continues it bipartisan consensus on techno-nationalism vis-à-vis China, with continued technological restrictions and threat of sanctions extending even to undersea cables, an unprecedented move. The evolution is from protecting legitimate security-related technologies to attempting to undercut China in all "foundational technologies," including biotechnology. It seems that there is no end to technological realms that can come under the nationalistic umbrella.

In short, as of early 2023, the trends outlined in this book appear to be solidifying. This suggests that we take a hard look at the negative implications of zero-sum thinking, attempt to reengage with multilateral institutions, recommit to global public goods provision and allow for open innovation systems. A secure and prosperous future depends on it.

Kenneth A. Reinert

BIBLIOGRAPHY

Abdelal, R. (2005) 'Nationalism and International Political Economy in Eurasia', in E. Helleiner and A. Pickel (eds.), *Economic Nationalism in a Globalizing World*, Cornell University Press, 21–43.

Acemoglu, D., D.H. Autor, D. Dorn, G.H. Hanson and B. Price (2016) 'Import Competition and the Great U.S. Employment Sag of the 2000s', *Journal of Labor Economics*, 34:S1, S141–S198.

Adelman, J. (2013) *Worldly Philosopher: The Odyssey of Albert O. Hirschman*, Princeton University Press.

Adorno, T.W., E. Frenkel-Brunswik, D.J. Levinson and R.N. Sanford (2019 [1950]) *The Authoritarian Personality*, Verso.

Agence French-Presse (2022) 'Holocaust Survivors Condemn Race Remarks by Hungary's Orbán', July 27.

Alderman, L. and M. Santora (2019) 'Hungary's Nationalist Policies Have Created a Labor Shortage. The Fix Isn't Helping,' *New York Times*, May 3.

Ali-Yrkkö, J., P. Rouvinen, T. Seppälä and P. Ylä-Anttila (2011) 'Who Captures Value in Global Supply Chains? Case Nokia N95 Smartphone', *Journal of Industry, Competition and Trade*, 11:3, 263–278.

Amiti, M., S.J. Redding and D.E. Weinstein (2019) 'The Impact of the 2018 Tariffs on Prices and Welfare', *Journal of Economic Perspectives*, 33:4, 187–210.

Anderson, B. (1991) *Imagined Communities: Reflections on the Origin and Spread of Nationalism*, Verso.

Antal, A. (2017) 'The Political Theories, Preconditions and Dangers of the Governing Populism in Hungary', *Czech Journal of Political Science*, 24:1, 5–20.

Appadurai, A. (2022) 'Modi's India Has Now Entered Genocidalism, the Most Advanced Stage of Nationalism', *The Wire*, January 10.

Arnold, J.M., B.S. Javorcik and A. Mattoo (2011) 'Does Services Liberalization Benefit Manufacturing Firms? Evidence from the Czech Republic', *Journal of International Economics*, 85:1, 136–146.

Arnold, J.M., B.S. Javorcik, M. Lipscomb and A. Mattoo (2015) 'Services Reform and Manufacturing Performance: Evidence from India', *Economic Journal*, 126:590, 1–39.

Arnorsson, A. and G. Zoega (2018) 'On the Causes of Brexit', *European Journal of Political Economy*, 55, 301–323.

Asakawa, K., J. Song and S.-J. Kim (2014) 'Open Innovation in Multinational Corporations: New Insights from the Global R&D Research Stream', in H. Chesbrough, W. Vanhaverbeke and J. West (eds.), *New Frontiers in Open Innovation*, Oxford University Press, 157–168.

Autor, D.H., D. Dorn and G.H. Hanson (2013) 'The China Syndrome: Local Labor Market Effects of Import Competition in the United States', *American Economic Review*, 103:6, 2121–2168.

Badinger, H. (2005) 'Growth Effects of Economic Integration: Evidence from the EU Member States', *Review of World Economics*, 141, 50–78.

Bairoch, P. (1982) 'International Industrialization Levels from 1750 to 1980', *Journal of European Economic History*, 11:2, 269–331.

Bairoch, P. (1989) 'European Trade Policy, 1815–1914', in P. Mathias and S. Pollard (eds.), *Cambridge History of Europe, Vol. VIII, The Industrial Economies: The Development of Economic and Social Policies*, Cambridge University Press, 1–60.

Baker, B. (2018) 'Use That Word!: Trump Embraces the Nationalist Label', *New York Times*, October 23.

Baldwin, R.E. (1989) 'The Growth Effects of 1992', *Economic Policy*, 4:9, 247–281.

Baldwin, R.E. (2016) *The Great Convergence: Information Technology and the New Globalization*, Harvard University Press.

Baldwin, R.E. and S.J. Evenett (2020) 'Introduction', in R.E. Baldwin and S.J. Evenett (eds.), *COVID-19 and Trade Policy: Why Turning Inward Won't Work*, Center for Economic Policy Research, 1–19.

Baron, J. and J. Jurney (2001) 'Confusion of Group Interest and Self-Interest in Parochial Cooperation on Behalf of a Group', *Journal of Conflict Resolution*, 45:3, 283–296.

Baron, J. (1993) 'Norms Against Voting for Coerced Reforms', *Journal of Personality and Social Psychology*, 64:3, 347–355.

Baron, J. and S. Kemp (2004) 'Support for Trade Restrictions, Attitudes, and Understanding of Comparative Advantage', *Journal of Economic Psychology*, 25, 565–580.

Barry, B. and R.A. Friedman (1998) 'Bargainer Characteristics in Distributive and Integrative Negotiation', *Journal of Personality and Social Psychology*, 74:2, 345–359.

Baughn, C.C. and A. Yaprak (1996) 'Economic Nationalism: Conceptual and Empirical Development', *Political Psychology*, 17:4, 759–778.

Beck, A. (2014) 'Drought, Dams, and Survival: Linking Water to Conflict and Cooperation in Syria's Civil War', *International Affairs Forum*, 5:1, 11–22.

Becker, G. (1971) *The Economics of Discrimination*, University of Chicago Press.

Berchin, I.I, I.B. Valduga, J. Garcia and J.B.S.O. de Andrade Guerra (2017) 'Climate Change and Forced Migrations: An Effort Towards Recognizing Climate Refugees', *Geoforum*, 84, 147–150.

Bernstein, S., R. Diamond, T. McQuade and B. Pausada (2019) 'The Contribution of High-Skilled Immigrants to Innovation in the United States', Unpublished Paper.

Bigliardi, B., G. Ferraro, S. Fillipelli and F. Gelati (2020) 'The Influence of Open Innovation on Firm Performance', *International Journal of Engineering Business Management*, 12, 1–14.

Bloom, N., K. Handley, A. Kurman and P. Luck (2019) 'The Impact of Chinese Trade on U.S. Employment: The Good, the Bad, and the Debatable', Unpublished Paper.

Bollyky, T.J. and C.P. Bown (2020) 'The Tragedy of Vaccine Nationalism: Only Cooperation Can End the Pandemic', *Foreign Affairs*, 99:5, 96–108.

Bouie, J. (2020) 'We Waited in Vain for a Repudiation That Never Came', *New York Times*, November 5.

Boutros-Ghali, B. (1992) *An Agenda for Peace: Preventative Diplomacy, Peacemaking and Peacekeeping*, United Nations.

Bown, C. and T. Bollykyl (2021) *The World Needs a COVID-19 Trade and Investment Agreement*, Peterson Institute for International Economics.

Bown, C.P. (2020) 'COVID-19: Demand Spikes, Export Restrictions, and Quality Concerns Imperil Poor Country Access to Medical Supplies', in R.E. Baldwin and S.J. Evenett (eds.), *COVID-19 and Trade Policy: Why Turning Inward Won't Work*, Center for Economic Policy Research, 31–47.

Bown, C.P. (2021) *US-China Phase One Tracker: China's Purchases of US Goods*, Peterson Institute for International Economics.

Bown, C.P. (2022) *China Bought None of the Extra $200 Billion of US Exports in Trump's Trade Deal*, Peterson Institute for International Economics.

Bown, C.P. and D.A. Irwin (2015) 'GATT's Starting Point: Tariff Levels Circa 1947', National Bureau of Economic Research Working Paper 21782.

Bown, C.P. and D.A. Irwin (2019) 'Trump's Assault on the Global Trading System: And Why Decoupling from China Will Change Everything', *Foreign Affairs*, 98:5, 125–137.

Bown, C.P. and S. Keynes (2020) 'Why Trump Shot the Sheriffs: The End of WTO Dispute Settlement 1.0', *Journal of Policy Modeling*, 42:4, 799–819.

Brenner, R. (1973) 'The Civil War Politics of London's Merchant Community', *Past and Present*, 58, 53–107.

Brewer, J. (1990) *The Sinews of Power: War, Money and the English State, 1688–1783*, Harvard University Press.

Brewster, R. (2020) 'Gender and International Trade Policy: Economic Nostalgia and the National Security Steel Tariffs', *Duke Journal of Gender Law and Policy*, 27:1, 59–68.

British Broadcasting Corporation (2013) 'David Cameron Promises In/Out Referendum on EU', January 23.

British Broadcasting Corporation (2018) 'Trump Threatens to Pull US Out of World Trade Organization', August 31.

Broadberry, S.N. (1998) 'How Did the United States and Germany Overtake Britain? A Sectoral Analysis of Comparative Productivity Levels, 1870–1990', *Journal of Economic History*, 58:2, 375–407.

Bruton, H.J. (1998) 'A Reconsideration of Import Substitution', *Journal of Economic Literature*, 36:2, 903–936.

Burns, A. (2023) 'Liz Truss Crashes the (Republican) Party', *Politico*, January 30.

Caliendo, L., M. Dvorkin and F. Parro (2019) 'Trade and Labor Market Dynamics: General Equilibrium Analysis of the China Trade Shock', *Econometrica*, 87:3, 741–835.

Campos, N.F., F. Coricelli and L. Moretti (2014) 'Economic Growth and Political Integration: Estimating the Benefits from Membership in the European Union Using the Synthetic Counterfactuals Method', *IZA Discussion Paper 8162*.

Carlson, T. (1997) 'The Intellectual Roots of Nativism', *Wall Street Journal*, October 2.

Chanda, R. (2017) 'Trade in Services', in K.A. Reinert (ed.), *Handbook of Globalisation and Development*, Edward Elgar, 36–58.

Chang, H.J. (2003) *Kicking Away the Ladder: Development Strategy in Historical Perspective*, Anthem.

Chen, F. (2021) 'China Set to Launch Locally Made mRNA Vaccine', *Asia Times*, August 5.

Chesbrough, H. and M. Bogers (2014) 'Explicating Open Innovation: Clarifying an Emerging Paradigm for Understanding Innovation', in H. Chesbrough, W. Vanhaverbeke and J. West (eds.), *New Frontiers in Open Innovation*, Oxford University Press, 3–28.

Child, J. (1692) *A New Discourse on Trade*, T. Sowle.

Chotiner, I. (2022) 'Why John Mearsheimer Blames the U.S. for the Crisis in the Ukraine', *The New Yorker*, March 1.

Cisneros-Montemayor, A.M. and U.R. Sumaila (2019) 'Busting Myths That Hinder Agreement to End Harmful Fisheries Subsidies', *Marine Policy*, 109, 103699.

Clark, D. (2021) 'The Tech Cold War's Most Complicated Machine That's Out of China's Reach', *New York Times*, July 4.

Colantone, I. and P. Stanig (2019) 'The Surge of Economic Nationalism in Western Europe', *Journal of Economic Perspectives*, 33:4, 128–151.

Coleman, D.C. (1988) 'Adam Smith, Businessmen, and the Mercantile System in England', *History of European Ideas*, 9:2, 161–170.

Condliffe, J.B. (1950) *The Commerce of Nations*, Norton.

Connor, W. (1973) 'The Politics of Ethnonationalism', *Journal of International Affairs*, 27:1, 1–21.

Connor, W. (2007) 'Ethnonationalism', in *Blackwell Encyclopedia of Sociology*, John Wiley and Sons.

Corbett, S. (2016) 'The Social Consequences of Brexit for the UK and Europe: Euroscepticism, Populism, Nationalism, and Societal Division', *International Journal of Social Quality*, 6:1, 11–31.

Cowhey, P.F. (1993) 'Domestic Institutions and the Credibility of International Commitments: Japan and the United States', *International Organization*, 47:2, 299–326.

Crafts, N. (2016) *The Growth Effects of EU Membership for the UK: Review of the Evidence*, Social Market Foundation.

Crane G.T. (1998) 'Economic Nationalism: Bringing the Nation Back In', *Millennium*, 27:1, 55–75.

Csehi, R. and E. Zgut (2021) 'We Won't Let Brussels Dictate Us: Eurosceptic Populism in Hungary and Poland', *European Politics and Society*, 22:1, 53–68.

Curtice, J. (2017) 'Why Leave Won the UK's EU Referendum', *Journal of Common Market Studies*, 55:S1, 19–37.

Daily Express (2013) 'Britain is Full and Fed Up', October 31.

Dalrymple, W. (2019) *The Anarchy: The East India Company, Corporate Violence, and the Pillage of an Empire*, Bloomsbury.

Davidai, S. and M. Ongis (2019) 'The Politics of Zero-Sum Thinking: The Relationship Between Political Ideology and the Belief That Life Is a Zero-Sum Game', *Science Advances*, 5:12, 1–10.

Davies, C. (2021) 'Duke of Edinburgh, Prince Philip, Dies Aged 99', *The Guardian*, April 9.

Davis, D.E. (2004) *Discipline and Development: Middle Classes and Prosperity in East Asia and Latin America*, Cambridge University Press.

Deardorff, A.V. (1998) 'Technology, Trade, and Increasing Inequality: Does the Cause Matter for the Cure?' *Journal of International Economic Law*, 1:3, 353–376.

Deb, S. (2021) '"They Are Manufacturing Foreigners": How India Disenfranchises Muslims', *New York Times*, September 15.

Debebe, G. (2017) 'Navigating the Double Bind: Transformations to Balance Contextual Responsiveness and Authenticity in Women's Leadership Development', *Cogent Business and Management*, 4:1, 1313543.

Debebe, G. and K.A. Reinert (2014) 'Leading with Our Whole Selves: A Multiple Identity Approach to Leadership Development', in M. Miville and A. Fergeson (eds.), *Handbook of Race, Ethnicity, and Gender in Psychology*, Springer, 271–293.

Dedrick, J., K.L. Kraemer and G. Linden (2010) 'Who Profits from Innovation in Global Value Chains: A Study of the iPod and Notebook PCs', *Industrial and Corporate Change*, 19:1, 81–116.

de Châtel, F. (2014) 'The Role of Drought and Climate Change in the Syrian Uprising: Untangling the Triggers of the Revolution', *Middle Eastern Studies*, 50:4, 521–535.

De Santis, R. and C. Vicarelli (2007) 'The 'Deeper' and the 'Wider' EU Strategies of Trade Integration: An Empirical Evaluation of EU Common Commercial Policy Effects', *Global Economy Journal*, 7:4, Article 4.

de Vries, J. (2003) 'Connecting Europe and Asia: A Quantitative Analysis of the Cape-Route Trade, 1497–1795', in D.O. Flynn, A. Giráldez and R. von Glahn (eds.), *Global Connections and Monetary History, 1470–1800*, Ashgate, 35–106.

Devare, A. (2011) *History and the Making of a Modern Hindu Self*, Routledge.

Diez, T. (1999) 'Speaking "Europe": The Politics of Integration Discourse', *Journal of European Public Policy*, 6:4, 598–613.

Dinan, D. (2014) *Europe Recast: A History of European Union*, Lynne Rienner.

Dinan, D. (2017) 'Governance and Institutions: The Insidious Effect of Chronic Crisis', *Journal of Common Market Studies*, 55:S1, 73–87.

Dinan, D. (2021) *The European Council in 2020: Overview of Dynamics, Discussions and Decisions*, European Parliamentary Research Service.

Donnelly, J. (2000) *Realism and International Relations*, Cambridge University Press.

Duckitt, J. (1989) 'Authoritarianism and Group Identification: A New View of an Old Concept', *Political Psychology*, 10:1, 63–84.

Dustmann, C. and T. Frattini (2014) 'The Fiscal Effects of Immigration to the UK', *Economic Journal*, 124:580, F593–F643.

Dyson, J. (2015) 'No Theresa May, We Need Those Foreign Graduates', *The Guardian*, January 4.

Earle, S. (2021) 'Britain's Heading into a Nightmarish Winter', *New York Times*, October 1.

Eaton, J. (2017) 'The Long Shadow That Ricardo Has Cast Over the Modern Analysis of Trade', in S.J. Evenett (ed.), *Cloth for Wine? The Relevance of Ricardo's Comparative Advantage in the 21st Century*, Center for Economic Policy Research, 21–31.

Eccleston-Turner, M. and H. Upton (2021) 'International Collaboration to Ensure Equitable Access to Vaccines for COVID-19: The ACT-Accelerator and the COVAX Facility', *Milbank Quarterly*, 99:2, 426–449.

Eichengreen, B. (2008) *Globalizing Capital: A History of the International Monetary System*, Princeton University Press.

Elmslie, B. (2015) 'Early English Mercantilists and the Support of Liberal Institutions', *History of Political Economy*, 47:3, 419–448.

Espitia, A., N. Rocha and M. Ruta (2020) *Trade in Critical COVID-19 Products*, World Bank.

European Parliament (2017) 'Implications of Brexit for EU Financial Services', IP/A/ ECON/2016-22.

Evenett, S. (2020) 'Flawed Prescription: Export Curbs on Medical Goods Won't Tackle Shortages', in R.E. Baldwin and S.J. Evenett (eds.), *COVID-19 and Trade Policy: Why Turning Inward Won't Work*, Center for Economic Policy Research, 49–61.

Fearon, P.A., F.M. Götz, G. Serapio-García and D. Good (2021) 'Zero-Sum Mindset and Its Discontents', Economic and Social Research Council, SM-WP-2021-1.

Feenstra, R. and A. Sasahara (2018) 'The China Shock, Exports and US Employment: A Global Input-Output Analysis', *Review of International Economics*, 26:5, 1053–1083.

Feenstra, R., H. Ma and Y. Xu (2019) 'US Exports and Employment', *Journal of International Economics*, 120, 46–58.

Findlay, R. and K.H. O'Rourke (2007) *Power and Plenty: Trade, War, and the World Economy in the Second Millennium*, Princeton University Press.

Fisher, M. (2020) 'From Ebola to Coronavirus, Trump Always Sees Disease as a Foreign Threat', *Washington Post*, March 20.

Flaaen, A. and J. Pierce (2019) 'Disentangling the Effects of the 2018–2019 Tariffs on a Globally-Connected U.S. Manufacturing Sector', *Finance and Economics Discussion Series 2019–086*, Board of Governors of the U.S. Federal Reserve System.

Food and Agriculture Organization (2020) *The State of World Fisheries and Aquaculture.*

Food and Agricultural Organization (2022) *Hunger Hotspots: FAO-WFP Early Warnings on Acute Food Insecurity.*

Francis, A.D. (1960) 'John Methuen and the Anglo-Portuguese Treaties of 1703', *The Historical Journal*, 3:2, 103–124.

Francois, J.F. and K.A. Reinert (1996) 'The Role of Services in the Structure of Production and Trade: Stylized Facts from a Cross-Country Analysis', *Asia-Pacific Economic Review*, 2:1, 1–9.

Freeman, R., K. Manova, T. Prayer and T. Sampson (2022) 'Unravelling Deep Integration: UK Trade in the Wake of Brexit', *Centre for Economic Performance Discussion Paper 1847.*

Freeman, R.B. (2015) 'Immigration, International Collaboration, and Innovation: Science and Technology Policy in the Global Economy', *Innovation Policy and the Economy*, 15, 153–175.

Fukuyama, F. (1995) *Trust: The Social Virtues and the Creation of Prosperity*, Free Press.

Furceri, D., S.A. Hannan, J.D. Ostry and A.K. Rose (2020) 'Are Tariffs Bad for Growth? Yes, Say Five Decades of Data from 150 Countries', *Journal of Policy Modeling*, 42:4, 850–859.

Gamio, L. and J. Glanz (2021) 'Just How Big Could India's Covid Toll Be?' *New York Times*, May 25.

Gao, H. (2021) 'Finding a Rules-Based Solution to the Appellate Body Crisis: Looking Beyond the Multiparty Interim Appeal Arbitration Arrangement', *Journal of International Economic Law*, 24:3, 534–5507.

Garamvolgi, F. and J. Borger (2022) 'Trump Shares CPAC Hungary Platform with Notorious Racist and Antisemite', *The Guardian*, May 21.

Gasiorek and Jerzewska (2020) 'The Unresolved Difficulties of the Northern Ireland Protocol', *UK Trade Policy Observatory, Briefing Paper 41.*

Gelles, D. (2020) 'The Husband-and-Wife Team Behind the Leading Vaccine to Solve Covid-19', *New York Times*, November 10.

Gereffi, G., P. Pananond and T. Pedersen (2022) 'Resilience Decoded: The Role of Firms, Global Value Chains, and the State in COVID-19 Medical Supplies', *California Management Review*, 64:2, 46–70.

Gest, J., T. Reny and J. Mayer (2018) 'Roots of the Radical Right: Nostalgic Deprivation in the United States and Britain', *Comparative Political Studies*, 51:13, 1694–1719.

Ghebreyesus, T.A. (2021) 'Vaccine Nationalism Harms Everyone and Protects No One', *Foreign Policy*, https://foreignpolicy.com/2021/02/02/vaccine-nationalism-harms-everyone-and-protects-no-one/.

Ghemawat, P. (2003) 'The Forgotten Strategy', *Harvard Business Review*, 81:11, 76–84.

Ghemawat, P. (2009) 'Why the "World Isn't Flat"', *Foreign Policy*, October 14. https://foreignpolicy.com/2009/10/14/why-the-world-isnt-flat/.

Ghemawat, P. (2017) 'Why Managers Still Need to Take Account of Comparative Advantage', in S.J. Evenett (ed.), *Cloth for Wine? The Relevance of Ricardo's Comparative Advantage in the 21st Century*, Center for Economic Policy Research, 87–93.

Gietel-Basten, S. (2016) 'Why Brexit? The Toxic Mix of Immigration and Austerity', *Population and Development Review*, 42:4, 673–680.

Gifford, C. (2006) 'The Rise of Post-Imperial Populism: The Case of Right-Wing Euroscepticism in Britain', *European Journal of Political Research*, 45:5, 851–869.

Gil, N. (2015) 'A Guide to the Government's New Rules for International Students', *The Guardian*, July 29.

Gil, S., R. Llorca and J.A. Martíniz-Serrano (2008) 'Assessing the Enlargement and Deepening of the European Union', *World Economy*, 31:9, 1253–1272.

Gilpin, R. (1987) *The Political Economy of International Relations*, Princeton University Press.

Glanz, J., M. Hvistendahl and A. Chang (2023) 'How Deadly Was China's Covid Wave?', *New York Times*, February 15.

Glencross, A. (2016) *Why the UK Voted for Brexit: David Cameron's Great Miscalculation*, Palgrave Macmillan.

Goldberg, M. (2021) 'Angela Merkel Was Right', *New York Times*, October 21.

Goldin, I. and K.A. Reinert (2012) *Globalization for Development: Meeting New Challenges*, Oxford University Press.

Goldstone, J. (2009) *Why Europe? The Rise of the West in World History, 1500–1850*, McGraw-Hill.

González, A. (2020) 'A Memo to Trade Ministers on How Trade Policy Can Help Fight COVID-19', *Trade Policy Watch*, Peterson Institute for International Economics.

Goodman, P.S., K. Thomas, S.-L. Wee and J. Gettleman (2020) 'A New Front Line for Nationalism: The Global Battle Against a Virus', *New York Times*, April 10.

Gorski, P. and S. Perry (2022) *The Flag and the Cross*, Oxford University Press.

Grampp, W.D. (1952) 'The Liberal Elements in English Mercantilism', *Quarterly Journal of Economics*, 66:4, 465–501.

Gray, C. (2006) *Irregular Enemies and the Essence of Strategy: Can the American Way of War Adapt?* U.S. Army War College Press.

Gray, R. (2018) 'A *Daily Caller* Editor Wrote for an "Alt-Right" Website Using a Pseudonym', *The Atlantic*, September 5.

Green, E. (2019) 'The Nationalists Take Washington', *The Atlantic*, July 17.

Gupta, P. (2017) 'Global Production Networks', in K.A. Reinert (ed.), *Handbook of Globalisation and Development*, Elgar, 153–168.

Gynawali, D.R. and B.-J. Park (2011) 'Co-opetition Between Giants: Collaboration with Competition for Technological Innovation', *Research Policy*, 40:5, 650–663.

Hall, D. (2005) 'Japanese Spirit, Western Economics: The Continuing Salience of Economic Nationalism in Japan', in E. Helleiner and A. Pickel (eds.), *Economic Nationalism in a Globalizing World*, Cornell University Press, 118–138.

Hall, E. (1989) *Inventing the Barbarian: Greek Self-Definition through Tragedy*, Oxford University Press.

Hall, J.M. (2015) 'Ancient Greek Ethnicities: Towards a Reassessment', *Bulletin of the Instituto of Classical Studies*, 58:2, 15 29.

Hall, R. (2021) 'UK "Tough Guy" Act on Northern Ireland Will End in Disaster, Says Irish Minister', *The Guardian*, November 12.

Harris, A.L. (1964) 'John Stuart Mill: Servant of the East India Company', *Canadian Journal of Economics and Political Science*, 30:2, 185–202.

Hawtrey, R.G. (1930) *Economic Aspects of Sovereignty*, Longmans.

Helleiner, E. (2005) 'Conclusion: The Meaning and Economic Significance of Economic Nationalism', in E. Helleiner and A. Pickel (eds.), *Economic Nationalism in a Globalizing World*, Cornell University Press, 220–234.

Helleiner, E. (2021) 'The Diversity of Economic Nationalism', *New Political Economy*, 26:2, 229–238.

Henley, D. (2012) 'The Agrarian Roots of Industrial Growth: Rural Development in South-East Asia and Sub-Saharan Africa', *Development Policy Review*, 30:S1, S25–S47.

Hirschman, A.O. (1945) *National Power and the Structure of Foreign Trade*, University of California Press.

Hoekman, B.M. and M. Kostecki (2009) *The Political Economy of the World Trading System: From GATT to WTO*, Oxford University Press.

Hoekman, B.M. and P.C. Mavroidis (2020) 'To AB or Not To AB? Dispute Settlement in WTO Reform', *Journal of International Economic Law*, 23:3, 703–722.

Holshek, C. (2013) 'Thinking Globally, Acting Locally: A Grand Strategic Approach to Civil-Military Coordination in the 21st Century', in V.C. Franke and R.H. Dorff (eds.), *Conflict Management and Peacebuilding: Pillars of a New American Grand Strategy*, U.S. Army War College Press, 193–239.

Hotez, P. and M.E. Bottazzi (2021) 'A COVID Vaccine for All', *Scientific American*, December 30, https://www.scientificamerican.com/article/a-covid-vaccine-for-all/.

Hsieh, C.T., E. Hurst, C.I. Jones and P.J. Klenow. 2019. 'The Allocation of Talent and U.S. Economic Growth', *Econometrica* 87: 1439–1474.

Hyde, L. (2019) 'How Nationalism Can Destroy a Country', *New York Times*, August 21.

Hyrtsak, Y. (2022) 'Putin Made a Profound Miscalculation on Ukraine', *New York Times*, March 19.

Ignatieff, M. (1993) *Blood and Belonging: Journeys into the New Nationalism*, Farrar, Straus and Giroux.

Ikenberry, G.J. (1992) 'A World Economy Restored: Expert Consensus and the Anglo-American Postwar Settlement', *International Organization*, 46:1, 289–321.

Iliasu, A.A. (1971) 'The Cobden-Chevalier Commercial Treaty of 1860', *The Historical Journal*, 14:1, 67–98.

Ince, O.U. (2016) 'Friedrich List and the Imperial Origins of the National Economy', *New Political Economy*, 21:4, 380–400.

Inikori, J.E. (2002) *Africans and the Industrial Revolution in England: A Study in International Trade and Economic Development*, Cambridge University Press.

Inkster, S. (2019) 'The Huawei Affair and China's Technology Ambitions', *Survival*, 61:1, 105–111.

Irwin, D. (1995) 'The GATT in Historical Perspective', *American Economic Review*, 85:2, 323–328.

Irwin, D. (1998) 'The Semiconductor Industry', *Brookings Trade Forum*, 173–200.

Irwin, D. (2001) 'Tariffs and Growth in Late Nineteenth Century America', *World Economy*, 24:1, 15–30.

Irwin, D. (2002) 'Interpreting the Tariff-Growth Correlation in the Late 19th Century', *American Economic Review*, 92:2, 165–169.

Irwin, D. (2017) 'Ricardo and Comparative Advantage at 200', in S.J. Evenett (ed.), *Cloth for Wine? The Relevance of Ricardo's Comparative Advantage in the 21st Century*, Center for Economic Policy Research, 7–13.

Irwin, D. (2020) *Free Trade Under Fire*, Princeton University Press.

Irwin, N. (2016) 'Donald Trump's Economic Nostalgia', *New York Times*, June 28.

Ivarsflaten, E. (2008) 'What Unites Right-Wing Populists in Western Europe? Reexamining Grievance Mobilization Models in Seven Successful Cases', *Comparative Political Studies*, 41:1, 3–23.

Johnson, B. (2013) 'We Must Be Ready to Leave the EU If We Don't Get What We Want', *The Telegraph*, May 12.

Johnson, C. and B. Williams (2020) 'Gender and Political Leadership in a Time of COVID', *Politics & Gender*, 16:4, 943–950.

Johnson, H.G. (1965) 'A Theoretical Model of Economic Nationalism in New and Developing States', *Political Science Quarterly*, 80:2, 169–185.

Johnson, R.C. and G. Noguera (2012) 'Accounting for Intermediates: Production Sharing and Trade in Value Added', *Journal of International Economics*, 86, 224–236.

Johnson, S.G.B., J. Zhang and F.C. Keil (2020) 'Win-Win Denial: The Psychological Underpinnings of Zero-Sum Thinking', *PsyArXiv*, April 30.

Jones, R.W. and J. Larner (2021) 'What About Wales? Brexit and the Future of the UK', https://discoversociety.org/2021/06/08/what-about-wales-brexit-and-the-future-of-the-uk/.

Kahl, C. and T. Wright (2021) *Aftershocks: Pandemic Politics and the End of the Old International Order*, St. Martins.

Kahneman, D. and S. Frederick (2002) 'Representativeness Revisited: Attribute Substitution and in Intuitive Judgement', in T. Gilovich, D. Griffin and D. Kahneman (eds.), *Heuristics and Biases: The Psychology of Intuitive Thought*, Cambridge University Press, 49–81.

Kaplan, S.D. (2020) 'America Needs Nationalism', *The American Conservative*, November 10.

Kaul, I. (2009) 'Global Public Goods', in K.A. Reinert, R.S. Rajan, A.J. Glass and L.S. Davis (eds.), *The Princeton Encyclopedia of the World Economy*, Princeton University Press, 550–555.

Kaul, N. (2017) 'The Rise of the Political Right in India: Hindutva-Development Mix, Modi Myth, and Dualities', *Journal of Labor and Society*, 20:4, 523–548.

Keating, M. (2022) 'Taking Back Control? Brexit and the Territorial Constitution of the United Kingdom', *Journal of European Public Policy*, 29:4, 491–509.

Keleman, R.D. (2020) 'Hungary Just Became a Coronavirus Autocracy', *Washington Post*, April 2.

Kemeny, R. (2020) 'Brazil is Sliding into Techno-Authoritarianism', *MIT Technology Review*, August 19.

Kennedy, P. (1987) *The Rise and Fall of the Great Powers: Economic Change and Military Conflict from 1500 to 2000*, Vintage.

Kennedy, S. (2020) *China's COMAC: An Aerospace Minor Leaguer*, Center for Strategic and International Studies.

Kerr, S.P. and W. Kerr (2020) 'Immigrant Entrepreneurship in America: Evidence from the Survey of Business Owners 2007 & 2012', *Research Policy*, 49:3, 103918.

Khan, A.J. (2021) 'UK Aims to Ease Trucker Shortage with Visas into 2022', *New York Times*, October 2.

Khan, S.S., T. Svensson, Y.A. Jogdand and J.H. Liu (2017) 'Lessons from the Past for the Future: The Definition and Mobilization of Hindu Nationhood by the Hindu National Movement of India', *Journal of Social and Political Psychology*, 5.2, 477–511.

Kim, J. (2022) 'Biden Visits Samsung's Chip Plant to Highlight Economic Security', *Nikkei Asia*, May 20.

Kirkpatrick, D.D. and J.M. León Cabrera (2020) 'How Trump and Bolsonaro Broke Latin America's COVID-19 Defenses', *New York Times*, October 27.

Kobayashi, U. (1922) *Military Industries of Japan*, Oxford University Press.

Kohn, H. (1944) *The Idea of Nationalism: A Study in Its Origins and Background*, Macmillan.

Komireddi, K. (2021) 'India, the World's Largest Democracy, Is Now Powered by a Cult of Personality', *Washington Post*, March 18.

Konstan, D. (1997) 'Defining Ancient Greek Ethnicity', *Diaspora*, 6:1, 97–110.

Koopman, R., J. Hancock, R. Piermartini and E. Bekkers (2020) 'The Value of the WTO', *Journal of Policy Modeling*, 42:4, 829–849.

Koopman, R., Z. Wang and S.-J. Wei (2014) 'Tracing Value-Added and Double Counting in Gross Exports', *American Economic Review*, 104:2, 459–494.

Krugman, P. (1998) 'Ricardo's Difficult Idea: Why Intellectuals Can't Understand Comparative Advantage', in G. Cook (ed.), *Freedom and Trade: The Economics and Politics of International Trade*, Vol. 2, Routledge, 22–36.

Lagman, J.D.N. (2021) 'Vaccine Nationalism: A Predicament in Ending the COVID-19 Pandemic', *Journal of Public Health*, 43:2, e375–e376.

Lampe, M. (2009) 'Effects of Bilateralism and the MFN Clause on International Trade: Evidence for the Cobden-Chevalier Network, 1860–1875', *Journal of Economic History*, 69:4, 1012–1040.

Larch, M., J.-A. Monteiro, R. Piermartini and Y.V. Yotov (2020) 'On the Trade Effects of GATT/WTO: They Are Positive and Large After All', Unpublished Manuscript.

Leal Farias, D.B., G. Casarões and D. Magalhães (2022) 'Radical Right Populism and the Politics of Cruelty: The Case of COVID-19 in Brazil Under President Bolsonaro', *Global Studies Quarterly*, 2:2, 1–13.

Leconte, C. (2015) 'From Pathology to Mainstream Phenomenon: Reviewing the Euroscepticism Debate in Research and Theory', *International Political Science Review*, 36:3, 250–263.

Lee, J.-W. (2001) 'Education for Technology Readiness: Prospects for Developing Countries', *Journal of Human Development*, 2:1, 115–151.

Lee, Y.-S. (2016) *Reclaiming Development in the World Trading System*, Cambridge University Press.

Lee, Y.-S. (2019) 'Three Wrongs Do Not Make a Right: The Conundrum of the US Steel and Aluminum Tariffs', *World Trade Review*, 18:3, 481–501.

Leung, K., A. Au, X. Huang, J. Kurman, T. Niit and K.K. Niit (2007) 'Social Axioms and Values', *European Journal of Personality*, 21:2, 91–111.

Levie, J. (2007) 'Immigration, In-Migration, Ethnicity and Entrepreneurship in the United Kingdom', *Small Business Economics*, 28:2–3, 143–169.

Lewis, H. (2022) 'The British Right Doesn't Want to Hear Doubts', *The Atlantic*, July 27.

Liebich, A. (2006) 'Searching for the Perfect Nation: The Itinerary of Hans Kohn (1891–1971)', *Nations and Nationalism*, 12:4, 579–596.

Lighthizer, R. (2020) 'The Era of Offshoring US Jobs is Over', *New York Times*, May 11.

Lind, M. (1999) *Vietnam: The Necessary War*, The Free Press.

Lind, M. (2019) 'The Return of Geoeconomics', *The National Interest*, October 13.

Liptak, K. (2020) 'Trump Rails Against Paris Climate Accord in Virtual G20 Event', *CNN Politics*, November 22.

List, F. (2017 [1885]) *The National System of Political Economy*, Pantianos Classics.

Luo, Y. (2022) 'Illusions of Techno-Nationalism', *Journal of International Business Studies*, 53:3, 550–567.

Mac Ginty, R. (2014) 'Everyday Peace: Bottom Up and Local Agency in Conflict-Affected Societies', *Security Dialogue*, 45:6, 548–564.

Maddison, A. (2001) *The World Economy: A Millennial Perspective*, Organization for Economic Cooperation and Development.

Maneschi, A. (2002) 'The Tercentenary of Henry Martyn's *Considerations Upon East India Trade*', *Journal of the History of Economic Thought*, 24:2, 233–249.

Mann, M. (2013) 'The Role of Nationalism in the Two World Wars', in J.A. Hall and S. Malešević (eds.), *Nationalism and War*, Cambridge University Press, 172–196.

Marjit, S. and B. Mandel (2017) 'Virtual Trade between Separated Time Zones and Growth', *International Journal of Economic Theory*, 13:2, 171–183.

Markel, H. (2014) 'Worldly Approaches to Global Health: 1851 to the Present', *Public Health*, 128:2, 124–128.

Martin, J.G. and F.R. Westie (1959) 'The Tolerant Personality', *American Sociological Review*, 24:4, 521–528.

Martin, W. and D. Mitra (2001) 'Productivity Growth and Convergence in Agriculture Versus Manufacturing', *Economic Development and Cultural Change*, 49:2, 403–422.

Martin, W. and K. Anderson (2012) 'Export Restrictions and Price Insulation During Commodity Price Booms', *American Journal of Agricultural Economics*, 94:2, 422–427.

Martin, W.J. and J.W. Glauber (2020) 'Trade Policy and Food Security', in R.E. Baldwin and S.J. Evenett (eds.), *COVID-19 and Trade Policy: Why Turning Inward Won't Work*, Center for Economic Policy Research, 89–101.

Martyn, H. (1701) *Considerations Upon the East India Trade*, Churchill.

Mason, R. (2015) 'Boris Johnson Says Low Immigration Could Lead to Economic Stagnation', *The Guardian*, October 14.

Mavroidis, P.S. and A. Sapir (2021) *China and the WTO: Why Multilateralism Still Matters*, Princeton University Press.

McCoy T. (2021) 'Bolsonaro Has Insulted the World. Now Brazil Needs Its Help', *Washington Post*, April 30.

McMahon, W.W. (1998) 'Education and Growth in East Asia', *Economics of Education Review*, 17:2, 159–172.

Mearsheimer, J.T. (1994–1995) 'The False Promise of Institutions', *International Security*, 19:3, 5–49.

Mehta, H. (2004) 'In Modi's Gujarat, Hitler Is a Textbook Hero', *Times of India*, September 30.

Mendi, P., R. Moner-Colonques and J.J. Sempere-Monerris (2020) 'Cooperation for Innovation and Technology Licensing: Empirical Evidence from Spain', *Technological Forecasting and Social Change*, 154, 119976.

Messerlin, P. (2006) 'Enlarging the Vision for Trade Policy Space: Special and Differentiated Treatment and Infant Industry Issue', *The World Economy*, 29:10, 1395–1407.

Meyer, H.C. (1955) *Mitteleuropa in German Thought and Action 1815–1945*, Martinus Nijhoff.

Milton, G. (1999) *Nathaniel's Nutmeg: The True Story and Incredible Adventures of the Spice Trader Who Changed the Course of History*, Penguin Books.

Miroudot, S. (2020) 'Resilience Versus Robustness in Global Value Chains: Some Policy Implications', in R.E. Baldwin and S.J. Evenett (eds.), *COVID-19 and Trade Policy: Why Turning Inward Won't Work*, Center for Economic Policy Research, 117–130.

Möllers, N. (2021) 'Making Digital Territory: Cybersecurity, Techno-Nationalism and the Moral Boundaries of the State', *Science, Technology, & Human Values*, 46:1, 112–138.

Moore, A. (2017) 'US Military Logistics Outsourcing and the Everywhere of War', *Territory, Politics, Governance*, 5:1, 5–27.

Moretti, E. (2012) *The New Geography of Jobs*, Houghton Mifflin Harcourt.

Muller, J.Z. (2008) 'Us and Them: The Enduring Power of Ethnic Nationalism', *Foreign Affairs*, 87:2, 18–35.

Mun, T. (2013) *The Complete Works: Economic and Trade*, Newton Page.

Murphy-Shigematsu, S. (1993) 'Multiethnic Japan and the Monoethnic Myth', *MELUS*, 18:4, 63–80.

Murray, D. (2017) *The Strange Death of Europe: Immigration, Identity, Islam*, Bloomsbury.

Naqshbandi, M.M. and S.M. Jasimuddin (2018) 'Knowledge Oriented Leadership and Open Innovation: Role of Knowledge-Based Capability in France-Based Multinationals', *International Business Review*, 27:3, 701–713.

Nash, J. (1950) 'The Bargaining Problem', *Econometrica*, 18:2, 155–162.

Navarro, P. and G. Autry (2011) *Death by China*, Prentice Hall.

Neale, M.A. and M.H. Bazerman (1985) 'Perspectives on Understanding Negotiation: Viewing Negotiation as a Judgmental Process', *Journal of Conflict Resolution*, 29:1, 33–56.

Nolan, S. and K.D. Singh (2022) 'India is Stalling the WHO's Efforts to Make Global Covid Death Toll Public', *New York Times*, April 16.

Noorani, A.G. (2002) *Islam and Jihad: Prejudice versus Reality*, Zed Books.

Nordås, H.K. and D. Rouzet (2015) 'The Impact of Services Trade Restrictiveness on Trade Flows: First Estimates', *OECD Trade Policy Papers No. 178*, Organization for Economic Cooperation and Development.

O'Rourke, K.H. (2000) 'Tariffs and Growth in the Late 19th Century', *Economic Journal*, 110:463, 456–483.

Outhwaite, W. (2019) 'Migration Crisis and Brexit', in C. Menjívar, M. Ruiz and I. Ness (eds.), *Oxford Handbook of Migration Crises*, Oxford University Press, 93–109.

Pain, N. and G. Young (2004) 'The Macroeconomic Impact of UK Withdrawal from the EU', *Economic Modelling*, 21:3, 387–408.

Palonen, E. (2018) 'Performing the Nation: The Janus-Faces Populist Foundations of Illiberalism in Hungary', *Journal of Contemporary European Studies*, 26:3, 308–321.

Parker, G. and K. Allen (2016) 'David Davis Brushes Off Brexit Retaliation Fears', *Financial Times*, October 10.

Parker, G., P. Stafford, C. Giles and J. Brundsen (2021) 'Brexit Will Strengthen City as Leading Financial Hub, Sunak Says', *Financial Times*, January 12.

Pereira, J.C. and E. Viola (2020) 'Climate Multilateralism Within the United Nations Framework Convention on Climate Change', *Oxford Research Encyclopedia of Climate Science*.

Perrotta, C. (2014) 'Thomas Mun's *England's Treasure by Forraign Trade*: The 17th Century Manifesto for Economic Development', *History of Economics Review*, 59:1, 94–106.

Phelan, J.G. and E. Richardson (1969) 'Cognitive Complexity, Strategy of the Other Player, and Two-Person Game Behavior', *Journal of Psychology*, 71:2, 205–215.

Pickel, A. (2003) 'Explaining, and Explaining with, Economic Nationalism', *Nations and Nationalism*, 9:1, 105–127.

Pickel, A. (2005) 'False Oppositions: Reconceptualizing Economic Nationalism in a Globalizing World', in E. Helleiner and A. Pickel (eds.), *Economic Nationalism in a Globalizing World*, Cornell University Press, 1–17.

Pietrowski, J., J. Różycka-Tran, T. Baran and M. Żemojtel-Piotrowska (2019) 'Zero-Sum Thinking as Mediator of the Relationship of National Attitudes with (Un)willingness to Host Refugees in Own Country', *International Journal of Psychology*, 54:6, 722–730.

Pinchis-Paulsen, M. (2020) 'Trade Multilateralism and U.S. National Security: The Making of the GATT Security Exceptions', *Michigan Journal of International Law*, 109–193.

Politi, J. (2020) 'US Trade Advisor Seeks to Replace Chinese Drug Supplies', *Financial Times*, February 12.

Prahalad, C.K. and K. Lieberthal (2008) *The End of Corporate Imperialism*, Harvard Business Press.

Prebisch, R. (1950) *The Economic Development of Latin American and Its Principal Problems*, United Nations.

Prebisch, R. (1963) *Towards a Dynamic Development Policy for Latin America*, United Nations.

Qian, I. and D. Pierson (2022) 'Tragic Battle: On the Front Lines of China's Covid Crisis', *New York Times*, December 27.

Raiffa, H. (1982) *The Art and Science of Negotiation*, Harvard University Press.

Rankin, J. (2023) 'EU Leaders Voice Hope Northern Ireland Deal Will Be Start of New Chapter with UK', *The Guardian*, February 27.

Ray, I. (2009) 'Identifying the Woes of the Cotton Industry in Bengal: Tales of the Nineteenth Century', *Economic History Review*, 62:4, 857–892.

Redlener, I., J.D. Sachs, S. Hansen and N. Hupert (2020) *130,000–210,000 Avoidable COVID-19 Deaths –And Counting– in the U.S.*, Earth Institute, Columbia University.

Reich, R.B. (1987) 'The Rise of Techno-Nationalism', *Atlantic Monthly*, 259, 62–66.

Reich, R.B. (1989) 'The Quite Path to Technological Preeminence', *Scientific American*, 261:4, 41–47.

Reich, A. (2018) 'The Effectiveness of the WTO Dispute Settlement System: A Statistical Analysis', in T. Kono, M. Hiscock and A. Reich (eds.), *Transnational Commercial and Consumer Law: Current Trends in International Business Law*, Springer, 1–43.

Reicher, S., S.A. Haslam and M. Hopkins (2005) 'Social Identity and the Dynamics of Leadership: Leaders and Followers as Collaborative Agents in the Transformation of Social Reality', *Leadership Quarterly*, 16:4, 547–568.

Reinert, K.A. (2017) 'Globalisation and Development: Introduction and Overview', in K.A. Reinert (ed.), *Handbook of Globalisation and Development*, Edward Elgar, 1–15.

Reinert, K.A. (2018) *No Small Hope: Towards the Universal Provision of Basic Goods*, Oxford University Press.

Reinert, K.A. (2021a) *An Introduction to International Economics: New Perspectives on the World Economy*, Cambridge University Press.

Reinert, K.A. (2021b) 'Mercantilism', in P. James (ed.), *Oxford Bibliographies in International Relations*, Oxford University Press.

Reinert, K.A. (forthcoming) 'Fisheries Subsidies and the WTO: A Concise History', *International Negotiation*.

Reinhart, C. and V. Reinhart (2020) 'The Pandemic Depression: The Global Economy Will Never Be the Same', *Foreign Affairs*, 99:5, 84–95.

Reuters (2018) 'Trump Tweets: "Trade Wars Are Good and Easy to Win"', March 2.

Reuters (2019) 'Who Pays Trump's Tariffs? China or US Customers and Companies?' May 21.

Reyes, J.A. and W.C. Sawyer (2016) *Latin American Economic Development*, Routledge.

Reyes, M. (2020) 'US Sees No Material Impact on Economy, Kudlow Says', *Bloomberg*, January 30.

Ricardo, D. (1951 [1817]) 'On the Principles of Political Economy and Taxation', in Piero Straffa (ed.), *The Works and Correspondence of David Ricardo*, Vol. 1.

Rim, C. (2019) 'The Real Reason Trump Wants to Ban Chinese College Students', *Forbes*, June 14.

Rodrik, D. (1998) 'Why Do More Open Economies Have Bigger Governments?', *Journal of Political Economy*, 106:5, 997–1032.

Rolfe, H., C. Rienzo, M. Lalani and J. Portes (2013) *Migration and Productivity: Employers' Practices, Public Attitudes and Statistical Evidence*, National Institute of Economic and Social Research.

Rommelse, G. (2010) 'The Role of Mercantilism in Anglo-Dutch Political Relations: 1650–74', *Economic History Review*, 63:3, 591–611.

Rose, A.K. (2004) 'Do We Really Know That the WTO Increases Trade?' *American Economic Review*, 94:1, 98–114.

Ross, T. (2016) 'Boris Johnson: The EU Wants a Superstate, Just as Hitler Did', *The Telegraph*, May 15.

Różycka-Tran, J., J.P. Piotrowski, M. Żemojtel-Piotrowska, P. Jurek, E.N. Osin, B.G. Adams, R. Ardi, S. Bălţăţescu, A.L. Bhomi, S.A. Bogomaz and J. Cieciuch (2021) 'Belief in a Zero-Sum Game and Subjective Well-Being Across 35 Countries', *Current Psychology*, 40:7, 4575–3584.

Różycka-Tran, J., P. Boski and B. Wojciske (2015) 'Belief in a Zero-Sum Game as a Social Axiom: A 37-Nation Study', *Journal of Cross-Cultural Psychology*, 46:4, 525–548.

Różycka-Tran, J., Paweł Jurek, Michał Olech, Jarosław Piotrowski and Magdalena Żemojtel-Piotrowska. (2019) 'A Warrior Society: Data from 30 Countries Show That Belief in a Zero-Sum Game Is Related to Military Expenditure and Low Civil Liberties', *Frontiers in Psychology*, 9, 2645.

Ruffin, R.J. (2002) 'David Ricardo's Discovery of Comparative Advantage', *History of Political Economy*, 34:4, 727–748.

Ruggie, J.G. (1982) 'International Regimes, Transactions, and Change: Embedded Liberalism in the Postwar Economic Order', *International Organization*, 36:2, 379–415.

Ruggie, J.G. (1992) 'Multilateralism: The Anatomy of an Institution', *International Organization*, 46:3, 561–598.

Samuels, R.J. (1994) *Rich Nation, Strong Army: National Security and the Technological Transformation of Japan*, Cornell University Press.

Samuelson, W. and R. Zeckhauser (1988) 'Status Quo Bias in Decisionmaking', *Journal of Risk and Uncertainty*, 1:1, 7–59.

Savarkar, V.D. (1969 [1928]) *Hindutva: Who Is a Hindu?* S.S. Savarkar.

Schaefer, M. (2002) 'Sovereignty, Influence, Realpolitik and the World Trade Organization', *Hastings International Comparative Law Review*, 25:3, 341–369.

Schaeffer, C. (2017) 'How Hungary Became a Haven for the Alt-Right', *The Atlantic*, May 28.

Schomberg, W. (2022) 'Truss Prepared Her Bonfire of the Regulations in a Bid to Boost UK Growth', *Reuters*, October 3.

Schott, J.J. and E. Jung (2019) *In US-China Trade Disputes, the WTO Usually Sides with the United States*, Peterson Institute for International Economics.

Scott, J. (2003) 'Good Night Amsterdam: Sir George Downing and Anglo-Dutch Statebuilding', *English Historical Review*, 118:476, 334–356.

Seeley, J.R. (1914 [1883]) *The Expansion of England*, Macmillan.

Sen, A. (2006) *Identity and Violence: The Illusion of Destiny*, Norton.

Sertić, M.B., A.C. Časni and V. Vučković (2017) 'The Impact of China's Imports on European Union Industrial Employment', *Economics of Transition and Institutional Change*, 25:1, 91–109.

Sevastopulo, D. and T. Mitchell (2018) 'US Considered Ban on Student Visas for Chinese Nationals', *Financial Times*, October 3.

Shaxson, N. (2021) 'The City of London Is Hiding the World's Stolen Money', *New York Times*, October 11.

Shih, G. and A. Gupta (2022) 'Religious Clashes across India Spark Fears of Further Violence', *Washington Post*, April 20.

Singer, P. (1972) 'Famine, Affluence and Morality', *Philosophy and Public Affairs*, 1:3, 229–243.

Singh, J.P. (2008) *Negotiation and the Global Information Economy*, Cambridge University Press.

Singh, J.P. (2017) *Sweet Talk: Paternalism and Collective Action in North-South Trade Relations*, Stanford University Press.

Singh, J.P. (2023) The Political Economy of North-South Relations: A View from the South', in E. Hannah and J. Ravenhill (eds.), *Global Political Economy*, Oxford University Press.

Slobodian, Q. (2018) 'You Live in Robert Lighthizer's World Now', *Foreign Policy*, August 6.

Smith, A. (1937 [1776]) *The Wealth of Nations*, Modern Library.

Smith, G., T. Zhuo and E. Goldberg (2023) 'White House Moves Closer to Total Ban on Sale of America Tech on Chinese Company', *Financial Times*, January 31.

Solender, A. (2020) 'Federal Watchdog Finds Trump Advisor Peter Navarro Repeatedly Violated Hatch Act', *Forbes*, December 7.

Sourvinou-Inwood, C. (2005) *Hylas, the Nymphs, Dionysos & Others: Myth, Ritual, Ethnicity*, Paul Forlag Astroms.

Specia, M. (2022) 'UK Plan to Send Asylum Seekers to Rwanda Stokes Anger and Fear', *New York Times*, May 2.

Spiegel, H.W. (1991) *The Growth of Economic Thought*, Duke University Press.

Stellinger, A., I. Berglund and H. Isakson (2020) 'How Trade Can Fight the Pandemic and Contribute to Global Health', in R.E. Baldwin and S.J. Evenett (eds.), *COVID-19 and Trade Policy: Why Turning Inward Won't Work*, Center for Economic Policy Research, 21–30.

Stevensen, A. (2022) 'These Vaccines Have Been Embraced by the World. Why Not in China?', *New York Times*, February 18.

Stiglitz, J.E. (1996) 'Some Lessons from the East Asian Miracle', *World Bank Research Observer*, 11:2, 151–177.

Stolper, W. and P.A. Samuelson (1941) 'Protection and Real Wages', *Review of Economic Studies*, 9:1, 58–73.

Stråth, B. (2008) 'Mitteleuropa: From List to Naumann', *European Journal of Social Theory*, 11:2, 173–183.

Subramanian, A. and S.-J. Wei (2007) 'The WTO Promotes Trade, Strongly But Unevenly', *Journal of International Economics*, 72:1, 151–175.

Sumaila, U.R., Ahmed Khan, Reg Watson, Gordon Munro, Dirk Zeller, Nancy Baron and Daniel Pauly (2007) 'The World Trade Organization and Global Fisheries Sustainability', *Fisheries Research*, 88:1–3, 1–4.

Sumaila, U.R., Naazia Ebrahim, Anna Schuhbauer, Daniel Skerritt, Yang Li, Hong Sik Kim, Tabitha Grace Mallory, Vicky W.L. Lam and Daniel Pauly (2019) 'Updates Estimates and Analysis of Global Fisheries Subsidies', *Marine Policy*, 109, 103695.

Sumption, M. and C. Vargas-Silva (2020) *Briefing: Net Migration to the UK*, Migration Observatory, University of Oxford.

Suranovic, S.M. (2000) 'A Positive Analysis of Fairness with Applications to International Trade', *World Economy*, 23:3, 283–307.

Swales, K. (2016) 'Understanding the Leave Vote', *NatCen Social Research*.

Syal, R. and M. Brown (2022) 'Home Office Staff Threaten Mutiny Over "Shameful" Rwanda Asylum Deal', *The Guardian*, April 20.

Szirmai, A. (2015) *Socio-Economic Development*, Cambridge University Press.

Taggart, P. (1998) 'A Touchstone of Dissent: Euroscepticism in Contemporary Western European Party Systems', *European Journal of Political Research*, 33:3, 363–388.

Tamir, Y. (2019) 'Not so Civic: Is there a Difference between Ethnic and Civil Nationalism', *Annual Review of Political Science*, 22, 419–434.

Tchernookova, A. (2021) 'Post-Brexit Financial Services Debate at a Standstill', *International Financial Law Review*, March 25.

Temple, J. (2004) 'The Long-Run Implications of Growth Theory', in D.A.R. George, L. Oxley and K.I. Carlaw (eds.), *Surveys in Economic Growth: Theory and Empirics*, Blackwell, 271–284.

The Economist (1998) 'A Taste of Adventure', December 17.

The Economist (2016a) 'The New Political Divide', July 30.

The Economist (2016b) 'Briefing: Globalization and Politics', July 30.

The Economist (2017) 'Politicians Cannot Bring Back Old-Fashioned Factory Jobs', January 14.

The Economist (2020a) 'The Revenge of Strategic Yogurt', October 3.

The Economist (2020b) 'Tariff Man', October 24.

The Economist (2020c) 'Realism and the Wrecking Ball', October 31.

The Economist (2020d) 'Democracy in India', November 28.

The Economist (2020e) 'The Brexit Endgame', December 5.

The Economist (2020f) 'The Taiwanese Economy', December 5.

The Economist (2021a) 'Why "Equivalence" Matters in Brexit Britain', January 15.

The Economist (2021b) 'England Speaks Up', March 20.

The Economist (2021c) 'The Pandemic in India', April 24.

The Economist (2021d) 'Mexico's Populist President', May 29.

The Economist (2021e) 'Brazil's Politics', May 29.

The Economist (2021f) 'The Pandemic in India', June 12.

The Economist (2021g) 'The UN's Refugee Convention at 70', August 7.

The Economist (2021h) 'The Fuel Crisis: Running on Empty', October 2.

The Economist (2021i) 'Brazil's Woes: President Anti-Vaxxer', October 23.

The Economist (2021j) 'The Northern Ireland Protocol: Groundhog Day', November 13.

The Economist (2022a) 'Brexit: Happy Now?' January 1.

The Economist (2022b) 'India: Stop Inciting Murder', January 15.

The Economist (2022c) 'Game of Chiplomacy', January 29.

The Economist (2022d) 'Radical Research: Health Curiosity', February 12.

The Economist (2022e) 'China Inc and Self-Reliance: The Techno-Independence Movement', February 26.

The Economist (2022f) 'Chipmaking: Crossing the Chokepoint', April 30.

The Economist (2022g) 'Vaccinating the World', May 15.

The Economist (2022h) 'The Food Catastrophe', May 21.

The Economist (2022i) 'Scapegoating Africans: Xenophobia in South Africa', June 11.

The Economist (2022j) 'Clownfall', July 9.

The Economist (2022k) 'Ethiopia: Falling Apart', August 27.

The Economist (2022l) 'Pandemic Controls: Covid Confusion', November 26.

The Economist (2022m) 'China v. Covid-19: Zero Options', December 3.

The Economist (2023a) 'Britain and the EU: Careful Assembly Required', January 7.

The Economist (2023b) 'Speak Softly, and Carry a Big Chip', January 21.

The Economist (2023c) 'Asian Chipmakers: Silicon Islands in the Storm', February 4.

The Lancet (2021) 'India's COVID-19 Emergency', *The Lancet*, 397:10286, 1683.

Thielmann, E. and D. Schade (2014) 'Buying into Myths: Free Movement of People and Immigration', *The Political Quarterly*, 87:2, 139–147.

Thomas, P.J. (1926) *Mercantilism and the East India Trade*, Frank Cass.

Thornton, B. (2000) *Greek Ways: How the Greeks Created Western Civilization*, Encounter Books.

Tolstoy, A. and E. McCarrray (2015) 'Mind Games: Alexander Dugin and Russia's War of Ideas', *World Affairs*, 177:6, 25–30.

Toynebee, P. (2020) 'Boris Johnson Will Get a Deal: But It Will Be a Betrayal of the Brexiters', *The Guardian*, November 30.

Tsai, R.L. (2019) 'Immigration Unilateralism and American Ethnonationalism', *Loyola University of Chicago Law Journal*, 51:523, 101–133.

United Nations High Commissioner for Refugees (2016) *Frequently Asked Questions on Climate Change and Disaster Displacement*.

United States Center for Naval Analysis Military Advisory Board (2014) *National Security and the Accelerating Risks of Climate Change*.

United States Trade Representative (2021) *Ambassador Katherine Tai's Remarks as Prepared for Delivery on the World Trade Organization*.

Usherwood, S. (2021) 'Our European Friends and Partners? Negotiating the Trade and Cooperation Agreement', *Journal of Common Market Studies*, forthcoming.

Van Boven, L., C.M. Judd and D.K. Sherman (2012) 'Political Polarization Projection: Social Projection of Partisan Attitude Extremity and Attitudinal Processes', *Journal of Personality and Social Psychology*, 103:1, 84–100.

Vanhaverbeke, W., J. Du, B. Leten and F. Aalders (2014) 'Exploring Open Innovation at the Level of R&D Projects', in H. Chesbrough, W. Vanhaverbeke and J. West (eds.), *New Frontiers in Open Innovation*, Oxford University Press, 115–131.

Varas, A., R. Varadarajan, J. Goodrich and F. Yinug (2021) *Strengthening the Global Semiconductor Supply Chain in an Uncertain Era*, Boston Consulting Group and Semiconductor Industry Association.

Venkataramakrishnan, R. (2015) 'The One Thing That Amartya Sen and Jagdish Bhagwati Agree On: Hindutva is Dangerous for India', *Scroll.in*, January 15.

Viner, J. (1930a) 'English Theories of Foreign Trade Before Adam Smith', *Journal of Political Economy*, 38:3, 249–301.

Viner, J. (1930b) 'English Theories of Foreign Trade Before Adam Smith (Concluded)', *Journal of Political Economy*, 38:4, 404–457.

Viner, J. (1948) 'Power Versus Plenty as Objectives of Foreign Policy in the Seventeenth and Eighteenth Centuries', *World Politics*, 1:1, 1–29.

Viner, J. (2014 [1950]) *The Customs Union Issue*, Oxford University Press.

von Neuman, J. (1928) 'Zur Theorie der Gesellschaftsspiele', *Mathematische Annalen*, 100, 295–320.

von Neuman, J. and O. Morgenstern (1953) *Theory of Games and Economic Behavior*, Princeton University Press.

Waibel, A. (2019) 'What is DARPA? How to Design Successful Technology Disruption', https://isl.anthropomatik.kit.edu/pdf/Waibel2019a.pdf.

Wall Street Journal (2018) 'The National Security Tariff Ruse', March 12.

Wang, V. (2022) 'As China Imposed More Covid Lockdowns, "Everyone is Scared"', *New York Times*, September 5.

Wang, Z., S.-J. Wei, X. Yu and K. Zhu (2018) 'Reexamining the Effects of Trading with China on Local Labor Markets: A Supply Chain Perspective', National Bureau of Economic Research Working Paper 24886.

Weaver, J.H., M.T. Rock and K. Kusterer (1997) *Achieving Broad-Based Sustainable Development*, Kumarian Press.

Wellings, B. (2010) 'Losing the Peace: Euroscepticism and the Foundations of Contemporary English Nationalism', *Nations and Nationalism*, 16:3, 488–505.

Wilson, C. (1957) *Profit and Power: A Study of England and the Dutch Wars*, Longmans.

Wilson, J. (2021) 'Australia Shows the World What Decoupling from China Looks Like', *Foreign Policy*, November 9.

Witt, M.A. (2019) 'Deglobalization: Theories, Predictions, and Opportunities for International Business Research', *Journal of International Business Research*, 50:7, 1053–1077.

Woo-Cumings, M. (2005) 'Back to Basics: Ideology, Nationalism, and Asian Values in Asia', in E. Helleiner and A. Pickel (eds.), *Economic Nationalism in a Globalizing World*, Cornell University Press, 91–117.

Woolhandler, S., D.U. Himmelstein, S. Ahmed, Z. Bailey, M.T. Bassett, M. Bird, J. Bor, D. Bor, O. Carrasquillo, M. Chowkwanyun and S.L. Dickman (2021) 'Public Policy and Health in the Trump Era', *Lancet*, 397:10275, 705–753.

World Bank (2020) *Global Economic Prospects: Slow Growth, Policy Challenges*.

World Trade Organization (2001) 'Report of the Working Party on the Accession of China', *WT/ACC/CHN/49*.

World Trade Organization (2021) 'Draft General Council Declaration on the TRIPS Agreement and Public Health in the Circumstances of a Pandemic', IP/C/W/681.

Xenos, N. (1996) 'Civic Nationalism: Oxymoron?' *Critical Review*, 10:2, 213–231.

Yack, B. (1996) 'The Myth of the Civic Nation', *Critical Review*, 10:2, 193–211.

Yadate, A.R. and E.T. Garoma (2015) 'The Role of Language in Constructing National Identity in the Contemporary Ethiopia', *International Journal of Research in the Social Science and Humanities*, 5:4, 118–137.

Yang, D.L. (2021) 'The COVID-19 Pandemic and the Estrangement of US-China Relations', *Asian Perspective*, 45:1, 7–31.

Yasir, S. (2021) 'As Hindu Extremists Call for Killing of Muslims, India's Leaders Keep Silent', *New York Times*, December 25.

Yuan, L. (2022) 'China's Zero-Covid Mess Proves Autocracy Hurts Everyone', *New York Times*, April 13.

Zedillo, E. (2017) 'Don't Blame Ricardo: Take Responsibility for Domestic Political Choices', in S.J. Evenett (ed.), *Cloth for Wine? The Relevance of Ricardo's Comparative Advantage in the 21st Century*, Center for Economic Policy Research, 81–86.

Zhang, C. (2019) 'How Much Do State-Owned Enterprises Contribute to China's GDP and Employment?' Unpublished Paper, World Bank.

Zoellick, R. (2003) 'Freeing the Intangible Economy: Services in International Trade', Speech Presented at the Coalition for Services Industries, December 2.

NOTES

1. Albert Hirschman's Forgotten Book

1 See Chapters 1–5 of Adelman's (2013) fascinating portrait of Hirschman.
2 Hirschman (1945), p. 12.
3 Hirschman (1945), p. 79.
4 Hirschman (1945), p. 79.
5 Hirschman (1945), p. 80.
6 Adelman (2013) reports that "*National Power* was instantly forgotten" (p. 215).
7 See Hoekman and Kostecki (2009), p. 138 and Bown and Irwin (2015).
8 See Koopman et al. (2020), for example.
9 Koopman et al. (2020), p. 835.
10 Bown (2020).
11 See Bown (2020). This was particularly in cases concerning what are known as safeguards and trade remedies.
12 As we will discuss in Chapter 4, this is Article XXI of the GATT and Section 232 of Section 232 of the 1962 Trade Expansion Act.
13 Kahl and Wright (2021), p. 10.
14 https://www.who.int/news/item/05-05-2022-14.9-million-excess-deaths-were-associated-with-the-covid-19-pandemic-in-2020-and-2021.
15 Abdelal (2005), p. 22.
16 Anderson (1991).
17 Crane (1998), p. 62.
18 See, for example, Colantone and Stanig (2019). These researchers note that economic nationalist narratives involve "appeals to national sovereignty, as well as the defense of traditional morality, cultural homogeneity, and the national way of life" (p. 131).
19 Some political economy researchers (e.g., Pickel, 2005; Helleiner, 2021) accuse economists of deploying "economism" for their ignoring social, cultural and historical factors. That is a bit like accusing political scientists of deploying "politicism." Indeed, modern international economics is quite scant in much of the contemporary research on economic nationalism. Here we attempt to find a middle ground between the fields of economics and political science.
20 In particular, we avoid the terms "neoliberalism" and "globalization discourse" as being too broad and vague to capture the fine-grained details of actual research on economic globalization. See, for example, Chapter 1 of Goldin and Reinert (2012) and Reinert (2017).
21 Gilpin (1987), p. 31.
22 Crane (1998), p. 61.

23 Hall (2005), p. 124.
24 See, for example, Pickel (2005) and Helleiner (2005, 2021).
25 Hall (2005), p. 124.
26 To take but one example, most economists would agree with Pickel (2003) that "given the continued significance of national economies, states remain the central actors of all political economies" (p. 113).
27 Pickel (2003), p. 118.
28 Although *The Authoritarian Personality* (Adorno et al., 2019, orig. 1950) was subsequently (and inevitably) criticized, it has become known as one of the most important books in social psychology.
29 See, for example, the early study by Martin and Westie (1959), as well as Duckitt (1989).
30 Pickel (2003) states that "the nationalising mechanism […] is the culturally grounded process of internal and external integration or disintegration of national political economies and societies" (p. 118). Pickel also includes "globalisation processes" as part of the nationalizing mechanism (p. 120).
31 Helleiner (2005), p. 226.
32 Pickel (2003), for example, states that the concept of civic nationalism has been "demolished." This book will suggest that it still has relevance.
33 The violence associated with ethnonationalism was notably considered by Ignatieff (1993).
34 Reinert (2018) provides a book-length consideration of the importance of basic goods provision.

2. Power and Plenty

1 See Chapter 3 of Milton (1999) and Chapter 1 of Dalrymple (2019).
2 Spiegel (1991), Chapter 5.
3 Findlay and O'Rourke (2007), pp. 227–228. Similarly, Thomas (1926) states that "the ideal before the Mercantilists was a wealthy and powerful nation, getting richer every year at the expense of other countries" (p. 73).
4 For an annotated bibliography of mercantilist writings, see Reinert (2021b). For insights into who the merchants were, see Brenner (1973).
5 Mun (2013, orig. 1664), p. 110. Here and elsewhere, I have changed spellings to the modern ones.
6 Mun (2013, orig. 1664), p. 134.
7 Mun (2013, orig. 1664), p. 113.
8 Mun (2013, orig. 1664), p. 154.
9 "Power and Plenty" was the title of a famous article by Viner (1948). It also became the title of the extraordinary book by Findlay and O'Rourke (2007).
10 Mun (2013, orig. 1664), p. 258.
11 Mun (2013, orig. 1664), p. 260.
12 Mun (2013, orig. 1664), p. 257.
13 Mun (2013, orig. 1664), p. 260.
14 Mun (2013, orig. 1664), p. 270.
15 Rommelse (2010), p. 591.
16 Regarding Downing, Scott (2003) observes: "Ideologically […] he was neither a republican nor a royalist. Pragmatically he was first one and then the other" (p. 339).

17 Wilson (1957), p. 95.
18 Scott (2003), p. 339.
19 Scott (2003), p. 347.
20 Findlay and O'Rourke (2007), p. 242.
21 Rommelse (2010), p. 601.
22 Brewer (1990).
23 Scott (2003), p. 356.
24 Findlay and O'Rourke (2007), pp. 175–176.
25 *The Economist* (1998).
26 As reported by Milton (1999), Coen was untroubled by his extermination of the Bandanese, stating that "they are indolent people of whom little good can be expected" (p. 317).
27 de Vries (2003) notes that "altogether, at least two million Europeans, overwhelmingly young men, embarked for Asia between 1500 and 1795" and that "it is doubtful that many as half of them ever returned to Europe" (p. 72).
28 Rommelse (2010), p. 592.
29 Rommelse (2010), p. 594.
30 Findlay and O'Rourke (2007), p. 183.
31 *The Economist* (1998).
32 Smith (1937, orig. 1776), p. 398.
33 On criticisms of Smith's conception of mercantilism, see, for example, Coleman (1988) who suggests that the "mercantile system" did not exist but was rather "a ragbag of devices which emerged from Parliament and Crown by a uniquely English process" (p. 164).
34 Smith (1937, orig. 1776), p. 550.
35 Smith (1937, orig. 1776), p. 555 and p. 581.
36 An early work in this iconoclastic tradition is Grampp (1952).
37 See Elmslie (2015).
38 Seeley (1914), p. 9.
39 Seeley (1914), p. 10.
40 See, for example, Harris (1964). The decidedly illiberal policies of the EIC in India are detailed in Dalrymple (2019) who called them "the supreme act of corporate violence in world history" (p. 394). Nonetheless, it is notable that Mill did not support slavery.
41 Thomas (1926), p. 21.
42 Thomas (1926), p. 24.
43 As has been subsequently recognized, many of Smith's arguments had been previously made by Henry Martyn (1701) in his *Considerations Upon East India Trade*. See, for example, Maneschi (2002). It is not clear, however, if Smith ever read the work.
44 Smith (1937, orig. 1776), p. 429.
45 Smith (1937, orig. 1776), p. 431.
46 Spiegel (1991), p. 146.
47 Thomas (1926) notes that "the usual calculations of the balance of trade had ceased to justify the East India Company" and that "by no manner of computation was its possible to show that there was a favourable balance for England from the East Indian trade" (p. 15).
48 Dalrymple (2019), p. xxv. To be fair, there was a principal–agent problem at play here. Dalrymple notes that "the directors consistently abhorred ambitious plans of

conquest, which they feared would get out of control and overwhelm them with debt. [...] Instead, what conquering, looting and plundering took place was almost always initiated by senior Company official on the spot" (p. 123n).

49 Dalrymple (2019), 394.
50 Thomas (1926) states: "When British commerce was established with the East early in the seventeenth century, India was the unrivalled centre of cotton manufacturing in the whole world. What silk was the China, linen to Egypt, wool to England, that was cotton to India" (p. 31).
51 Thomas (1926), pp. 71–72.
52 To again quote Thomas (1926): "There is no use enumerating the inconsistencies. [...] They were but practical men forced by circumstances to take up a position against orthodox mercantilism [...] they were but mercantilists trying to adjust that system to their convenience and self-interest" (p. 82).
53 Thomas (1926), p. 138.
54 In examining this history, Ray (2009) states that "Bengal's cotton textiles were [...] severely discriminated against in the international market because of the consolidation of their trade under the aegis of the East India Company" (p. 863).
55 Viner (1930a, b).
56 The first researcher to point out liberal elements in mercantilism was Grampp (1952) who saw mercantilism as a "predecessor" of classical liberalism.
57 See, for example, Elmslie (2015).
58 Findlay and O'Rourke (2007), p. 229.
59 See Francis (1960).
60 Again, see Francis (1960).
61 See Ruffin (2002).
62 Irwin (2017), p. 7.
63 This term was introduced by Krugman (1998).
64 This is embedded in the Stolper–Samuelson theorem of Stolper and Samuelson (1941). In the words of Deardorff (1998), "One might have thought and hoped that the broader gains from trade [...] might have allowed both abundant and scarce factors to gain from trade. [...] But alas no, Stolper and Samuelson showed this is not the case" (p. 364).
65 Eaton (2017), p. 29.
66 Thomas (1926), p. 3. P. J. Thomas would go on to be the first economic adviser to independent India and was a signatory of the Bretton Woods agreement.

3. Industry and War

1 Gilpin (1987), p. 33.
2 Bairoch (1982), Table 10.
3 Findlay and O'Rourke (2007), p. 320.
4 Findlay and O'Rourke (2007) note that "the key technological innovations were clearly the work of British inventors and entrepreneurs, operating within a broader European environment in which new techniques and applications were rapidly diffused from country to country and from one branch of industry to another" (p. 337).
5 Findlay and O'Rourke (2007) note that "it was (the) influx of machine-made Lancashire cotton textiles that brought about the deindustrialization of India" (p. 334).

6   This received a book-length treatment by Inikori (2002). See in particular, Table 4.7.

7   Helleiner (2021), p. 230.

8   For a succinct biography, see Chapter 9 of Condliffe (1950).

9   Ince (2016), p. 381.

10 List (2017, orig. 1885), p. 54.

11 List (2017, orig. 1885), 161.

12 List (2017, orig. 1885), p. 60.

13 Here is just one of his lists: "the Christian religion, monogamy, abolition of slavery and of vassalage, hereditability of the throne, invention of printing, of the press, of the postal system, of money, weights and measures, of the calendar, of watches, of policy, the introduction of freehold property, of means of transport" (p. 63).

14 List (2017, orig. 1885), p. 65.

15 Ince (2016), p. 384.

16 Condliffe (1950) observes: "In the last quarter of the nineteenth century, the rise of German industry was phenomenal. Its foundation had been security laid in the educational and social system" (p. 279).

17 Smith (1937, orig. 1776), pp. 347–348. This passage has been criticized, for example, by Chang (2003) and Lind (2019).

18 Chang (2003) interprets this passage as a stern warning of "the Americans against any attempt at infant industry promotion" (p. 5). Lind (2019) states that "if American leaders had followed the advice of Adam Smith, the United States in the twenty-first century would still be an agrarian economy, shipping cotton, corn and wheat abroad while importing all factory-made goods on unfavorable terms from industrial nations in Europe and Asia." These might not be the only interpretations.

19 Smith (1937, orig. 1776), p. 347.

20 Smith (1937, orig. 1776), p. 6.

21 List (2017, orig. 1885), p. 55.

22 See, for example, Davis (2004), Henley (2012) and Martin and Mitra (2001).

23 List (2017, orig. 1885), p. 60.

24 List (2017, orig. 1885), p. 54.

25 List (2017, orig. 1885), p. 75. This imperial tendency of List is discussed in Ince (2016).

26 List (2017, orig. 1885) addresses the freedom of "negroes," stating that their "freedom merely leads to idleness" and refers to "a miserable, drunken, lazy, vicious, mendicant horde called free negroes" (p. 159). He suggests that slavery in the New World be replaced by a system of serfdom rather than actual freedom.

27 List (2017, orig. 1885), p. 76.

28 Condliffe (1950), p. 278. The same influence can perhaps be found in Vladimir Putin's 2022 invasion of Ukraine.

29 See Irwin (2001), for example.

30 Irwin (2001) concludes that "the mundane non-traded sectors, such as utilities, distribution, and other services, accumulated capital more rapidly than manufacturing, achieved higher rates of (total factor productivity) growth than manufacturing, and boosted US–UK relative labor productivity in such a way as to help the United States overtake the United Kingdom in in per capital GDP" (p. 29).

31 Chang (2003), p. 32.

32 Chang (2003), p. 35. Economic historian Paul Bairoch (1989), whose work is cited by Chang, writes that, by the mid-1870s, "Germany had virtually become a free trade country" (p. 41).

33 See Broadberry (1998) whose empirical analysis concludes: "Both Germany and the United States overtook Britain in terms of aggregate labor productivity largely by shifting resources out of agriculture and by improving comparative labor productivity in services rather than by improving comparative labor productivity in manufacturing" (p. 376).

34 See O'Rourke (2000) and Irwin (2002).

35 See, for example, Furceri et al. (2020).

36 Prebisch (1963), p. 71.

37 See, for example, Chapter 6 of Reyes and Sawyer (2016).

38 Bruton (1998) states: "To accept learning and knowledge accumulation both as the bottom line of growth and as having deep roots in the ethos and history of a society requires that explanation and policy prescription probe these precincts that are so alien to mainstream thinking. This is the great message of the histories of technological knowledge accumulation and of the stories of the failures of import substitution" (p. 933).

39 Chang (2003), p. 49.

40 This point receives an extraordinary, book-length treatment in Davis (2004).

41 List (2017, orig. 1885), p. 162.

42 Chang (2003), pp. 127–128.

43 Chang (2003), p. 141.

44 Messerlin (2006), p. 1400.

45 See, for example, Lee (2016) for the current, expansive agenda.

46 See Lee (2016), Chapter 3.

47 List (2017, orig. 1885), p. 31.

48 Interestingly, it is also sometimes attributed to the historian Paul Kennedy who uses it in his book *The Rise and Fall of the Great Powers* (1987). It might be that this is something List should have said or that it appeared in one of his early pamphlets.

49 List (2017, orig. 1885), p. 34.

50 Spiegel (1991), Chapter 5.

51 The alleged link from military production to economic boon is actually much more nuanced than often alleged. See, for example, Chapter 1 of Samuels (1994).

52 Meyer (1955), p. 11 and 15.

53 Stråth (2008), p. 175. Here is List (2017, orig. 1885) on the case of Holland: "We from *a national point of view* say and maintain that Holland is in reference to its geographical position, as well as with in respect [...] to the origin and language of its inhabitants, a German province [...] without whose reincorporation in the German Union Germany may be compared to a house the door of which belongs to a stranger" (p. 155, emphasis added).

54 Stråth (2008), p. 177.

55 Stråth (2008), for example, states: "Bismarck's policy represented a crucial shift in the wake of the 1848 revolution. The national and Central European question was [...] discussed [...] in terms of power politics, defined in military, economic and geopolitical terms. On this point, there was clear continuity with the thoughts of Friedrich List" (p. 179).

56 Putin's essay on the "historical unity of Russians and Ukrainians" is not very different in tone from List's claims about *Mitteleuropa*. See http://www.en.kremlin.ru/misc/66182.

57 Woo-Cumings (2005), p. 100.

58 Samuels (1994) states: "Friedrich List [...] anticipated the mercantilist thread in Japanese technology ideology. List's argument that a nation's independence and security depend on the independence and vitality of its manufacturers is isomorphic to Japan's relentless acceleration toward autonomy and its unflagging commitment to nurturance and technological diffusion" (p. 56).

59 Kobayashi (1922), pp. 161–162.

60 Samuels (1994), p. 319.

61 Mann (2013), p. 193.

62 The term "techno-military paradigm" is due to Samuels (1994).

63 Lind (2019).

64 It is perhaps worth mentioning that Lind (1999) describes the Vietnam War (in which approximately two million Vietnamese citizens perished) as a "necessary war" because of its "symbolism" (p. 62). This raises the question of how many civilian deaths we are willing to tolerate for symbolic ends.

65 An early and oft-cited work on this is Francois and Reinert (1996).

66 Chanda (2017), p. 45. Chanda also states that: "As countries seek to increase their participation in global value chains, instead of a "services versus goods" approach, they must adopt a "services and goods" based trade and development strategy, which recognises the backward and forward linkages between the two sectors" (p. 55).

67 See, for example, Arnold, Javorcik and Mattoo (2011), Arnold et al. (2015) and Nordås and Rouzet (2015). Nordås and Rouzet (2015) find that restrictiveness in services trade suppresses manufacturing exports across a sample of 40 countries.

68 Moore (2017), p. 7. As Moore emphasizes, this sector also involves large and globalized workforces.

69 There is a military saying that "Amateurs talks tactics, but professionals talk logistics."

70 See, for example, Ali-Yrkkö et al. (2011) for the case of the Nokia N95 smartphone and Dedrick, Kraemer and Linden (2010) for the case of the Apple iPod.

71 Moretti (2012), p. 69.

72 Johnson and Noguera (2012) and Koopman, Wang and Wei (2014). Koopman, Wang and Wei (2014) provide a more comprehensive treatment of the issue. For a simple introduction, see also Chapter 11 of Reinert (2021a).

4. Zero-Sum Thinking

1 von Neuman (1928).

2 von Neuman and Morgenstern (1953).

3 For example, Davidai and Ongis (2019) state: "Although pure zero-sum situations are rare, many people perceive non-zero-sum situations as zero-sum, believing that one person's gains are balance by another person's loss" (p. 2).

4 Fearon et al. (2021), p. 3.

5 These assumptions are that there is perfect competition, no externalities, no public goods, perfect information and no labor market discrimination.

6 Johnson, Zhang and Keil (2020), p. 3.

7 This goes back to the work of Nash (1950).

8 Johnson, Zhang and Keil (2020), p. 4.

9 Krugman (1998), an appreciator of difficult ideas and an economist who has spent a great deal of effort at communicating them, nevertheless expresses a great deal of frustration on this matter.

10 Baron and Kemp (2004), p. 567.
11 See the results of Baron and Kemp (2004), for example.
12 For a discussion of this, see Goldin and Reinert (2012) and Reinert (2017).
13 This idea was introduced by Kahneman and Frederick (2002).
14 Findlay and O'Rourke (2007), p. 387.
15 See Chapter 1 of Eichengreen (2008).
16 See Samuelson and Zeckhauser (1988).
17 See, for example, Baron and Kemp (2004).
18 See Baron and Jurney (1993).
19 Suranovic (2000), p. 295.
20 Różycka-Tran, Boski and Wojciske (2015), p. 526.
21 See Leung et al. (2007). Cross-cultural psychologists have measured this tendency in multi-country studies. Indeed, there is even a tested belief in zero-sum game scale with some evidence of validity. See Różycka-Tran, Boski and Wojciske (2015).
22 See, for example, Chapter 5 of Reinert (2021a).
23 As noted by Irwin (2020), for example, "standard estimates of the gains from trade [...] largely overlook the benefits to consumers from exposure to a greater variety of goods. [...] Yet the few intriguing attempts to explore this benefit have suggested that it is tremendously important" (p. 53).
24 See, for example, Chapter 14 of Reinert (2021a).
25 https://www.federalregister.gov/documents/2017/04/05/2017-06968/omnibus-report-on-significant-trade-deficits.
26 This is due to Raiffa (1982).
27 Neale and Bazerman (1985), p. 36.
28 See, for example, Baron (2001).
29 Hoekman and Kostecki (2009), p. 152.
30 Neale and Bazerman (1985), p. 37.
31 Baron and Kemp (2004), p. 566.
32 Hoekman and Kostecki (2009), pp. 179–180.
33 Hoekman and Kostecki (2009), Chapter 4.
34 Phelan and Richardson (1969) and Neale and Bazerman (1985).
35 Barry and Friedman (1998), pp. 356–357.
36 Ghemawat (2003), p. 78. On corporate imperialism, see the corporate strategists Prahalad and Lieberthal (2008).
37 Ghemawat (2009). He goes on to state the Friedman's arguments are "mostly characterized by emotional rather than cerebral appeals, a reliance and prophecy, [...] and [...] a clamor for attention."
38 Ghemawat (2017), p. 89.
39 Różycka-Tran et al. (2019).
40 Holshek (2013), p. 227.
41 Holshek (2013), p. 196.
42 Gray (2006), p. 5.
43 Hrytsak (2022).
44 See, for example, Fearon et al. (2021).
45 Fearon et al. (2021), p. 8.
46 Van Boven, Judd and Sherman (2012).
47 See, for example, Fearon et al. (2021).
48 Fearon et al. (2021), p. 24.

49 Fukuyama (1995).
50 Johnson, Zhang and Keil (2020), p. 5.

5. Battleground WTO

1   Ruggie (1992), p. 568.
2   Ruggie (1992), p. 568.
3   See Lampe (2009). Lampe states that "the Cobden-Chevalier Treaty came closer to 'moderate protection' than 'free trade,' as substantial duties remained" (p. 1017).
4   Irwin (1995), p. 323.
5   See Ruggie (1992), p. 581 and Findlay and O'Rourke (2007), p. 396. Another source was the 1934 US Reciprocal Trade Agreements Act (RTAA). As stated by Irwin (2020), "the United States aimed to convert the piecemeal, bilateral RTAA approach into a broader, multilateral system based on nondiscrimination and the reduction of trade barriers" (p. 260).
6   Hoekman and Kostecki (2009), p. 42.
7   Ruggie (1992), p. 586, emphasis added.
8   See, for example, Ikenberry (1992).
9   Singh (2008) reports that "at (a) 1982 meeting in Geneva, which included 82 ministers and 800 official delegates, the USTR [...] was especially aggressive on the services issue" (p. 97).
10 Zoellick (2003). The text of this speech has been subsequently removed from the USTR website.
11 See Singh (2017), pp. 141–142.
12 See Schott and Jung (2019). These authors show that, of the 23 complaints the United States brought to the WTO against China between 2002 and 2018, nine were settled in consultation. Of the remaining 14, 11 were ruled in the favor of the United States.
13 British Broadcasting Corporation (2018).
14 Rose (2004).
15 See, for example, Subramanian and Wei (2007) who use the more appropriate import variable rather than average of imports and exports and who correct for several other relevant factors, as well as Larch et al. (2020).
16 Koopman et al. (2020), p. 830.
17 Mavroidis and Sapir (2021) note that "the main factor behind the protracted negotiations was the special nature of China's foreign trade regime. The China regime, when compared to those prevailing in most of the WTO members, was idiosyncratic and, for incumbents, a major cause of concern" (p. 23).
18 Feenstra and Sasahara (2018), p. 1054.
19 http://www.oecd.org/industry/ind/TIVA-2018-China.pdf.
20 Johnson and Noguera (2012) report that "the U.S.-China deficit is approximately 30–40% smaller when measured on a value added basis" (p. 225). Koopman, Wang and Wei (2014) also put this figure at approximately 40 percent.
21 Koopman, Wang and Wei (2014) show that, from a value-added perspective, "a significant portion of China's trade surplus to the United States in gross trade terms reflects indirect value-added exports that China does on behalf of Japan, Korea and Taiwan" (p. 461).
22 Autor, Dorn and Hanson (2013).

23 Acemoglu et al. (2016).
24 On EU effects, see Sertić, Ĉasni and Vuĉković (2017).
25 Feenstra and Sasahara (2018) and Feenstra, Ma and Xu (2019).
26 See Bloom et al. (2019).
27 Caliendo, Dvorkin and Parro (2019).
28 See, for example, Wang et al. (2018).
29 World Trade Organization (2001), pp. 1–2.
30 Mavroidis and Sapir (2021), p. 39.
31 Zhang (2019).
32 See, for example, Reich (2018).
33 Bown and Irwin (2019), p. 125. These authors include former Trump adviser Steve
    Bannon as a force for economic nationalism in the early days of the administration.
    After he left the administration and shortly after he was arrested on fraud charges
    only to be pardoned by President Trump, Bannon announced a new Institute for
    Populism and Economic Nationalism.
34 Pinchis-Paulsen (2020), p. 111.
35 It is worth noting that the Trump administration supported Russia in using the same
    national security arguments at the WTO.
36 Pinchis-Paulsen (2020), p. 191. Pinchis-Paulsen also states that "the (US) State
    Department advocated that trade multilateralism was a necessary ingredient for
    national security" (p. 193).
37 *Wall Street Journal* (2018). The editorial board of this conservative newspaper referred
    to the use of Section 232. Section 232 of the 1962 Trade Expansion Act in this case
    as a "stunt."
38 See Lee (2019).
39 Lee (2019), p. 490. Lee also correctly points out that what the Trump administration
    was doing was applying tariffs to put pressure on trading partners to sign bilateral
    quota arrangements, another problematic action from the point of view of WTO
    agreements.
40 Johnson (1965), p. 170.
41 Irwin (2016).
42 See, for example, Flaaen and Pierce (2019). Irwin (2020) reports that the US steel
    industry "employs about 147,000 workers, while there are roughly 2.3 million workers
    in steel-using industries" (p. 102).
43 See, for example, Furceri et al. (2020). These authors state that "the negative effect
    of tariffs (on growth) seems to arise from an increase in the costs of (imported) inputs
    owing to tariffs" (p. 856).
44 Iliasu (1971), p. 92.
45 See Irwin (2020), p. 125, footnote 11. His source here is the American Iron and Steel
    Institute!
46 See Irwin (2016) and Brewster (2020).
47 Brewster (2020), p. 64. Relatedly, "nostalgic deprivation" was identified as an
    important variable in explaining right-wing movements by Gest, Reny and Mayer
    (2018).
48 Bown and Irwin (2019) note that the USMCA "is hardly a major rewrite of NAFTA.
    It preserves NAFTA's requirements of duty-free access, would slightly open up
    Canadian dairy markets to U.S. farmers, and incorporates a host of new provi-
    sions from the TPP" (pp. 129–130). It was, in their view, "an unnecessary exercise"
    (p. 130).

49 Navarro and Autry (2011). Autry is on the Board of the Coalition for a Prosperous America, and the book was endorsed by Ian Fletcher, an economist with that organization. Navarro is not a trade economist, Autry specializes in the commercial use of space, and Ian Fletcher's background is in industry. None of these individuals seems to have much professional specialization in trade issues, either law or economics. In 2018, Navarro claimed on television that there would not be retaliation against increased US steel and aluminum tariffs. He was, of course, wrong.

50 Bown and Irwin (2019), p. 134.

51 Reuters (2018).

52 Lee (2019).

53 Irwin (2020), p. 111.

54 Bown (2021, 2022).

55 See Reuters (2019).

56 See, for example, Amiti, Redding and Weinstein (2019).

57 Gao (2021).

58 For a detailed analysis, see Gao (2021).

59 As discussed in Hoekman and Mavroidis (2020), the EU has led the effort to put a Multiparty Interim Appeal Arbitration Arrangement to function in place of the Appellate Body, but this is a plurilateral arrangement representing a small fraction of WTO membership. These authors provide a thorough discussion of potential avenues of reform but note that the approach of the United States to sabotaging the system is "unquestionably indefensible" (p. 721).

60 United States Trade Representative (2021).

61 *The Economist* (2020b).

62 Bown and Irwin (2019), p. 134.

63 Iliasu (1971), pp. 75–76. Indeed, it seems that peace was foremost in Cobden's mind. Iliasu writes: "Cobden on the whole shared Gladstone's motives for supporting the negotiations, particularly the one concerned with drawing the two countries closer. But he hoped to realize something more than improving Anglo-French relations. He hoped that once the treaty was concluded, there would be sufficient grounds for urging the governments of the two countries to end their arms race. This was, in fact, Cobden's chief interest in urging Napoleon the sign the treaty" (p. 91). In the end, this hope was not realized.

64 Mavroidis and Sapir (2021), p. 148.

65 Mavroidis and Sapir (2021), p. 151.

66 Mavroidis and Sapir (2021) state that "the current crisis can *partly* be addressed through better enforcement of existing rules, including commitments taken by China in its Protocol of Accession" (p. 206, emphasis added).

67 Mun (2013, orig. 1664), p. 257.

68 FAO (2020), p. 5.

69 FAO (2020).

70 Sumaila et al. (2019).

71 Cisneros-Montemayor and Sumaila (2019), p. 2.

72 See, for example, Sumaila et al. (2007) and Reinert (forthcoming).

73 https://www.wto.org/english/news_e/spno_e/spno28_e.htm.

74 Some of these points are made by Koopman et al. (2020). Mavroidis and Sapir (2021) note that trade "provides a very appropriate mechanism to avoid conflict by increasing the existing level of cooperation" and that "the WTO is undeniably the most far-reaching institutional arrangement promoting cooperative attitudes" (p. 216).

6. The Ethnicity Trap

1　This chapter will not delve deeply into the Trump-led ethnonationalism of the United States. See Gorki and Perry (2022) who state: "White Christian nationalism is a form of what is often called 'ethno-nationalism.' [...] It reinforces a narrow ethno-nationalist definition of 'the people'" (pp. 114–115).

2　"Stochastic violence" is usually called "stochastic terrorism," but the latter seems to be a more restrictive term. In both cases, there appears to be a dearth of research on an increasingly common phenomenon.

3　Connor (1973), p. 3. For example, when President Donald Trump repeatedly attacked an elected Somali member of the US Congress in his campaign rallies, he intuitively drew on this structure of thought.

4　Baughn and Yaprak (1996), p. 763.

5　Baughn and Yaprak (1996), p. 763.

6　*The Economist* (2016b).

7　In the US context, for example, Gorski and Perry (2022) state: "The goal is to forever redeem and restore a lost world corrupted by 'outsiders.' That won't happen without a fight. So white Christian nationalism marches its adherents toward a bloody battle" (p. 7).

8　Connor (2007), p. 1. Similarly, Konstan (1997) states that: "The relevant question is whether, and to what extent, groups affirm their ethnic identity on the basis of one or another kind of marker, irrespective of its ostensible truth as decided by modern scientific methods. The idea that ethnicity is a discursive phenomenon means just that it is dependent on ideology, not of facts as such" (p. 99).

9　Samuels (1994), p. 331. Samuels notes that, in this tradition, "Japanese bones, the Japanese brain, Japanese intestines, even Japanese snow are exceptional" (p. 331).

10　Murphy-Shigematsu (1993).

11　Tamir (2019), p. 423, emphasis added. Fairness in quotation requires mentioning Tamir's following statement that "many of the rudimentary concepts of political theory [...] are equally ridden with ambiguity" (p. 423).

12　Boutros-Ghali (1992), p. 18.

13　Yadate and Garoma (2015).

14　See, for example, *The Economist* (2022k).

15　For example, Johnson (1965) emphasizes the "psychic satisfaction derived from the community at large from gratification of the taste for nationalism" (p. 177).

16　Johnson (1965), p. 183.

17　*The Economist* (2020a).

18　Becker (1971).

19　Mun (2013, orig. 1664), p. 270.

20　Kaplan (2020).

21　Gorski and Perry (2022). These authors refer to US-based white Christian nationalism as "a mythological version of history" (p. 4) and as "us vs. them tribalism" (p. 7) supported by "a cottage industry that spreads historical misinformation" (p. 25).

22　https://nationalconservatism.org/natcon-dc-2019/.

23　Green (2019).

24　See Gray (2018).

25　To be fair to Mr. Carlson, he once raised issues about extreme forms of ethnonationalism in the United States (Carlson 1997) but seems to have abandoned his own position on this.

26 *The Economist* (2016a, b). *The Economist* (2016b)) states that: "From Warsaw to Washington, the political divide that matters is less and less between left and right, and more and more between open and closed."
27 Reicher, Haslam and Hopkins (2005), p. 564.
28 Gorski and Perry (2022), pp. 112–113.
29 Komireddi (2021).
30 Reicher, Haslam and Hopkins (2005), p. 564.
31 The term "Hindutva" comes from its two roots "Hindu" and "Tattva," the latter meaning "principles."
32 Devare (2011), p. 201.
33 See Khan et al. (2017).
34 https://archive.org/details/hindutva-vinayak-damodar-savarkar-pdf/mode/2up.
35 Savarkar (1969), p. 24.
36 Savarkar (1969), p. 89, emphasis in original. Singh (2023) notes the "diminishing of Gandhian legacy with the rise of extremist Hindu movements in India."
37 Savarkar (1969), p. 139.
38 Savarkar (1969), p. 84. As noted by Khan et al. (2017), Savarkar uses the term "Jati." These authors state that he "used *Jati* to denote identity in terms of racial characteristics" (p. 490).
39 See, for example, Appadurai (2022).
40 Khan et al. (2017), p. 492.
41 Khan et al. (2017). At the time of this writing, the website savarkar.org features a Hindutva flag with a swastika on it. The choice to do this in the current era is surprising to say the least.
42 Khan et al. (2017), p. 496.
43 This is reported in Mehta (2004).
44 This is a *short* list based on Kaul (2017) and *The Economist* (2020d). As described in Deb (2021), the new citizenship law has rendered stateless approximately two million residents of Assam.
45 See Yasir (2021) and *The Economist* (2022b).
46 Shih and Gupta (2022). These authors report Hindu-nationalist mobs marching through Muslim neighborhoods with weapons in six Indian states with hundreds of individuals being injured.
47 This was pointed out by Johnson (1965), for example.
48 Venkataramakrishnan (2015).
49 See Nolan and Singh (2022) for these suppressed WHO estimates.
50 Antal (2017) characterizes the new Hungarian constitution as follows: "the restriction of the Constitutional Court's power, which was the main counterweight institution of the Government's power; the reinforcement of the Government's power; the stabile majority of the Government in the Parliament; the control over the Parliament by the Government; the power of Government to overrule the decisions of the Constitutional Court, raising the dilemma of an unconstitutional constitution; the concentration of powers instead of the separation of powers" (p. 13).
51 Palonen (2018) states that "Orbán managed to define the Hungarian and European liberals as the enemy and rearticulate the nation as the basis of legitimacy" (p. 316).
52 For example, in the Hungarian context, Csehi and Zgut (2021) state that: "'The elite' is defined as a group that acts against the will of 'the people' in different realms of everyday life, from politics, through economics, and even academia. Given that 'the people' are pure and uncorrupted whereas 'the elites' are dishonest and fraudulent, a

normative as well as practical struggle between the two groups is inevitable" (p. 55). The same language is used among ethnonationalists in the United States.

53 Csehi and Zgut (2021), p. 60.

54 Csehi and Zgut (2021), p. 60.

55 Dinan (2017), p. 76.

56 Murray (2017). Interestingly, Murray is an atheist, but nonetheless a supporter of Christianity as an *identity*.

57 Schaeffer (2017).

58 https://arktos.com.

59 https://counter-currents.com.

60 Tolstoy and McCarrray (2015), p. 25. These authors also state that "Dugin is the intellectual who has Vladimir Putin's back in the emerging ideological conflict between Russia and the West. [...] No individual better represents the tactics of the current Russian regime" (p. 25).

61 In August 2022, Dugin's daughter, Darya Dugina, was killed by a car bomb after she and her father participated in the Russian nationalist "Traditions" festival outside of Moscow. This seemed to be related to her father's support of the Russian invasion of Ukraine.

62 See Alderman and Santora (2019).

63 See https://www.europarl.europa.eu/doceo/document/TA-8-2018-0340_EN.html ?redirect. The text of the resolution specifically mentions and discusses the following concerns: functioning of the constitutional and electoral system, independence of the judiciary, corruption and conflicts of interest, privacy and data protection, freedom of expression, academic freedom, freedom of religion, freedom of association, right to equal treatment, minority rights, rights of migrants and refugees and economic and social rights.

64 https://www.europarl.europa.eu/news/en/press-room/20220304IPR24802/rule-of -law-conditionality-commission-must-immediately-initiate-proceedings. EU scholar Desmond Dinan reports that "the EU specifically linked the allocation of NextGenEU funding to respect for rule of law, with Hungary and Poland in mind, in the course of the arduous negotiations on the COVID recovery package in 2020" (private communication).

65 https://www.statista.com/chart/18794/net-contributors-to-eu-budget/.

66 Garamvolgi and Borger (2022). Bayer has referred to Jewish people as "stinking excrement," called Roma people "animals" and used a notorious racist term to describe Black people.

67 Agence French-Presse (2022).

68 Hsieh et al. (2019).

69 Bouie (2020).

70 Connor (1973), p. 18. As indicated in Reicher, Haslan and Hopkins (2005), both Hitler and Mussolini were self-identified performance artists.

71 Pickel (2003), p. 122.

72 Muller (2008), p. 20.

73 Muller (2008), p. 31.

74 Dinan (2014), p. 1.

75 Yack (1996), p. 202.

76 Debebe and Reinert (2014).

77 For example, Sen (2006) states that "the diminution of human beings involved in taking note only of one membership category for each person (neglecting all others) expunges at one stroke the far-reaching elements of our manifold affinities and involvements" (pp. 176–177).

78 Singer (1972).
79 https://www.nbcnews.com/politics/donald-trump/here-s-full-text-donald-trump-s
-speech-poland-n780046. The choice of Poland as a location for this speech was not
accidental on the part of the Trump administration but rather reflected the illiberal
tendencies of the Polish government and an attempt to intervene in its conflict with
the EU as described by Dinan (2017).
80 Thornton (2000), p. 11. Thornton is a frequent contributor to David Horwitz's
online *FrontPage Magazine*, considered by most serious researchers to be a bit beyond
the pale.
81 Sourvinou-Inwood (2005), p. 25.
82 Hall (2015), p. 18, emphasis added.
83 Hall (2015) citing Anderson (1991). Hall states that "it is not sufficient to identify [...]
what *we* see as the fundamental characteristics of Greek culture; rather, what has to
be demonstrated is a conscious [...] abstraction of ideas, beliefs, and practices as the
specific expression of a Hellenic community rather than of the *polis* or *ethnos*" (p. 27,
emphasis in the original).
84 Hall (1989), p. viiii.
85 Hall (2015), p. 22.
86 Goldstone (2009) notes that: "There has been a tendency to see modern science
and mathematics as a European invention based on ideas originated by the ancient
Greeks. [...] We now realize, however, that this picture is almost entirely false" (p.
137). He states that "before 1500, the greatest mathematicians, astronomers, chem-
ists, and physicists in the world were probably the Arabs and other Muslims" (p.
138) and that "their discoveries laid the foundations for almost all higher work in
mathematics in Europe since the Renaissance" (p. 139). For a modern assessment
of Islam and the West, see Noorani (2002), particularly Chapter 5 on human rights
and Chapter 6 on *ijtihad*.
87 UNHCR (2016).
88 Berchin et al. (2017), p. 149.
89 de Châtel (2014) and Beck (2014).
90 *The Economist* (2022i) reports how these tendencies in South Africa are taking a violent turn.
91 *The Economist* (2021g). This article notes that "among Donald Trump's first acts
as America's president was to shut the doors to refugees from some Muslim countries, prompting Germany's chancellor, Angela Merkel, to explain the convention
to him."
92 Tsai (2019), p. 105, 115 and 116–117.
93 Outhwaite (2019), p. 101.
94 Goldberg (2021).
95 See, for example, Davidai and Ongis (2019) and Pietrowski et al. (2019).
96 See, for example, Liebich (2006) and Tamir (2019).
97 See, for example, Connor (2007).
98 Ignatieff (1993), p. 6 and 7, emphasis added. Note Ignatieff's use of the term "patriotic." Relatedly, Gorski and Perry (2022) state that "patriotism is understood in
terms of constitutional ideals and democratic institutions and citizenship is not
based on racial, ethnic, or religious identity" (p. 9).
99 Yack (1996), p. 198 and p. 207.
100 Xenos (1996).
101 Tamir (2019), p. 431.

102 Yack (1996), p. 206.
103 Palonen (2018), p. 312.
104 Tamir (2019), p. 432.
105 Mac Ginty (2014), p. 553 and p. 552. Mac Ginty also states that "such everyday peace and diplomacy activity can provide the social glue that prevents a society from tipping over the edge" (p. 561).
106 Ignatieff (1993), p. 243.
107 Hyde (2019).
108 Ignatieff (1993), p. 245. He further states that "it is almost as if the quotient of crude historical fiction, violent moral exaggeration, ludicrous caricature of the enemy is in direct proportion to the degree to which the speaker himself is aware that it is all really a pack of lies" (p. 245).
109 In the Hungarian context popular with US ethnonationalists, Csehi and Zgut (2021) state that: "Populists believe that representative institutions failed to carry out the general will of 'the people' as they served the interests of the 'corrupt elite.' As these institutions are not considered to be the right representatives of the right people, populists often advocate a majoritarian takeover of the existing polity" (p. 55).

7. The Brexit Blunder

1   British Broadcasting Corporation (2013).
2   Glencross (2016).
3   See Corbett (2016), Gifford (2006), Leconte (2015) and Taggart (1998).
4   See Leconte (2015).
5   Corbett (2016), p. 20.
6   Leconte (2015), p. 255.
7   Diez (1999), p. 606.
8   Wellings (2010).
9   The monetary union initiative began in 1970 when a commission chaired by the then prime minister of Luxembourg, Pierre Werner, issued a report providing a detailed plan for a step-by-step movement to a EMU by 1980 but it only came into effect in 1999.
10 *The Economist* (2020e).
11 Johnson (2013).
12 Mun (2013, orig. 1664), p. 258.
13 Johnson (2013). Johnson states that "in or out of the EU, we must have a clear vision of how we are going to be competitive in the global economy."
14 Curtice (2017), p. 25.
15 Ross (2016).
16 See Swales (2016).
17 See, for example, Keating (2022) who offers a different view, namely that the UK is "not a unitary state but a union of nations" (p. 492).
18 *Daily Express* (2013).
19 See Sumption and Vargas-Silva (2020).
20 See Curtice (2017).
21 Gietel-Basten (2016), p. 676.
22 Mason (2015).

23 See, for example, Dustmann and Frattini (2014).
24 See Thielmann and Schade (2014), published shortly before the Leave vote. These authors state: "Overall, while it is indeed the case that the UK has seen a considerable increase in the number of foreigners, including EU migrants, living in the country, its situation is by no means unique. Furthermore, the weight of the evidence suggests that EU migrants contribute more to the UK's public coffers than they take out. Any suggestions that migration patterns to the UK are unique, or that such migration is creating unsustainable pressures for the UK welfare system, need to be treated with caution" (p. 142).
25 Tony Blair's speech in March 2003 to the British House of Commons on the eve of the Iraq invasion, with its invocation of non-existent weapons of mass destruction and past appeasement to Hitler, has not aged well.
26 *The Economist* (2022j).
27 See the analysis by Curtice (2017), for example.
28 See, for example, De Santis and Vicarelli (2007) and Gil, Llorca and Martíniz-Serrano (2008).
29 See, for example, Baldwin (1989).
30 Temple (2004) has expertly considered long-run growth rate versus level effects and found the latter to be more important from a welfare standpoint.
31 See, for example, Badinger (2005) and Campos, Coricelli and Moretti (2014).
32 Pain and Young (2004).
33 On productivity, see Rolfe et al. (2013). On fiscal contributions, see Dustmann and Frattini (2014).
34 Crafts (2016).
35 Curtice (2017), p. 27.
36 Gietel-Basten (2016), p. 678.
37 Gest, Reny and Mayer (2018), p. 1701.
38 Gest, Reny and Mayer (2018), p. 1695, emphasis added.
39 See, for example, Ivarsflaten (2008).
40 Gest, Reny and Mayer (2018), p. 1698.
41 Gest, Reny and Mayer (2018), p. 1701.
42 Toynbee (2020).
43 Usherwood (2021), p. 5.
44 Parker and Allen (2016).
45 See Earle (2021) and Khan (2021).
46 *The Economist* (2021h).
47 *The Economist* (2021h).
48 https://yougov.co.uk/topics/politics/survey-results/daily/2021/09/29/ad945/1?utm _source=twitter%20&utm_medium=daily_questions&utm_campaign=question_1 and *The Economist* (2023a).
49 Freeman et al. (2022).
50 European Parliament (2017), p. 9.
51 *The Economist* (2021a).
52 Parker et al. (2021).
53 See, for example, Shaxson (2021).
54 Quoted in Tchernookova (2021).
55 *The Economist* (2021a).
56 *The Economist* (2022a).

57 *The Economist* (2021b).

58 *The Economist* (2021b).

59 Keating (2022) explains: "The Northern Ireland settlement has a transnational dimension. Citizens in Northern Ireland are invited to define themselves as British, Irish or any combination of these. People born in Northern Ireland have a right to Irish, and thus European, citizenship on the same basis as those in the Republic of Ireland" (p. 493).

60 See Jones and Larner (2021).

61 Gasiorek and Jerzewska (2020), p. 2.

62 See Gasiorek and Jerzewska (2020), particularly Table 1.

63 As reported in Dinan (2021), in October 2020, the European Council president, Charles Michel, stated that the EU "stands in full solidarity with Ireland and this is especially true when it comes to the full implementation of the Withdrawal Agreement and the Protocol on Ireland and Northern Ireland. This text has been negotiated for three years. Each word, each comma has been debated for hours and hours. It has been ratified by both parties. There is simply no question on its full implementation. This is a matter of law, a matter of trust" (p. 18).

64 *The Economist* (2021j).

65 See, for example, Hall (2021).

66 *The Economist* (2021j) noted that Boris Johnson's "team is fostering the delusion that he was forced to accept the protocol by pro-European MPS who tied his hand in the Brexit talks, and they the ineptitude of his predecessor, Theresa May. This skates over the fact that Mr. Johnson himself chose to create the border in the Irish Sea. [...] He then railroaded the Brexit deal through."

67 See Rankin (2023).

68 See Specia (2022).

69 https://www.unhcr.ca/news/un-refugee-agency-opposes-uk-plan-to-export-asylum/.

70 Syal and Brown (2022).

71 Usherwood (2021), pp. 7–8.

72 *The Economist* (2022j) reported that "in the end the government had so many vacancies that it could no longer function."

73 Truss seems to have learned very little from her experience with the financial markets, choosing instead to confer with tax-cutting afficionados in the United States. See Burns (2023).

74 Lewis (2022). This author notes that "Brexit is now less a policy than a vibe."

75 See, for example, Schomberg (2022).

76 Colantone and Stanig (2019) conclude that "many promises of Leave campaigners were unrealistic, and Brexit [...] is likely to backfire on the vulnerable segments of British society who have supported it" (p. 147).

8. Pandemic Nationalism

1 World Bank (2020).

2 Reinhart and Reinhart (2020), p. 84.

3 Lighthizer (2020).

4 See Politi (2020). Note that, despite his role, Peter Navarro had no background in trade policy. As reported in Solender (2020) and elsewhere, he also repeatedly violated

the US Hatch Act, which prohibits US Federal Government employees from performing political tasks in their official roles. In June 2022, he was arrested for being in contempt of the US Congress for refusing to testify about his role in 6 January 2021 insurrection.

5 In Taiwan, where mask wearing was near universal, and contract tracing effective, economic recovery was much quicker. See *The Economist* (2020f).

6 Gelles (2020). A member of the German parliament noted that this potentially revolutionary innovation is just the thing that the ethnonationalistic Alternative for German party would have prevented from taking place with its proposed immigration policies.

7 *The Economist* (2022g).

8 Markel (2014), p. 125. Markel notes that "economic interests, politics, and bad behaviour trumped all such debates and little substantive policy was accomplished in terms of regulatory control. But [...] the International Sanitary Conventions' [...] historical achievement was the establishment of an international forum for the discussion and adjudication of health matters that would only grow in importance over time" (p. 125).

9 Markel (2014), p. 125.

10 Markel (2014), p. 127.

11 At its height, the United States was spending US$8 billion *each month* on the Iraq war.

12 Kahl and Wright (2021), p. 159.

13 Kahl and Wright (2021), p. 85, emphasis added. These authors state that the Chinese authorities "knew they had a problem but kept it under wraps, because they did not want to disrupt the tourist season during the Lunar New Year in January 2003" and that "the Chinese media [...] was banned from reporting on the outbreak" (p. 85).

14 See Yang (2021) who details the rising tide of nationalism in China as a result of the trade war that reached a level of a "desire for revenge" (p. 10).

15 Yang (2021). This researcher stated: "Although the novel coronavirus epidemic was in the first instance a public health emergency requiring an urgent response, its handling [...] was fundamentally political. Xi Jinping personally took leadership of and credit for the official response as he launched a multifaceted campaign that went far beyond public health" (p. 14).

16 Reyes (2020).

17 Yang (2021), pp. 23–24.

18 See Wilson (2021).

19 Baker (2018).

20 Kahl and Wright (2021), p. 190.

21 Kahl and Wright (2021), p. 161.

22 Kahl and Wright (2021), p. 2, 14 and 134.

23 Redlener et al. (2020).

24 Woolhandler et al. (2021). Unusually for a medical journal, this study also emphasized that Trump's "appeals to racism, nativism, and bigotry have emboldened white nationalisms and vigilantes, and encouraged police violence and, at the end of his term in office, insurrection" (p. 705).

25 Fisher (2020).

26 *The Economist* (2021c) and *The Lancet* (2021).

27 *The Economist* (2021c).

28 *The Economist* (2021f).

29 Nolen and Singh (2022) who note that "science in India has been increasingly politi-
    cized over the course of the pandemic."
30 Quoted in McCoy (2021).
31 Kirkpatrick and León Cabrera (2020).
32 Kirkpatrick and León Cabrera (2020). These authors also state that "public health
    experts say the Pan-American Health Organization—with offices inside every health
    ministry and nearly 120 years of experience tackling epidemics—was uniquely posi-
    tioned to confront Covid-19."
33 Kahl and Wright (2021), p. 166.
34 Leal Farias, Casarões and Magalhães (2022). These authors conclude that "President
    Bolsonaro's dismissal of the suffering of fellow countrymen and women caused by the
    virus has remained a constant staple of his political repertoire" (p. 2). These authors
    explicitly compare him to Trump and Hungary's Orbán.
35 *The Economist* (2021e).
36 *The Economist* (2021i).
37 Kemeny (2020).
38 See, for example, Debebe (2017).
39 See Keleman (2020).
40 Johnson and Williams (2020).
41 Kahl and Wright (2021), p. 6.
42 See, for example, Gamio and Glanz (2021).
43 See the statistical analysis at: https://www.npr.org/sections/health-shots/2021/12
    /05/1059828993/data-vaccine-misinformation-trump-counties-covid-death-rate.
44 Stellinger, Berglund and Isakson (2020), p. 21.
45 See Bown (2020) and Evenett (2020).
46 Baldwin and Evenett (2020), p. 8.
47 See Espitia, Rocha and Ruta (2020).
48 Goodman et al. (2020). Note that these authors refer to this as "zero-sum mentality."
49 Bown (2020) states that "global PPE markets are in chaos, with reports of piracy,
    defective products, hoarding and price gouging, in addition to the shortages" (p. 32).
50 Stellinger, Berglund and Isakson (2020).
51 For one review of GVCs in medical products, see Gereffi, Pananond and Pedersen
    (2022). These authors conclude: "For policymakers, while it is tempting to think of
    GVC resilience as a standard concept that can be applied uniformly in national econ-
    omies, in fact, value chains are product-specific and overgeneralization may lead to
    higher risks and reduced security" (p. 65).
52 Baldwin and Evenett (2020), p. 16.
53 Evenett (2020), p. 50.
54 See, for example, Stellinger, Berglund and Isakson (2020). These authors suggest
    building upon the 1994 WTO Pharmaceutical Tariff Elimination Agreement as
    part of this process.
55 This is not a new insight. For example, in a discussion of globalization and develop-
    ment, Goldin and Reinert (2012) stated: "Improving the health outcomes of poor
    people usually involves imports of medicines and medical products. It is simply not
    possible for small developing countries to produce the entire range of even some of
    the more basic medical supplies, much less more advanced medical equipment and
    pharmaceuticals" (pp. 47–48). This was reiterated in Bown (2020).
56 See, for example, Lagman (2021).
57 Ghebreyesus (2021).

58 https://www.wto.org/english/news_e/spno_e/spno15_e.htm.
59 Bollyky and Bown (2020), pp. 96–97.
60 Bollyky and Bown (2020), p. 97, emphasis added.
61 See Kaul (2009). She states that "it primarily means that governments in many countries have to act, individually as well as collectively, and in many instances also together with private and civil society actors––in concert, so that all the various inputs fit together and the global public good actually emerges" (p. 552).
62 https://covid19gap.org/.
63 https://www.gavi.org/gavi-covax-amc.
64 Eccleston-Turner and Upton (2021), p. 444.
65 See, for example, the April 2021 statement by Doctors without Borders: https://www.doctorswithoutborders.org/what-we-do/news-stories/news/us-trade-representatives-encouraging-statements-access-covid-19.
66 https://ustr.gov/about-us/policy-offices/press-office/press-releases/2021/may/statement-ambassador-katherine-tai-covid-19-trips-waiver.
67 World Trade Organization (2021).
68 See Hotez and Bottazzi (2021). These authors state: "This new COVID vaccine has several distinct features that make it particularly suitable for use in resource-poor settings: it is safe, effective and can be locally produced at very high quantities. CORBEVAX is easy to store and inexpensive. […] CORBEVAX is made using technology that has been employed worldwide for decades, meaning that manufacturing processes are generally already well-known and won't require a steep learning curve."
69 Yuan (2022). This author notes that the cities under lockdown "account for 26 percent of China's population and 40 percent of its economic output." For the situation as of September 2022, see Wang (2022) who reports that over thirty Chinese cities were in lockdown.
70 See, for example, Stevensen (2022).
71 *The Economist* (2022l).
72 *The Economist* (2022m).
73 Qian and Pierson (2022).
74 For a review of scientific articles on China's post zero-COVID death toll, see Glanz, Hvistendahl and Chang (2023).
75 This is discussed in González (2020).
76 Miroudot (2020), p. 117.
77 https://www.wto.org/english/news_e/spno_e/spno15_e.htm.
78 Bown and Bollykyl (2021).
79 For the call by ministers of health, see https://www.bmj.com/content/375/bmj.n2879.

9. Techno-Nationalism

1 The 1980s imbroglio between the United States and Japan over semiconductors resulted in several trade policy actions by the United States against Japan. See Irwin (1998).
2 Reich (1987), no page numbers.
3 Reich (1987), no page numbers.
4 Reich (1987), no page numbers.
5 Samuels (1994), p. 31. Samuels goes further, calling techno-nationalism an ideology, "a force that precedes and informs the institutions of an entire national economy" (p. 31).

 6 Reich (1989).
 7 Samuels (1994), p. 30. Samuels also notes that "Japan's defense industry is very small: defense production comprises barely one half of one percent of total industrial production, sales equal to those of the nation's sushi shops" (pp. 319–320). Chapter 9 of Samuels' book makes as stark contrast between the US and Japanese approaches to the military that support Reich's claims.
 8 Luo (2022), pp. 550–551.
 9 Luo (2022), p. 553.
10 Foreign direct product rules are now part of the United States Export Administration Regulations and extend the extraterritorial coverage of US export controls to specified items produced outside of the United States. They constitute an evolving legal thicket for international business.
11 Witt (2019), p. 1067.
12 See, for example, Witt (2019).
13 Waibel (2019), no page numbers.
14 See Waibel (2019).
15 See *The Economist* (2022d).
16 https://www.gov.uk/government/publications/advanced-research-and-invention -agency-aria-statement-of-policy-intent/advanced-research-and-invention-agency -aria-policy-statement.
17 *The Economist* (2022c).
18 Inkster (2019), p. 109.
19 Smith, Zhuo and Goldberg (2023).
20 See https://ec.europa.eu/commission/presscorner/detail/en/statement_21_4951.
21 See https://ec.europa.eu/commission/presscorner/detail/en/statement_21_4951.
22 Clark (2021).
23 *The Economist* (2022c) reported that "Applied Materials, a Californian firm that makes machines used to etch minute circuits on silicon wafers, sold tools worth $5 billion to China in 2020, more than to any other market."
24 See also Chapter 11 of Reinert (2021a).
25 Varas et al. (2021), p. 4.
26 See *The Economist* (2022f).
27 *The Economist* (2022f).
28 *The Economist* (2023c) reports: "After much cajoling, Japan (and the Netherlands) reportedly signed on to America's export controls against China."
29 *The Economist* (2023b). Interestingly, like in the perennial case of steel, *The Economist* reports a significant amount of semiconductor *oversupply*.
30 *The Economist* (2023c).
31 Luo (2022), p. 554.
32 For example, Samuels (1994) stresses the role of cooperation among Japanese firms since the end of World War II and notes that, beginning in the 1990s, this practice began to cross national borders.
33 Luo (2022), p. 560.
34 See, for example, Gynawali and Park (2011). These researchers state that "collaborations provide timely access to knowledge and resources that are otherwise unavailable, and firms can combine each other's resources in pursing innovation projects that involve high risks and require heavy investments" (p. 651) and that "by learning from partners, firms can facilitate their own product/technological development and leverage the knowledge across related business within the firms" (p. 652).

35 Chesbrough and Bogers (2014), p. 16.
36 Vanhaverbeke et al. (2014), p. 127.
37 Gynawali and Park (2011), p. 657.
38 For some empirical evidence on this, see Mendi, Moner-Colonques and Sempere-Monerris (2020).
39 *The Economist* (2022e) reported that this goal is part of China's 14th five-year plan.
40 See Chen (2021).
41 See Kennedy (2020) and *The Economist* (2022e). Kennedy provides an impactful diagram of the extent to which the C919 is dependent on imported components.
42 *The Economist* (2022e).
43 Baldwin (2016), p. 6.
44 Möllers (2021), p. 116. Möllers considers the case of Germany in some detail. As part of this, she states: "For the German state, the materiality of information infrastructure has become a key problem for state power in the digital age. What is at stake for the government is reclaiming what they see as lost sovereignty from American hegemony" (p. 118).
45 See again Baldwin (2016) as well as Marjit and Mandel (2017).
46 Reich (1989), p. 46.
47 For the East Asian case, see Stiglitz (1996), McMahon (1998) and Lee (2001). Weaver, Rock and Kusterer (1997) noted that "in each of the East Asian (newly industrializing countries), the earliest emphasis was on expanding primary enrollment. This was followed with timed expansion of the secondary and then the tertiary systems" (p. 166).
48 Weaver, Rock and Kusterer (1997) noted that "no country since 1850 has achieved self-sustaining growth without first achieving universal primary education" (p. 166). The Commission on Growth and Development (2008) concluded that "every country that sustained high growth for long periods put substantial effort into schooling its citizens and deepening its human capital" (p. 37). In an extensive review, Szirmai (2015) concluded that "there is not a single case of successful catch-up in the world economy since the last quarter of the nineteenth century, where *advances in educational levels did not precede subsequent economic growth*. Education is indeed one of the necessary conditions for economic development" (p. 249, emphasis in original).
49 Szirmai (2015), p. 153.
50 Szirmai (2015), p. 152.
51 Lee (2001), p. 116.
52 Gill (2015).
53 Dyson (2015).
54 Freeman (2015) discusses this trend, stating: "Companies locate R&D around the world in part to be near the markets of consumers of their products or to be close to the production plants of their firm or its major suppliers. But the key factor in the spread of multinational research factories worldwide is the new availability of qualified scientific and engineering workers in developing countries at lower wages than in advanced countries" (p. 159).
55 See, for example, Freeman (2015). This author states: "The United States remains the lead country in R&D worldwide, but global catch-up has shrunk the US advantage and is likely to continue to do so into the foreseeable future. Whether or not China surpasses the United States in R&D spending in the next 10–15 years, as trend extrapolations suggest, the globalization of basic and applied science and of product development has created a new world of knowledge creation and application to the economic world" (p. 160).

56 Freeman (2015), p. 171.
57 Sevastopulo and Mitchell (2018). The author of the proposal was the avowedly eth-
    nonationalist Trump adviser and speechwriter Stephen Miller.
58 https://www.federalregister.gov/documents/2020/06/04/2020-12217/suspension
    -of-entry-as-nonimmigrants-of-certain-students-and-researchers-from-the-peoples
    -republic.
59 Rim (2019). This author also states: "It should be unacceptable to even the most
    nationalistic to deliberately undermine our higher education system, one of the areas
    where the United States is indisputably the best in the world."
60 Kim (2022).
61 Luo (2022), p. 563, emphasis added.

10. Beyond Zero Sum

1 And once again, the work of Viner (1930a, b) remains relevant here.
2 For example, in her chapter on economic nationalism, Woo-Cumings (2005) states:
   "The political enemy need not be morally evil or aesthetically ugly; he need not
   appear as an economic competitor, and it may even be advantageous to engage with
   him in business transactions. But he is, nevertheless, the stranger, the Other. […] He
   is existentially something different and alien, so that in the extreme case he can be
   killed" (p. 99).
3 https://www.who.int/news/item/05-05-2022-14.9-million-excess-deaths-were-
   associated-with-the-covid-19-pandemic-in-2020-and-2021.
4 To take but one example, Zedillo (2017) states that "the economics profession has long
   warned against a simplistic application of the Ricardian model to justify unreserved
   free trade. […] Recommendations of trade liberalisation must always be accompanied
   by other policy prescriptions if the distributional effects of open markets deemed
   undesirable are to be mitigated" (pp. 82–83).
5 Lind (2019).
6 Zedillo (2017), p. 83.
7 To just cite one of many sources on the role of policies in globalization processes, see
   Chapter 8 of Goldin and Reinert (2012) including Table 8.2.
8 Zedillo (2017) notes that "a better job must […] be done to understand why a dispro-
   portionate share of the benefits, not only of trade but of growth in general, end up
   being captured by a small proportion of the population, probably because of policies
   over which the rich minority has an overwhelming influence" (p. 86).
9 See, for example, Calantone and Stanig (2019). These authors state: "Plenty of voters
   have seen companies in their communities shutting down or offshoring activities to
   low-wage countries. Entire manufacturing regions have lost prosperity of time. All
   this provides fertile ground for the electoral success of parities promising protectionism" (p. 136). Note that these authors also attribute this to the "China shock" discussed in Chapter 5 but, like most such discussions, only focus on the import side as if
   countries don't also export to China.
10 Spiegel (1991), Chapter 5.
11 Eaton (2017), p. 29.
12 List (2017, orig. 1885), p. 54.

13 See Ruggie (1992). As described in Adelman (2013, Chapter 8), Albert Hirschman, who we met in Chapter 1, would play a small role in this in the US government as part of the Economic Cooperation Administration.

14 Ruggie (1992), p. 590, emphasis added.

15 See Cowhey (1993).

16 See, for example, Rodrik (1998).

17 In some interpretations, this is considered to be a failure of the "embedded liberalism" model of Ruggie (1982). See, for example, Colantone and Stanig (2019).

18 For a sense of the process, see https://www.wto.org/english/thewto_e/acc_e/a1_chine_e.htm.

19 *The Economist* (2020c).

20 Davies (2021).

21 On the provision of basic goods and services, see Reinert (2018).

22 *The Economist* (2017).

23 For example, in his book on economic nationalism and techno-nationalism in Japan, Samuels (1994) states that "even in global economies, national interests lie in enhancing the *skills* and *welfare* of citizens within their geographic boundaries" (p. 32, emphases added). Most economic nationalists lose sight of these priorities.

24 See, for example, Singh (2017).

25 Singh (2023).

26 Gelles (2020).

27 Asakawa, Song and Kim (2014), p. 157.

28 Naqshbandi and Jasimuddin (2018), p. 701.

29 Kerr and Kerr (2020) and Bernstein et al. (2019).

30 See, for example, Levie (2007).

31 For a review of the effects of open innovation on firm performance, see Bigliardi et al. (2020).

32 On the definition and importance of global public goods, see Kaul (2009).

33 Liptak (2020).

34 Despite the prominent role of climate change skeptics in the United States, the United States Center for Naval Analysis Military Advisory Board (2014) issued a warning about the "threat multipliers" inherent in climate change. It stated: "In many areas, the projected impacts of climate change will be more than threat multipliers; they will serve as catalysts for instability and conflict. In Africa, Asia, and the Middle East, we are already seeing how the impacts of extreme weather, such as prolonged drought and flooding—and resulting food shortages, desertification, population dislocation and mass migration, and sea level rise—are posing security challenges to these regions' governments" (p. 2).

35 See, for example, Pereira and Viola (2020).

36 Pereira and Viola (2020), for example, conclude: "Regardless of how one looks at different carbon budgets and mitigation scenarios, immediate, unprecedented mitigation efforts are needed if humanity is to stand any chance of achieving the temperature targets of the Paris Agreement. However, it seems highly unlikely that the mid- and long-term processes can prevent dangerous climate change" (p. 14).

37 As another example of the fact that international economists are not market fundamentalist or exclusively "free trade," Douglas Irwin (2020) supports a multilateral agreement to address climate change via taxation. He states: "Such a tax would

reduce trade, but more trade is not always the goal. Effective environmental and safety regulations should not be avoided simply because they reduce international trade. The notion that all trade must be kept free at all costs is simply wrong" (p. 322).

38 Reinert (2018), p. 76.

39 https://www.fsinplatform.org/sites/default/files/resources/files/GRFC%202022 %20KM%20ENG%20ARTWORK.pdf and *The Economist* (2022h).

40 Food and Agriculture Organization (2022).

41 For example, Martin and Anderson (2012) estimated that during the 2007–8 crisis, export restrictions accounted for 45 percent of the increase in the price of rice and 30 percent of the increase in the price of wheat. Martin and Glauber (2020) also state: "An export restriction may affect access indirectly by lowering domestic prices, making net food buyers better off and lowering the cost of their food. But if it does this successfully, it will make net food sellers worse off and may, increase poverty and worsen food security" (p. 94).

42 *The Economist* (2022h).

43 https://www.worldbank.org/en/programs/debt-statistics.

44 In the case of the United States, Gorski and Perry (2022) have analyzed the role of "righteous violence" (p. 7) in white Christian nationalism as "the ultimate source of order" (p. 102).

45 Donnelly (2000), p. 9.

46 Mearsheimer (1994–1995), p. 9.

47 Donnelly (2000), p. 133. Donnelly has characterized Mearsheimer's arguments as set of non sequiturs.

48 Koopman et al. (2020), p. 830.

49 Chotiner (2022). Mearsheimer states that "we should be working overtime to create friendly relations with the Russians." Mearsheimer is correct that the threat to expand NATA into Ukraine pursued by the US Bush administration was misguided, but he extends this same logic to potential Ukraine membership in the EU, a process that began for Ukraine in the early 2000s. And it is difficult to create "friendly relations" with Russia while it occupies parts of both Ukraine and Georgia, contributes to atrocities in both Syria and Sudan, and supports a global network of illicit businesses.

50 See Schaefer (2002), for example, who states that "no nation gives direct effect or self-executing status to all treaties in their domestic legal system" (p. 344). This author rightly points out that WTO Panel and Appellate Body reports "do not have any effect in the U.S. domestic legal system." That is also the case for other WTO members.

INDEX

5G networks 139, 142–43
1700 Act 20

Abogen Biosciences 149
absorption capacity 151
Acer 40
Adorno, Theodor 6, 54; *Authoritarian Personality, The* 6, 54
Advanced Research and Innovation Agency (ARIA) 141
Advanced Research Projects Agency (ARPA) 140–42
Advisory Committee on Trade Policy Negotiations 60
African American citizens 94
Agenda for Peace (Boutros-Ghali) 79
Agreement on Subsidies and Countervailing Measures (ASCM) 64
agriculture 29–30
ahimsa (nonviolence) 82
Amboyna Massacre (1623) 14
American ethnonationalism 87
American Iron and Steel Institute 71
Amnesty International 83, 114
Anglo-American conservatism 80
Anglo-Dutch war 14, 15
anti-immigrant policies 85
anti-Muslim riots (2002) 83
anti-trade attitudes 45
Appellate Body 3
Applied Materials 146
Arab Spring (2006–10) 92, 104
Ardern, Jacinda 127
ARIA, *see* Advanced Research and Innovation Agency
Arktos Media 85
ARPA, *see* Advanced Research Projects Agency
ASCM, *see* Agreement on Subsidies and Countervailing Measures

ascribed identity 89
Asia 13–14
ASML 144, 146
AstraZeneca 124
Athenian law 91
Athenians 90
Australia 122
Australian government 121
authoritarianism 55, 125, 150
Autor, David 63
avowed identity 89

Babri mosque 83
Baffin, William 9
balance of payments 21–22, 157
Baldwin, Richard 129–30, 150; *Great Convergence: Information Technology and the New Globalization, The* 150
Banda archipelago 14
Bank of England 101
Bannon, Steve 84, 97
BATNA, *see* best alternative to a negotiated agreement
Bayer, Zsolt 86
Becker, Gary 80
beef ban 83
Bengal 18–20
Bengal Famine (1943) 123
Bengali textile industry 20–21
best alternative to a negotiated agreement (BATNA) 168
Bhagwati, Jagdish 83
Bharatiya Janata Party (BJP) 82–83
Biden, Joe 156
Biden administration 65, 71, 73, 133, 143–44, 146, 165
bigoted culture 95
bilateral trade 41; balances 10–11, 46–47; relations 62; treaties 58
bilateralism 58, 65

BioNTech 118, 164
Bismarck, Otto von 38
BJP, *see* Bharatiya Janata Party
Bogers, Marcel 148
Bollyky, Thomas 131, 135
Bolsonaro, Jair 124–26
Bolsonaro government 125
Bombay (Mumbai) 18
Boston Consulting Group 144
Bouie, Jamelle 87
Boutros-Ghali, Boutros 79
Bown, Chad 3, 65, 69–70, 72, 131, 135
Brazil 124–26, 128
Bretton Woods Conference (1944) 161
Brexit 142, 171; assessing blunder 114–16;
    asylum seekers to Rwanda 114; came
    into effect 107–8; campaign 99;
    disunited Kingdom 111–13; economics
    of EU Membership 105–6; entry
    of Johnson 101–2; fish over finance
    110–11; impacts 108–9; nostalgic
    deprivation 106–7, 163; sovereignty
    and immigration 102–5; vote 99–100,
    102, 105–6, 110, 112, 115, 153
Britain/British 11, 16–17, 25, 27, 30,
    37, 99, 111–13, 141–42; attack on
    Dutch settlements 15; cloth exports
    in Portugal 22; conquering India 19;
    economic thought 28; government
    19; identity 107; imperial grip 29; in
    Industrial Revolution 30; military
    power 12; nationalism 100; sovereignty
    100, 103, 104, 171; tariffs reduction 58;
    woolens sector 19, 25
British Chambers of Commerce 109
British East India Company (EIC) 9,
    11–13, 15–21
British Parliament 15
Broadberry, Stephen 32
Broadcom 143
Brussels 108
Bruton, Henry 34
Budapest 84–85
Business Roundtable 97

Calcutta 18
calico controversy (1696–1700) 19–20
calico imports 20
calico printing industry 20
Cameron, David 99, 102–3, 115
Cameron government 154
Canada 4, 66, 128
Cape of Good Hope 13–14

Capitol insurrection 81, 97
Carlson, Tucker 80, 85–86
CCP, *see* Chinese Communist Party
Center for Disease Control, Taiwan 120
Centre for Economic Performance,
    London School of Economics 109
Chanda, Rupa 39
Chang, Ha-Joon 32–35; *Kicking Away the
    Ladder* 32–33, 35
Charles (prince) 114
Charles II 12
Chesbrough, Henry 148
Chevalier, Michel 72
Child, Josiah 18–20; *New Discourse of Trade,
    A* 18–19
China 25, 69–70, 72–73, 120–21, 129,
    133–34, 139, 144–46, 154, 173–74;
    accession to World Trade Organization
    62–65, 162; achievement of "great
    power" status 169; government 134,
    149–50, 155; Protocol of Accession
    65, 73; technology development 143;
    trade and technology war with United
    States 4, 121, 142–45, 155, 174; trade
    relationship with United States 62, 72
China shock 63–64
China Standards (2035) 149
Chinese Communist Party (CCP) 120,
    149
Chinese Ministry of Foreign Affairs 173
Chip 4 Alliance 147
CHIPS Act (2022) 146
Citizenship Amendment Act (2019) 83
civic activities 96
civic institutions 94–95
civic nationalism 7–8, 94–97, 167–68
civil war 92
climate change 73–74, 91–92, 94, 165–67,
    169, 173
climate refugees 92
Clive, Robert 18–19
Coalition of Service Industries (CSI) 60
Coalition of the Willing 104
Cobden, Richard 72
Cobden-Chevalier Treaty (1860) 23,
    58–59, 68, 72
Coen, Jan Pieterszoon 13–14
coercive power 54
cognitive complexity 51–52, 54, 56
colonialism 29
COMAC, *see* Commercial Aircraft
    Corporation of China
"Command Paper" 113

commerce and conflict 13–16
Commercial Aircraft Corporation of
    China (COMAC) 149
Common Agricultural Policy 60
Common Framework for Debt
    Treatments 167, 173
communal conflict 89
comparative advantage 23, 45, 47–48, 50,
    53, 158
compulsory licensing 133
Condliffe, John Bell 32
Confederation of British Industry 113
Conservative Party 109, 111, 115
Conservative Political Action Committee
    (CPAC) 86–87
constituencies 50–51
Contagious Disease National Direct
    Reporting System 120
Convention Relating to the Status of
    Refugees (1951) 92–93
coopetition 141, 158
CORBEVAX 133
Corbin, Jeremy 102
Cornwallis, Charles 19
corporate imperialism 52
corporate lobbying 21
cosmopolitical economy 28
cotton: good production 25–26; import
    from colonies 26; textiles 19; unprinted
    cotton prohibition 19
COVAX AMC, see COVID-19 Vaccines
    Advance Market Commitment
COVAX Facility 132–33
COVID GAP, see COVID Global
    Accountability Platform
COVID Global Accountability Platform
    (COVID GAP) 132
COVID-19 117, 166; back to
    multilateralism 134–36; Bolsonaro's
    failure 124–25; deaths in US and India
    117–18, 122, 128; Delta variant 124;
    Modi's failure 123–24; multilateralism
    in health 119–20; nationalism and
    populist leadership 125–29, Omicron
    variant 134; origins and tensions
    120–22; pandemic 4, 7, 73, 81, 83, 87,
    97, 101, 117, 118, 122, 125, 126–27, 129,
    131, 133, 141, 155; personal protective
    equipment (PPE) and medical supplies
    129–31; recovery funds 86; Trump's
    failure 122–23; vaccine nationalism
    133–34; vaccines 118, 131–33; virus as
    Wuhan virus/Kung flu 121

COVID-19 Trade and Investment
    Agreement 135
COVID-19 Vaccines Advance Market
    Commitment (COVAX AMC) 132–33,
    135
Cox, Jo 100
CPAC, see Conservative Political Action
    Committee
CPI, see parliamentary commission of
    inquiry
Crafts, Nicholas 105
Crane, George 5
Cromwell, Oliver 12
cross-border collaborative activities 147
cross-licensing 147, 149
CSI, see Coalition of Service Industries
cultural identities 89

Daily Express 103
Dalrymple, William 18; Anarchy, The 18
DAO, see discrete analog and other
DARPA, see Defense Advanced Research
    Projects Agency
Davis, David 108–9
Debebe, Gelaye 89
debt crisis 34, 166
decolonization 21
de-conflicting 141
Defense Advanced Research Projects
    Agency (DARPA) 140–43
Defense Production Act (DPA) 129
deglobalization 140
deindustrialization 26
Democratic Party 85
democratic processes 54–56
demonetization 83
Denmark 31
development-facilitation tariff (DFT) 36,
    157
DFT, see development-facilitation tariff
Diez, Thomas 100
digital territory 150–51
digital trade 151
Dinan, Desmond 04, 00, Europe Recast 00
discourse power 121
discrete analog and other (DAO) 145
discrimination 77, 80, 87, 89; taste for 80
discriminatory measures 83
Disease X 120
Dispute Settlement Understanding (DSU)
    71
distributive bargaining 51–57
Doha Round 3, 72

domestic legal systems 171
domestic politics 45–46, 161
Donnelly, Jack 168–69
Dorn, David 63
Downing, George 12, 13, 16
DPA, *see* Defense Production Act
DSU, *see* Dispute Settlement Understanding
Dugin, Alexander 85
Duke University 132
Dutch 11–12; British attack on settlements 15; citizens relocation 12; control over spices 14, 15; economic practice 12; execution of British nationals 14; government 13
Dyson, James 154

Earth Institute, Colombia University 122
East Asia 30, 34, 145, 151
East India trade 20
Eaton, Jonathan 23, 160
Ebola crisis 123
EC, *see* European Community
Eccleston-Turner, Mark 133
ECJ, *see* European Court of Justice
economic development/growth 28, 30, 32, 48, 67, 87, 167–68
economic globalization 45, 149–50, 159, 162
economic nationalism 4–6; *see also individual entries*
economic nationalist(s) 7, 8, 23–24, 27, 39, 57, 130; agendas 45; in high-income countries 41; ideology 4; modern 10, 21, 30, 34; movements 114, 160; policies 4, 158; US 143
economic nostalgia 68
economic power 6, 53
economic self-sufficiency 25
economic sovereignty 171
economic symbolism 79
economic warfare 16, 37, 160
economic welfare 46, 50
Economist, The 13, 15, 71, 78, 93, 109–11, 123, 125–26, 142, 144, 146, 150, 162–63
EDA, *see* electronic design automation
EDPs, *see* environmentally displaced persons
EEC, *see* European Economic Community
EIC, *see* British East India Company
Eichengreen, Barry 46

Eisenhower administration 140
electronic design automation (EDA) 144
employment 22, 48, 63, 67–68, 83
EMU, *see* European Monetary Union
England/English 10–12, 18, 25, 58, 72, 111; colonial products export to 12–13; governments 15; nationalism 111; trade with Portugal 22
environmental policies 57
environmentally displaced persons (EDPs) 91
ethical responsibilities 89–90
Ethiopia 79
ethnic cleansing 14
ethnic community 89
ethnic consciousness 89
ethnic purity 78
ethnicity 4, 79, 90–91, 97
ethnonationalism 6, 7, 77, 114, 123, 126, 162–63; assessing 87–90; civic nationalism 94–97; and economic nationalism 97; ethnonationalist leaders and 81; Hindutva 82–84; Hungary 84–87; nation, definition 78–81; performance and policy 87; refugees 91–94; Western 90–91
ethnonationalists 88–89, 91, 93
ethnopsychology 79
EU, *see* European Union
EU Commission 129
EU workers 109
Europe 25–26, 34, 88, 94, 161
European Central Bank 110
European Commission 108
European Community (EC) 105
European Council 104
European Court of Justice (ECJ) 86, 113
European Economic Community (EEC) 99
European International Sanitary Conferences 119
European Monetary Union (EMU) 101
European nationalism 88
European Parliament 86, 110
European Union (EU) 60, 63, 65, 100–106, 108, 110–13, 133, 139, 144, 164; Hungary joining 86, 115; Japan and 70
Euroscepticism 99–102
Euro-speak 100
EU-US Trade and Technology Council (TTC) 144
Evenett, Simon 129–30

exclusive companies 16

fair trade 48, 108
FAO, *see* Food and Agriculture Organization
Farage, Nigel 99, 101
fascism 1, 54
FDI, *see* foreign direct investment
Federal Agency for Disruptive Innovation (SPRIN-D) 141
Feenstra, Robert 63
Fidesz government 84
Fidesz party 84, 86
financial services 39, 110–11
Findlay, Ronald 9, 12–13, 15, 21, 26, 45; *Power and Plenty* 45
First World Climate Conference (1979) 165
fiscal-military state 13
fisheries subsidies 74–75
fishing rights 108
fishing sector 110
Flag and the Cross, The (Gorski and Perry) 80
Food and Agriculture Organization (FAO) 74
food shortages 109
forced labor 44
forced technology transfer 49, 70, 73
foreign direct investment (FDI) 105, 139, 144, 152, 156, 169
foreign markets 27
foreign policy 59
foreign trade 1, 10
foreign trading partners 57
fossil fuel subsidies 166
France 15, 58, 72, 129
free trade 17, 20, 58, 147, 159, 161; agreement 109
Freeman, Richard 154–55
French government 129
Friberg, Daniel 85
Friedman, Thomas 52; *Lexus and the Olive Tree: Understanding Globalization, The* 52; *World Is Flat: A Brief History of the 21ˢᵗ Century, The* 52
Frost, David 113
fukoku kyōhei (rich nation, strong army) 38
Fukuyama, Frances 55
fustian 26
Future of Europe Conference (2018) 84

G20 meetings 165, 167

game theory 43
Gandhi, M. K. 82
Gao, Henry 71
GATS, *see* General Agreement on Trade in Services
GATT, *see* General Agreement on Tariffs and Trade
GDP 36, 62–64, 68, 83, 101, 105, 134
General Agreement on Tariffs and Trade (GATT) 2–3, 23, 35, 60–61, 162; Article I 58–59; Article XVIII 36; Article XVIIIa 35; Article XVIIIc 35; Article XXI 65–67; Article XXVIII 35
General Agreement on Trade in Services (GATS) 60, 110
general equilibrium effects 63, 67
Generalized System of Preferences (GSP) 61
German Bund 31
German civilization 94
German education system 29
German expansionism 31
German Socialist Party 1
Germany 27–29, 31–32, 34, 37–38, 57, 62–63, 93, 95, 129
Gest, Justin 106–7
Getulio Vargas Foundation 124
Ghebreyesus, Tedros Adhanom 131
Ghemawat, Pankaj 52–53
Gilpin, Robert 5, 25
Ginty, Roger Mac 96
Global Compact on Refugees (2018) 93
global economy 2, 6, 40, 52, 140, 161
global financial crisis (2009) 117
global food security 74–75, 166
global public goods 75, 93, 132, 158, 165–66, 171, 174
global public health 7, 8, 74–75, 119, 128, 133–34, 136
global trade 3, 57
global value chains (GVCs) 36, 40–41, 130, 134, 142, 144–48, 150, 154
globalism 122, 124
globalization 5, 52, 118, 139, 159–60, 164
Göring, Herman 1
Gorski, Philip 80
Great Depression 117, 161
Greek ethnicity 90
gross trade values 41
Group of 7 (G7) meeting 122, 127–28
GSP, *see* Generalized System of Preferences
Guardian, The 108, 154

Gujarat model 83
Gujarat State Board of Textbooks 83
GVCs, *see* global value chains

The Hague 12, 13
Hall, Derek 5
Hall, Edith 91
Hanson, Gordon 63
hard power 54
Hastings, Warren 19
Health Committee 119
hegemonism 173
Helleiner, Eric 6, 27
heuristic substitution 45, 46, 48, 68, 158
Highnam, Peter 141
Hindutva movement 82–84, 123–24
Hirschman, Albert 1, 2, 4, 6–7, 9, 30–2,
    57, 171; *National Power and the Structure of
    Foreign Trade* 1, 2, 9, 57, 171
"His Majesty's Seas" 11–14, 80
HIV-AIDS 133
Hoekman, Bernard 51, 59
Holland 31
Holshek, Christopher 54
Horizon Europe program 141
hostile attribution bias 54
Huawei 142–43
human rights 114
Hungarian Order of Merit (2016) 86
Hungary 83–87, 93, 128; Chamber of
    Commerce 85; government 86

IBM 60
ICT, *see* information and communication
    technologies
Ignatieff, Michael 94, 96
illiberal democracy 84, 86
illiberalism 85, 126
imagined community 5, 90
IMF, *see* International Monetary Fund
imperial Germany 157
imperial Japan 157
inclusive citizenship 95
inclusive nationalism 80
India 18–21, 25, 29, 77, 82, 95, 123–24,
    126, 128, 133, 154
Indonesia 58
industrial capacity 38–39
Industrial Revolution 25–27, 30, 34, 40
industrialization 25–26
infant industry protection 28–29, 32–36
information and communication
    technologies (ICT) 150, 152

in-group solidarity 77
inherited culture 95
Inkster, Nigel 143
Institute of International and Strategic
    Studies, Peking University 150
institutional multilateralism 165
institutionalized xenophobia 91
integrative bargaining 51–52, 54
Intel 137, 143, 146
intellectual property (IP) 3, 36, 45, 60–61,
    65, 70, 133, 143–44, 155
Intellectual Property Committee 60
Intergovernmental Panel on Climate
    Change (IPCC) 165
international cooperation 74
international economic(s) 22; policy 21;
    relations 1, 2, 43, 50–51, 53, 60, 119;
    transactions 43
international finance 45–46
international institutions 2, 23, 35, 59, 169
International Labor Organization 57
international markets 44
International Monetary Fund (IMF) 2,
    115, 171, 173–74
international relations 75, 151, 161, 168
international trade 2, 10, 23, 38, 56, 61–
    62, 150, 159; agreements 48; economic
    psychology of 44–48; German 57;
    politics of 51; system 59
International Trade Organization (ITO)
    2
intra-industry trade 47
intranational conflict 46
IP, *see* intellectual property
IPCC, *see* Intergovernmental Panel on
    Climate Change
Irwin, Douglas 23, 32, 58, 65, 69–70, 72
Islamofascism 85
ITO, *see* International Trade
    Organization
Ivarsflaten, Elisabeth 107

Japan 38, 58, 70, 78, 95, 127, 138–39, 143,
    146–47, 151, 156
Japanese government 38, 139
Japanese nationalists 78
Johnson, Boris 101–2, 107, 110, 112–16
Johnson, Carol 126
Johnson, Harry 67, 79
Johnson, Robert 41
Johnson government 108–10, 112–14
Jones, Jonathan 113
Jóźwik, Arkadiusz 103

Kahl, Colin 4, 120, 122, 127
K-Chips Act 146
Kissinger, Henry 94
KLA 146
Kohn, Hans 94; *Idea of Nationalism, The* 94
Kohn's dichotomy 94
Koopman, Robert 41, 169
Korean government 137
Kostecki, Michel 51, 59
Krasiński Square 90
Kudlow, Larry 121
Kumbh Mela festival 123
Kushner, Jared 69
Kwarteng, Kwasi 115
Kyoto Protocol (1997) 165

labor markets 63, 64
Labour Party 102
Lam Research 146
Lancet, The 123
Latin America 33–34
Latin American governments 33
LCD, *see* liquid crystal display
le grand remplacement (great replacement theory) 86
League of Nations 119
Lee, Jong-Wha 152
Lee, Yong-Shik 36, 66
Lee Jae-yong 137, 156
Lee Kun-hee 137
liberal democracy 84
liberal economic policy 21
liberalization 160
liberty 17
licensing 149
Lighthizer, Robert 3, 118
Lind, Michael 38–39, 159
liquid crystal display (LCD) 148
List, Friedrich 4, 27–32, 34, 41, 48, 157, 160–61; *National System of Political Economy, The* 27, 32, 37, 39; and war 36–39
LMICs, *see* low- and middle-income countries
localization 52
logic 145
London 110–11
London School of Economics (LSE) 1
low- and middle-income countries (LMICs) 41, 67, 89, 93, 130, 133, 152, 163, 166
LSE, *see* London School of Economics
Luo, Yadong 139, 147–48, 156

Maastricht Treaty (1992) 99–100
macroeconomic principles 49
Made in China (2025) 149
Madras 18
Mandetta, Luiz Henrique 124
manufacturing and services 39–41
manufacturing capacity 29, 36, 53
manufacturing power 27, 28
Markel, Howard 119
market fundamentalism 160
market systems 97
market transactions 44, 50
masculine leadership 125, 126, 128
mass murder 83
Mavroidis, Petros 64, 72–73; *China and the WTO: Why Multilateralism Still Matters* 72
May, Theresa 102, 107, 153–54
Mayer, Jeremy 106–7
Mearsheimer, John 168–69, 170
medical nationalism 129
Meiji government 38
memory 145
mercantile rivalry 15
mercantilism 4, 9–10, 13, 15–18, 21–24, 46, 157
mercantilist thinking 21, 24
mercantilist trading structures 26, 27
merchant oligarchy 13
Merkel, Angela 93, 127
Messerlin, Patrick 35
Methuen, John 22
Methuen Treaty (1703) 22, 23, 58
Mexico 66
MFN, *see* most-favored nation
militarization 53
military industry 38
military power 25, 39
military technology 138
Mill, John Stuart 17, 21; *On Liberty* 17
Milton, Giles 14; *Nathaniel's Nutmeg* 14
miniaturization 89
Mitteleuropa 32, 37
MNEs, *see* multinational enterprises
Moderna 141, 149
Modi, Narendra 77, 81–83, 87, 97, 123–24, 126
Modi government 83, 123
Modi-Hindutva movement 83
Möllers, Norma 150
Mölnlycke 129
Monarch-in-Parliament 102
monopolistic trading companies 16

monopolization 18, 20, 29
monopoly control 10
monopoly profits 10
monopoly rights 9
Moretti, Enrico 41
Morgan, John 85
Morgenstern, Oskar 43; *Theory of Games and Economic Behavior* 43
most-favored nation (MFN) 58–59, 62, 72
MPIA, *see* Multiparty Interim Appeal Arbitration Arrangement
mRNA biotechnology 133–34, 149
MTNs, *see* Multilateral trade negotiations
Mughal Empire 19, 20
Muller, Jerry 88–89
multilateral cooperation 4, 58
multilateral institutions 7, 8, 59
multilateral trade 72; agreements 35; cooperation 3; system 4, 23, 59, 72, 75, 130, 136, 159, 161, 163
multilateral trade negotiations (MTNs) 2, 3, 51
multilateralism 7, 57–60, 65, 71–74, 118–20, 124, 129, 134–36, 158, 160–63, 168, 171, 173
multinational enterprises (MNEs) 51, 63, 138, 140, 147–48, 150, 160, 164
Multiparty Interim Appeal Arbitration Arrangement (MPIA) 71
Mun, Thomas 9–12, 16–21, 74, 80, 101, 110; *England's Treasure by Forraign Trade* 10
Murphy-Shigematsu, Stephen 78
Murray, Douglas 85; *Strange Death of Europe: Immigration, Identity, Islam, The* 85
Muscovy trade 14
Muslim Indian citizens 83, 95

NAFTA, *see* North American Free Trade Agreement
Bonaparte, Louis-Napoléon, 68
nation 77–81, 88
National Association of Manufacturers 97
national consciousness 78
National Conservatism 80
National Conservatism Conference (2019) 82
national defense 17, 18
national economy 28
national identity 5, 79–80, 82, 88
national labor market 22
national power 1, 2, 6, 36

national security 3, 25, 38, 54, 65–67, 71, 155
national sovereignty 30, 150
nationalism 7, 8, 38, 77, 79–80, 94, 125–29
nationalistic politics 79
nationality 31, 79
nationalizing mechanism 6
nationhood 79
Navarro, Peter 69, 118, 129; *Death by China* 69
Navigation Act (1651) 12, 13, 15, 17
Nazi Germany 57
Nazi government 57
Naziism 82–83
negative reciprocity fairness 47
negotiations theory 50–52
neo-mercantilist policies 18, 37, 43, 45, 47
new nationalism 7
New World 15, 26
New York Times 52, 144
Newly industrialized countries (NICs) 30
new-right movements 85
NICs, *see* Newly industrialized countries
Nigeria 79
Noguera, Guillermo 41
non-zero-sum approaches 168
non-zero-sum games 43
North American Free Trade Agreement (NAFTA) 64, 69
Northern Ireland 112–13
Northern Ireland Protocol 113
nostalgic deprivation 106–7, 163

Obama, Barack 73, 123
Obama administration 64, 71
Office International d'Hygiène Publique (OIHP) 119
OIHP, *see* Office International d'Hygiène Publique
Okonjo-Iweala, Ngozi 131, 135
open innovation 7, 53, 147–49, 156, 158, 163–64
open market system 64
open trading system 65, 134
open-economy macroeconomics 48
Operation Warp Speed vaccine development program 118
Orbán, Viktor 84–87, 91, 97, 115, 126
Organisation of Semiconductor Exporting Countries (OSEC) 143–47
Organization for Economic Cooperation and Development 63

organized violence 95
O'Rourke, Kevin 9, 12–13, 15, 21, 26, 32, 45; *Power and Plenty* 45
Osborne, George 103, 154
OSEC, *see* Organisation of Semiconductor Exporting Countries
out-group hostility 77
overall balance of trade 10

PAHO, *see* Pan-American Health Organization
Palonen, Emilia 95
Pan-American Health Organization (PAHO) 119, 124
Pan-American Sanitary Bureau 119
pandemic nationalism 87, 122, 125, 130; *see also* COVID-19
Pandemic Treaty 135
pandemics and economic nationalism 118
Paris Accord 73; 2015 165; 2017 165
parliamentary commission of inquiry (CPI) 125
parochialism 50
partialism 90
Patel, Priti 114
Peace Treaty (1667) 15
Pennsylvania Association for the Promotion of Manufacturing Industry 27
People's Liberation Army (PLA) 149, 155
People's Republic of China (PRC) 155
performative nationalism 87, 127–28, 165
Peron, Evita 117
Perry, Samuel 80
personal protective equipment (PPE) 129–31
Pfizer 60, 118, 125, 163–64
phase-one deal 70
Philip (prince) 162
Pickel, Andreas 6, 87
PLA, *see* People's Liberation Army
plurilateral agreement 73, 130
plurilateral mechanism 135–36
political economy 5, 25, 27, 28, 140
political ideology 15
political psychology 77
political violence 55
populism 99–100, 114, 127, 159
Port Wine Treaty 22
Portugal 22, 58
Portuguese wines 22
positive reciprocity fairness 47
PPE, *see* personal protective equipment

PRC, *see* People's Republic of China
Prebisch, Raul 33; *Economic Development of Latin American and Its Principal Problems, The* 33
preferential trade agreements 106
prejudice 77
presidential election (2020) 81
productive power 28, 30, 37
pro-market economic policies 83
property rights 21, 64
public finance 21
Putin, Vladimir 38, 54, 85, 125, 173

"the Quad" 72
Qualcomm 143
"Quintet" 72, 75, 166

race 82–83, 90, 91
race mixing 87
racism 80
Rashtriya Swayamsevak Sangh (National Volunteer Organization, RSS) 82
ratio reasoning 45
RCUK, *see* Research Councils UK
R&D, *see* Research and Development
Reagan-Thatcher revolution (1980s) 161
realism 140, 151–52, 168–71
reciprocal fairness 46–47, 51
re-exports 21
refugees 91–94
Reich, Robert 138–39, 151
Reinhart, Carmen 117
Reinhart, Vincent 117
religious bigotry 83
Reny, Tyler 106–7
replacement theory 80
representative democracy 84
representative governments 55–56
Republic of Ireland 112
Republican Party 81, 111
Research and Development (R&D) 40–41, 53, 138–39, 148
Research Councils UK (RCUK) 142
Reserve Bank of India 87
Ricardo, David 22–23, 45, 48, 53, 158, 160
Rommelse, Gijs 13, 15
Roosevelt administration 161
Rose, Andrew 61
RSS, *see* Rashtriya Swayamsevak Sangh
Ruffin, Roy 22
Ruggie, John 57, 59, 161, 168
rules-based trading system 3, 31, 57, 59

Russia 54, 125, 140, 166, 170, 173

Samsung Electronics 137, 145, 148–49, 156
Samuels, Richard 38, 138–39; *Rich Nation, Strong Army* 38, 138
Sapir, André 64, 72–73; *China and the WTO: Why Multilateralism Still Matters* 72
SARS epidemic (2002–3) 120
Savarkar, Vinayak Damodar 82–83; *Hindutva: Who Is a Hindu?* 82
scale economies 35, 53
Schengen Agreement 103
Scotland 112
Scottish National Party (SNP) 112
Seeley, J. R. 17; *Expansion of England, The* 17
SEMATECH, *see* Semiconductor Manufacturing Technology
Semiconductor Industry Association 144
Semiconductor Manufacturing International Company (SMIC) 146, 149
Semiconductor Manufacturing Technology (SEMATECH) 143–47
semiconductors 137–38, 144–45
Sen, Amartya 83; *Identity and Violence* 89
Serum Institute of India 124
servicification 39, 40
Shah Alam (Mughal emperor) 19
shared civic practices 95–96
shared social identity 81
Shih, Stan 40
shokusan kōgyō (industrial promotion) 38
"significant trade deficits" report 48
Singer, Peter 89
Singh, J. P. 163
Sinopharm 133
Sinovac 133
slavery 27
slave(s): emancipation 31; labor 26; law 86
SMIC, *see* Semiconductor Manufacturing International Company
smile curve 40–41
Smith, Adam 16–18, 29–31, 36; division of labor 28; *Wealth of Nations, The* 16–17
Smythe, Thomas 9
SNP, *see* Scottish National Party
social axiom 47
social safety nets 97, 159, 161–62
SOEs, *see* state-owned enterprises
soft power 54

Sony 148
South Africa 133
South Korea 146–47, 149, 151, 156, 164
sovereignty 124, 171–72
Spain 11
Spanish Civil War 1
spice islands 14
spice race 14, 18
spice trade 14
Spiegel, Henry William 9, 18, 37, 160
spinning 40
SPRIN-D, *see* Federal Agency for Disruptive Innovation
Staples Act (1663) 12
state-owned enterprises (SOEs) 64, 70, 73
status quo effect 46
Steel Manufacturers Association 71
stochastic violence 77, 86, 97
strategy of differences 52–53
Stuenkel, Oliver 124
Sturgeon, Nicola 112
Sunak, Rishi 110–11, 115
Suranovic, Steven 47
Syria 92
Syrian refugee crisis (2015) 84–85, 92
Syrian refugees 91, 93, 100, 103–4
Szirmai, Adam 152

Tai, Katherine 71
Taiwan 120, 146–47, 149, 151, 164
Taiwan Chips Act 146
Taiwan Semiconductor Manufacturing Company (TSMC) 137, 145–47, 149
Tamir, Yael 78, 95
tariff(s) 2–4; duties 34; policy 32, 33; unilateral 70
TCA, *see* Trade and Cooperation Agreement
techno-authoritarianism 125
techno-independence 149–50
technological capabilities 53
technological diffusion 26, 29
technological learning 34
techno-military paradigm 38
techno-nationalism 4, 53, 137, 174; Advanced Research Projects Agency (ARPA) 140–42; conventional and new 139; Defense Advanced Research Projects Agency (DARPA) 140–42; digital territory 150–51; emergence 138–40; Huawei 142–43; international students and high-skilled immigrants 153–55; multinational enterprises

(MNes) 140; open innovation and 156; Organisation of Semiconductor Exporting Countries (OSEC) 143–47; quality of basic education and technological development 151–53; Semiconductor Manufacturing Technology (SEMATECH) 143–47; techno-independence and 149–50; zero-sum global technology vs. open innovation 147–49

TEU, see Treaty on European Union

Thomas, P. J. 17, 24

Thornton, Bruce 90

Tigray province conflict (2020–22) 79

Tokyo Electron 146

Tory conference (2022) 115

Tory Party 115

Toynbee, Polly 108

TPP, see Trans-Pacific Partnership

trade: autonomy 2; coercion measures 122; facilitation 36; law 36; liberalization 58, 105; mercantilist 58; policies 21, 35–36, 38, 48, 50, 71; relations 3, 57–58; wars 46, 61, 70

Trade and Cooperation Agreement (TCA) 108–11, 113

Trade Expansion Act (1962) 66; Section 232 66, 71

Trade Facilitation Agreement (2013) 3

Trade-Related Aspects of Intellectual Property Rights (TRIPS) 60, 133

Trans-Pacific Partnership (TPP) 64, 69

Treaty of Breda 15

Treaty on European Union (TEU, 2007) 84; Article 2 86; Article 7(1) 86

TRIPS, see Trade-Related Aspects of Intellectual Property Rights

Trump, Donald 3, 61, 67, 69–71, 77, 86, 114, 117–18, 120–28, 162, 165, 171; administration 3, 48–49, 52, 64–73, 81, 85, 87, 90, 93, 97, 120–21, 129, 142–44, 155, 162; movement 106, 111, 114, 160

Truss, Liz 115

Tsai, Robert 93

TSMC, see Taiwan Semiconductor Manufacturing Company

TTC, see EU-US Trade and Technology Council

Turkish immigration 103

two-way trade 47–48

UK, see United Kingdom

UK Home Office 114

UK Independence Party (UKIP) 100, 102–3, 107

UK Office of Budget Responsibility 101

UKIP, see UK Independence Party

Ukraine 40, 54, 115, 125, 140, 166, 170, 173

Ukrainian refugees 91, 114

UK's Office of Budget Responsibility 115

UN Refugee Convention 114

unfair trade 48

unfair/discriminatory practices 48

UNHCR, see United Nations High Commissioner of Refugees

unilateralism 73–74

United Kingdom (UK) 62–63, 93, 102–13, 115, 141, 154

United Nations 33, 79, 119, 120, 173

United Nations Environment Program 165

United Nations High Commissioner of Refugees (UNHCR) 57, 91–92, 114

United States (US) 2, 23, 27, 32, 48–50, 52, 59–60, 77, 80, 87, 93, 97, 106, 111, 114, 119, 122, 126–29, 139, 142, 147, 154, 161, 164–65, 170; bilateral and multilateral trade relationship with China 62, 72; Center for Disease Control and Prevention 120; Chamber of Commerce 97; Chinese graduate students in 154–55; COVID-19 deaths in 117–18, 122, 128; Department of Commerce 66; Department of Defense 66; Department of State 66; and dispute settlement system 61; economy 60, 64, 68; employment 67–68; Federal Reserve 87; funding 143–44; government 3, 49, 137, 143, 146; higher education service 155; interest in services trade liberalization 60; labor markets in 63–64; military 54; and multilateral system 75; National Economic Council 121; Pentagon 141; steel industry 3; technological development 143; trade and technology war with China 4, 121, 142–45, 155, 174; unilateral tariffs on China 70

United States-Mexico-Canada Agreement (USMCA) 64

United Steelworkers 71

Universal Declaration of Human Rights (1948) 92

universal free trade 31

universal secondary education 152

University of California 1, 32

University of Tübingen 27

Upton, Harry 133
US, *see* United States
USMCA, *see* United States-Mexico-
  Canada Agreement

vaccine nationalism 131–34, 149, 165
value added values 41
value-added exports 63
value-added trade 63
vegetarianism, politicization of 83
Vereenigde Oost-Indische Compagnie
  (VOC) 13–16
Vienna Convention on the Law of
  Treaties (1969) 171
Viner, Jacob 21
VOC, *see* Vereenigde Oost-Indische
  Compagnie
von der Leyen, Ursula 108
von Neumann, John 43; *Theory of Games
  and Economic Behavior* 43
voting rights 55

Wales 112
Wang, Zhi 41
Washington, George 19
weaving 25, 26, 40
Wei, Shang-Jin 41
Wellesley, Richard 19
Wellings, Ben 100
Western civilization 85, 90–91
Western Europe 32–33, 58
WHA, *see* World Health Assembly
white Christian nationalism 80, 81
White working-class communities 106
whiteness 91, 107
WHO, *see* World Health Organization
Williams, Blair 126
Wilson, Harold 99
Windsor Framework 113
win-lose default 56
win-win denial 44
Woo, Meredith 38
woolen weavers 20
World Bank 2, 36, 117, 171
World Health Assembly (WHA) 135–36
World Health Organization (WHO)
  119–20, 122–23, 134–35, 165

World Meteorological Organization 165
World Trade Organization (WTO) 2, 3,
  23, 31, 34–36, 48, 57–59, 110, 122, 130,
  133, 135–36, 157–58; Appellate Body
  71; assessment 75; China's accession
  to 62–65, 162; Dispute Settlement
  Body 3; dispute settlement system 3,
  61, 64–65, 73, 143, 162, 171; evidence
  61–62; fish consumption and fisheries
  74–75; Ministerial Meeting (2022) 75;
  public international law of 171; return
  to multilateralism 71–74; threats 65–71;
  US and 59–61; violation 4; Working
  Party 162
World War I 58
World War II 59, 88, 95–96, 117, 119,
  122, 151, 162, 169
Wright, Thomas 4, 120, 122, 127
WTO, *see* World Trade Organization
Wuhan 120

Xenos, Nicholas 95
Xi Jinping 120–21, 173

Yack, Bernard 89, 95
Yang, Dali 121
Ying Bo 149
Yoon Suk-yeol 156
YouGov 109

Zedillo, Ernesto 159
zero-Covid policy 134
zero-sum belief 47, 54
zero-sum global technology 147–49
zero-sum military approach 39, 156
zero-sum thinking 5–7, 24, 41, 57, 94,
  131, 157–58, 160, 171; corporate
  strategy perspective 52–53; democratic
  processes 54–56; economic psychology
  of international trade 44–48; intuitive
  psychological appeal 56; market
  transactions 44; military analogy
  53–54; negotiations theory 50–52;
  trade balances and 48–50
Zhao Lijian 121
Zoellick, Robert 60
ZTE Corporation 142

Ingram Content Group UK Ltd.
Milton Keynes UK
UKHW012002070723
424689UK00003B/51